VEGETABLE GARDENING

by

W.E. SHEWELL-COOPER

N.D.H., F.L.S., F.R.S.A., F.R.H.S., Dip. Hort. (Wye)
Director, The Horticultural, Educational and Advisory Bureau
and The Principal of the Horticultural Training Center
Sometime H. Superintendent, Swanley Horticultural College
Sometime Horticultural Adviser to the Warwickshire and
Cheshire County Councils
Sometime Garden Editor, B.B.C. North Region
Command Horticultural Officer, S.E. and Eastern Commands 1940–1948

BIOTECH

2005

Biotech Books

Delhi - 110 035

2005 (W.E. Shewell-Cooper)
Original Title: The A.B.C. of Vegetable Gardening
© Reserved

ISBN 81-7622-126-0

Published by	:	**BIOTECH BOOKS** 1123/74, Tri Nagar, DELHI – 110 035 Phone: 27382765 e-mail: biotechbooks@yahoo.co.in
Showroom	:	4762-63/23, Ansari Road, Darya Ganj, NEW DELHI - 110 002 Phone: 23245578, 23244987
Printed at	:	**Chawla Offset Printers** New Delhi – 110 052

PRINTED IN INDIA

CONTENTS

AUTHOR'S THANKS
AND PREFACE

This book has travelled all over the world. It has helped students and allotment holders, house-holders and parksmen ; it did its part in the " Grow More Food Campaign " during the 1939–45 war, now it comes out in a new guise to win the peace.

This new and revised edition owes much of its improvement to the keenness of Miss Gweneth Wood, Dip. Hort. (Swanley), who has combed it through vigorously.

Thank you, readers, for your kind letters of appreciation, and best wishes to all those who are gardening with the A.B.C. series.

I should like to record my thanks to Miss Grace Brydon, B.Sc. (Hort.) and Miss Marion Huntbach, N.D.H., for helping to correct the proofs, and to Mr. John Featherstone, M.Sc., for advice freely given on Chapter II: also to Miss Diana Marks who prepared the drawings for the original volume.

The photographs are the copyright of the Horti-cultural Photo Supply Service.

W. E. S.-C.

Director,
The Horticultural Educational and Advisory Bureau,
Essex

ILLUSTRATIONS

PLATES

CHAPTER I

SOILS AND THEIR CULTIVATION

As we have got to work in soil to do our gardening we had better know something about :—

1. The different kinds of soils we may have to deal with.
2. How to drain the land to prevent its being waterlogged.
3. How to dig properly so as to get the best results.
4. How to hoe and the importance of it.
5. When it is necessary to tread or roll.
6. How some crops are earthed up.

It would not be suitable in a book of this kind to go into great details as to how the soils in our country have been produced. We, as gardeners, have to accept them as we find them. We have to work in them and get the best out of them, and, furthermore, we should try to improve them. Those who wish to go into the geology of the subject may get their information elsewhere.

Only those who have had to garden in different parts of Great Britain know how soil can influence the growth of plants. The light gravels over chalk suffer from drought very quickly, and to grow the best vegetable crops in soils of this character is most difficult. On the other hand, the light loams, rich in humus, that are of a good depth and have perfect drainage, can produce crops of show standard comparatively easily.

The soil chemist and the soil surveyor would attempt to divide soils into a very large number of groups. This again is not really necessary in our case, and it will be sufficient to take one or two typical soils as examples and explain how they should be worked to the best advantage.

A CLAY SOIL

The clay soil is retentive of moisture, but it is difficult to cultivate because of its heaviness, and, furthermore, it is apt

9

to crack badly in the summer if it is allowed to dry out.   During drought periods clay soils need hoeing constantly, and it is only hoeing that can prevent these fissures from appearing.   Clay soils need draining properly.   A vegetable garden with soil of a clayey character that is badly drained is almost impossible to work in the autumn and winter.   Crops die out because of waterlogging.

A clay soil needs digging and leaving rough in the autumn so as to expose the greatest surface of soil possible to the frost and winds.   The frost does pulverise the soil, and makes it possible to produce a fine seed-bed in the spring.   Lime is very necessary on clays because it prevents the particles from clogging together and so makes the soil less sticky and binding. In the olden days farmers improved the texture of clay soils by making large rubbish-heaps and burning quantities of clay on them.   This burnt clay was then returned to the soil and some improvement effected, because the burnt clay had lost its sticky nature.

Clay is a blessing during a hot, dry summer, but can be a great nuisance during a wet season.   A soil of this character should not be worked when it is wet or there is a danger that it may " pan down " hard, like cement.

Clay soils may be improved and opened up by the addition of strawy farmyard manure, spent hops, wool shoddy, and other similar organic material.   Burnt rubbish, wood ashes, flue dust, and inert matter of this kind help to improve workability.   Clay soils are generally rich in potash, but are frequently deficient in nitrogen.

An important advantage possessed by clay soil is that it does not easily part with plant foods in the drainage water : potash and phosphates, for example, are almost completely retained by the clay particles.

A MARLY SOIL

Marly soil is really a type of chalky clay.   Where clay predominates it is called a clay marl, and where chalk, it is known as chalky marl.   Marls may contain from 5 per cent to 20 per cent calcium carbonate.

A SANDY SOIL

Most people like a sandy soil because it is easy to work at any time of the year. It is not usually badly drained, and so plants do not die in the winter through waterlogging. It is a soil that warms up quickly in the spring, and sandy soils usually produce earlier crops than clay soils for this reason. On the other hand sandy soils dry out quickly in the summer, and so plants may suffer badly from drought.

Sandy soils can be too loose, and in extreme cases large quantities of such soils may be removed by winds. There are very bad cases of this in America at the present time. Such soils are very hungry, and large quantities of farmyard manure can be applied every year. They need such compost and organic material in order to help them retain moisture. Peat may be applied where farmyard manure is difficult to obtain. After all, the sandy soils in Holland and round about Paris have been made to produce some of the finest vegetable crops known.

Sands are usually lacking in potash and phosphates, though they are high in silica. It is not usual to apply lime in such heavy dressings as it is for clay soils.

Sand has practically no retentive power for plant foods, so that there is always a steady loss of such materials as lime, potash, and nitrates in the drainage water.

A PEATY SOIL

In some parts of England—i.e. in Lincolnshire, parts of Cheshire and Lancashire, etc.—peaty soils are found which consist largely of organic matter. A soil of this character has probably been produced by the growth and decay of aquatic plants over a very long period. Such soils may be badly drained, and they cannot be worked satisfactorily until this difficulty has been tackled. They are deficient in lime, and if the acid produced by the decaying vegetable matter is not counteracted the crops are poor. It may be necessary to apply lime every year on such soils at the rate of 7 oz. to the sq. yd.

Such soils are very easy to work and need not have quantities of organic manure added to them. Concentrated or other artificial manures are quite suitable. There is little necessity to apply nitrogen, but phosphates and potash are necessary.

A LOAMY SOIL

Most people find difficulty in understanding what the word loam means. Experts so often instruct the amateur to obtain some loam when making up a potting mixture of some sort, or a book may instruct a beginner to sow particular seeds in a loam. Actually a loam is an ideal mixture of the three soils already mentioned. When clay, sand, and well-rotted vegetable matter are mixed in certain proportions a loam is produced. Loams are ideal because they do not dry out quickly owing to the clay they contain. They do not " pan down " hard like cement because of the sand they contain. They are easily worked ; they are highly productive ; and they support nearly all crops satisfactorily.

Some soils of this character with a preponderance of clay are known as clayey loams, and others having more sand than clay may be described as sandy loams. It should be the aim of all gardeners to turn their soil into a loam. This can be done by continuous cultivation, by the addition of organic matter, and by efficient drainage. The ideal loam provides the roots of growing plants with a " balance " of air and water, both of which are necessary to sustain life.

SUBSOILS

Subsoils play almost as important a part in the success of vegetable culture as do the actual soils ; some people would suggest an even more important part. For instance, should the subsoil be chalk then the drainage will be perfect, and the chalk brought to the surface during deep cultivations will prevent the soil from becoming acid and will obviate the necessity of applying lime. Chalk itself is an unpleasant material to work in, and when cultivating on soils over chalk, care should be taken not to bring large quantities of the subsoil to the surface. During dry years the chalk acts as such a perfect " drain " that the soil overlying it is dried out quickly and the crops suffer in consequence.

Should the subsoil be clay, then an impenetrable barrier may be formed through which water cannot pass. This soon produces surface waterlogging. Such subsoils need draining carefully, and in the small garden it may be possible to bury large clinkers deeply, in order to help drainage. Occasionally the gardener may come across a hard redsand formation just below the top 9 in. or so of soil, and this substance seems to inhibit perfect growth above ; if the vegetable grower is to achieve success on a soil over such formation, he must break up that subsoil with a pickaxe.

DRAINING

Many gardens and allotments are already drained before the occupier takes them over. Sometimes these drains are blocked and a blocked drain is worse than no drain at all. The drain should be traced to its outlet, and, if it is found that the water is not running freely, then the drain should be " rodded," and, if this is of little value, it should be dug down to and the line followed, the agricultural drain-pipes removed, cleaned, and put down again.

The main function of the agricultural drain is to remove excess soil-water. The effect is to allow air to penetrate throughout the soil, and by the removal of excess moisture to make it possible for the soil to become warmer. Many plants will not grow satisfactorily on cold soils, and so the question of soil temperature is important. Experiments have shown that a drained soil may be 6 degrees F. warmer than a similar soil undrained.

Amateurs will probably find it difficult to lay down their own drains, and should in consequence consult their County Horticultural Adviser at the County Council Offices. As a general rule, drains should not be deeper than 2 ft. 6 in. and the drain-pipes should not be farther than 15 in. apart ; 3 in. drain-pipes are quite suitable for sub-mains, but 4 in. drains at least should be used for the mains.

It is a good plan to cover agricultural drain-pipes with clinkers or coarse brick rubbish, as this prevents the pipes from becoming sealed up.

Drain-pipes may get blocked by the roots of trees, grass, and plants, and that is the reason they have to be examined if it is found that they are not working properly.

Where it is impossible to use drain-pipes either on the score of expense or for some other reason, large stones and clinkers may be buried 18 in. or 2 ft. down to help to get the excess soil-water away. If, say, a 4 in. thickness of such stones can be buried 2 ft. down and in strips 3 ft. wide, it should be possible to carry the excess water down this home-made " culvert " to the lowest point in the garden or to some ditch outside.

VARIOUS METHODS OF DIGGING

There are four recognised forms of digging : (1) single digging ; (2) bastard trenching ; (3) true trenching ; and (4) ridging or ridge trenching. Each of such operations has its advantages, though all of them cannot be brought into use on all soils. The object of the cultivator should be to cultivate the soil to increase the area open to the roots to seek out soil foods. An ideal vegetable soil is one of a depth of 2 ft. Under ideal conditions and on special soils after years of trenching the soil might be extended to the depth of 3 ft.

Single Digging. This merely consists of inserting the spade into the soil, digging up the " spit," and inverting it ahead of the work. Usually a shallow trench is got out first of all and the soil taken to the other end of the plot as in bastard trenching, thus the surface of the soil is kept level all the way through. Single digging is usually done in the spring or at any time throughout the summer in order to prepare the soil for a particular crop, or after one crop has been harvested before the next one is sown.

Bastard Trenching (or Double Digging). The use of the term " bastard trenching " indicates that the soil is always left in its original layers. Thus, the top spit remains the top spit, the second spit the second spit, and the last spit the

PLANNING YOUR DIGGING

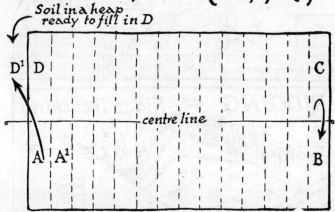

Soil in a heap
ready to fill in D

D¹ D   C

centre line

A A¹   B

Soil from A put on D¹
Soil from A¹ put on A
Soil from C put on B
and so on until
Soil from D¹ fills D

DOUBLE DIGGING or Bastard Trenching

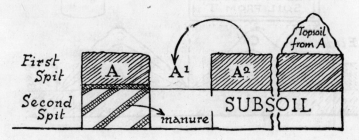

First Spit   A   A¹   A²   Topsoil from A

Second Spit   SUBSOIL

manure

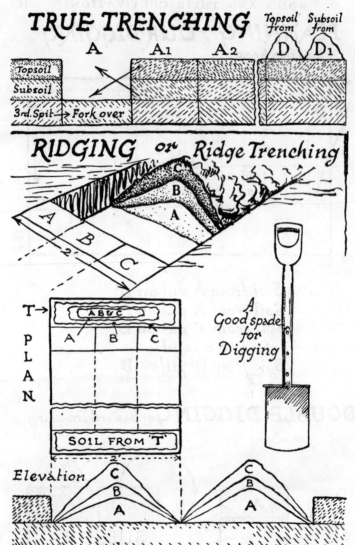

TRUE TRENCHING

Topsoil from Subsoil from

A   A₁   A₂   D D₁

Topsoil

Subsoil

3rd. Spit → Fork over

RIDGING or Ridge Trenching

C
B
A

A
B
C
2

T →

P
L
A
N

A B C

AB&C

SOIL FROM 'T'

A
Good spade
for
Digging

Elevation

C
B
A

C
B
A

2'

bottom spit, if bastard trenching is done to that depth.
Normally bastard trenching is done to two spits only.

A trench should be dug out 2 ft. wide and a spade's depth
at one end of the plot and the soil from this trench taken to the
other end of the plot, or the plot may be divided up into two
portions as in the diagram and the soil from A deposited at
D¹. The gardener will then work from A to B and from C to
D, putting the top soil from the end of C into the bottom of B
and so finding the soil at D¹ to fill the last trench at D.   When
trench A has been made, the gardener should get down into
the bottom of the trench and should fork the second spit over.
If it is desired to add manure, this should be forked in at the
same time so as to enrich the soil and/or another layer may be
put on top.   Then the soil from A¹ is put into the trench A
on top of the manure, and, of course, on top of the forked lower
soil, and when this is done the gardener gets into the bottom
of trench A¹ and forks over the bottom soil as in trench A, and
covers this in at A².

In this way the gardener cultivates the whole of his soil to
the depth of 18 in., incorporates all the organic material he
requires, and aerates the soil and improves the soil atmosphere.

Such digging should be done in the autumn, and the surface
soil should be left cloddy and rough so that the frost may act
upon it.

True Trenching.   This operation is seldom done to-day.
When true trenching, the land should be prepared in the same
way as for bastard trenching and the original trench dug out,
but not only has the first spit to be dug and placed at D, but
the second spit has to be removed and placed in a heap beyond
D as well.   In true trenching the positions of the lower soil
and the top soil are reversed.

Thus the top soil at A¹ goes into the bottom of trench A, and
the second spit of A¹ goes on to the top of trench A.   It can
thus be seen that the soil and subsoil of spit A¹ have been
reversed and are now in trench A.   The operator then puts
the top spit of A² into the bottom of trench A¹ and the second
spit of A² on to the top of this.

Ridge Trenching.   Ridging is *very useful* for all heavy soils.

It should be done in the autumn, and when complete it will be found that the greatest possible extent of surface has been exposed to the action of the weather. Ridges should never be too wide, and if they are kept as described, the channels will help to remove excess surface moisture and the soil in the ridges themselves will be found easily workable after one or two drying days in the spring.

Ridging should be commenced in the same way as for bastard trenching—that is, by the original trench being opened out. After this, however, the digging operation differs. A strip 2 ft. wide should be marked out running the whole length of the plot. Within this strip it should be possible to remove three separate spadefuls of soil. The first spit, A, is placed into the centre of the trench, spadeful B on top of this, and spadeful C on top of spadeful B. It will be seen from the drawing that in this way a ridge is made.

It is a pity that ridging is not done more. Clay soils derive a tremendous amount of benefit from it, and there are many allotments throughout the country which ought to be ridged every year. It is possible to ridge, bastard trench, and manure at the same time if necessary. To do this the bottom of the trench should be forked over before the spits A, B, or C are removed and the manure placed on the bottom of the forked-up trench. If this is done throughout the plot, a manured, bastard trenched, and ridged garden will result.

SPRING AND AUTUMN CULTIVATION

When carrying out autumn cultivations, the gardener's idea is to help drainage, ensure aeration, incorporate organic manures, ensure the thorough penetration of moisture, and so get the soil into a workable condition for the spring.

When the spring comes, the gardener needs to get the soil warm as early as he can, and if the frosts have done their job the soil should be friable. At this time of the year forking and raking will produce the fine tilth required for seed-sowing. It has been said that the soil in a seed bed should be such that every particle is no larger than a grain of wheat.

During the summer, constant hoeing is done to provide what is known as a dust mulch—a loose surface of dusty soil which prevents the evaporation of the soil moisture below. If the soil is firm up to the surface, then the sun is able to draw up the moisture and, together with the wind, cause its evaporation.

Hoeing ensures the keeping down of weeds and assists the plants by the aeration and warmth of the soil.

Both the Dutch hoe and the draw hoe play their part. The Dutch hoe is a favourite tool because with it the work can be done quickly, and as it is used whilst walking backwards the operator's footmarks are covered up. Hoeing should always be carried out before weeds appear and not afterwards. If it is done frequently enough, weeds need never be present at all.

In addition to dust mulching, many crops appreciate a mulching with an organic material. Peas, for instance, and runner beans like their roots to be kept cool, and so if lawn mowings or spent hops are placed along the rows to a depth of an inch or so, and for 6 in. to 9 in. on either side of the rows, another form of " mulching " is practised. Other substances used for mulching are straw, granulated peat, strawy manure, or rotted leaves.

OTHER OPERATIONS

The only other operations that might be mentioned are those of earthing-up and consolidation ; for crops like onions it may be necessary to tread or roll the soil. Light soils are more often treated in this way than the clays. Crops like Brussels sprouts and onions will appreciate the fact that the soil has been trodden or rolled before the crops are sown or planted out. After the rolling, of course, the top inch or so needs cultivating to produce a surface tilth.

Some vegetable crops like celery, leeks, and potatoes have to be earthed up in the summer so as to bleach them. This earthing-up prevents the green colouring-matter being produced in the stems, which in the case of these crops may cause bitterness, and in the case of potatoes and celery, at any rate, may produce a poison. Such earthing-up not only bleaches, but helps to produce more tender, succulent crops.

Seakale, chicory, and rhubarb are often forced or bleached by earthing-up or covering the earth with strawy manure. Pots or whitewashed continuous cloches are sometimes used to cover the crowns, though seakale and chicory can be produced by the ordinary earthing-up methods to the depth of 12 ins.

CHAPTER II

MANURING AND ARTIFICIAL FERTILISERS

I am often asked " What manure shall I use ? " I therefore give advice in this chapter on :—

1. Farmyard manure and suitable substitutes.
2. The use of artificial manures under their various headings.
3. The danger of using coal ashes.
4. Dual-purpose plant foods.
5. Special mixture of artificials to use with special crops.
6. The importance of lime.

IT is very difficult to lay down hard and fast rules on the subject of the manuring of vegetables, especially in view of the fact that few experiments have been done on the manuring of such crops. It can be said that inorganic manures can never replace organic manures entirely. Many workers, however, believe in addition that humus is extremely important for vegetables, and if the food value, flavour, and quality of vegetables are to be kept at a high level, the application of organic manures each year is an absolute necessity.

Organic manures, whether animal manures or efficient substitutes, assist in the aeration of soil and help to produce a better mechanical and physical condition. It is said that, owing to the lack of humus and the constant application of artificial fertilisers, many of the best soils in England have been turned into what may be described as desert lands.

At any rate there are certainly 250,000,000 acres in America which will never grow food again owing to erosion—and there are vast acreages in India, South Africa, New Zealand, etc. which also have been ruined.

Under poor soil conditions insect pests and diseases are generally rife, and it is far more difficult to control them. If a plant is growing well, is healthy, and has sufficient

21

room for development, then it is not attacked as badly—or at any rate it has the robustness that can withstand an attack. It is the same with the human body.

The main aim, then, of the gardener in the vegetable garden should be to try and supply sufficient humus, and to cultivate regularly. Once the organic material has been provided, the artificial fertilisers may play a useful part in stimulating crops and in supplying deficiencies. The main aim of a book of this kind should be to encourage everyone to produce vegetables of a high standard which can surely play an important part in preventing the diseases to which men are subject.

In the past, market gardeners had little difficulty in obtainin large quantities of farmyard manure, but to-day they find that there is a scarcity. The man with a small garden has always had a difficulty in getting the quantities he requires, and in many districts to-day it can truly be said that farmyard manure is almost unprocurable. As this commodity is expensive and scarce, it is a grand thing to know that experimental work has been done which has resulted in finding a really satisfactory substitute for it, e.g. compost. Humus is necessary to soil, and therefore different substitutes are given later on, together with details for their use.

FARMYARD MANURE

Many people use the term " farmyard manure " in a general way. It more usually applies, however, to cow and pig manure rather than to horse manure, which is usually sold separately.

Animal manures undoubtedly are valuable, not only for their content of organic material, but for the way in which they assist in liberating plant foods already present in soils. They differ greatly, however, in the amount of plant foods they contain. This is due to various factors : firstly to the amount of straw or other litter used, secondly to the method in which the animals are kept, and lastly to the way the manure has been stacked and stored. Manure-heaps that are exposed to the atmosphere lose much of their value through leaching by rain. Overheating, too, has a similar effect, causing the loss of nitrogen as ammonia.

Fresh manure, when dug in, seems to have a harmful effect on soils—scientists call it a de-nitrifying effect. It is important, therefore, to see that such manure is turned at least once before it is dug in. Well-rotted manure is more valuable from the gardener's point of view, even though it may not be quite so rich in plant foods as manure more freshly made. On the other hand, there is no need for the manure to be reduced to dust before it is applied, and, in fact, strawy manure will decompose in the soil, and during such decomposition will cause the temperature of the soil to rise ; this is quite an important point. Not only is the soil temperature raised, but the soil under such conditions is better aerated and kept more open.

It is difficult to give exact amounts of farmyard manure that should be used owing to the conditions mentioned above, but, roughly speaking, one good barrow-load of well-rotted manure should be sufficient for 10 sq. yds.

THE COMPOST HEAP

A very good substitute for dung may be made by the gardener with all the vegetable refuse from the garden or allotment. Many experiments have been and are being done on this very vital and interesting work. But, as a matter of fact, composting is no new method of fertilising the soil. It has been practised for hundreds of years by the Chinese, who are experts at the intensive culture of vegetables.

It is impossible to go into details of all the processes, but one, which has given excellent results and used at The Horticultural Advisory Bureau for a number of years, is as follows :—

A bin made of wood and covered with a corrugated iron roof is used to hold all the vegetable refuse from the house and garden—potato peelings, tea leaves, dead flowers, rotting leaves, hedge clippings, etc., and litter from the rabbit hutches and poultry runs.

These materials are put in to a depth of 6 inches and are well trodden. Calcium Cyanamide or sulphate of ammonia is then sprinkled on at the rate of 2 ozs. per sq. yd. after watering the material. The quantity of water added being con-

COMPOST HEAP

FEEDING ONIONS with FISH MANURE

DIGGING IN COMPOST

trolled by the dampness of the material composted ; it should never be sodden, but thoroughly moist. (Water should not ooze out of the compost when squeezed in the hand.) Successive layers are made in this manner as material becomes available. At the end of 3—6 months, depending on the material composted and the time of the year (quicker in spring and summer, slower in winter when the temperature is low), the compost is ripe, being then a dark, black, sweet-smelling substance, containing ample plant foods and providing the necessary glutinous physical property for binding the soil particles together.

Where no protection is available, heaps made in the open are quite successful, but take longer to mature for the sun dries out the moisture, the winds lower the temperature, and heavy rains give excess moisture. When sulphate of ammonia is used a dusting of lime (preferably powdered quick lime) should be given for every 2 feet. Brittle material, such as straw and the dead stems of herbaceous plants, should be sandwiched between layers of fresh green material, such as grass mowings and cabbage leaves. Where a large quantity of green material is to be composted, it should be allowed to wilt first, otherwise the water content of the heap will be too high and an acid slime will be produced, excluding air and retarding the work of the bacteria. Cabbage stumps and the like should be bashed up with the back of an axe on a chopping block before being used.

Testing for Condition

To test the condition of the compost, make a hole with a trowel in the side of the heap. If it is slimy, wet and sour-smelling, it will be as well to strip off the covering and turn the heap and add drier material and a sprinkling of lime. If it is brittle and smells musty, either add dilute liquid manure or water, or, if possible, turn the heap during rain. The compost is ready for use when it has a pleasant, earthy smell and is of a dark brown colour.

PEAT

This should be forked into the top 2 or 3 inches at the rate of half a bucketful to the square yd. If the soil is dry it is better to soak the peat well first. Peat is an excellent organic aid when de-acified. It should be used more.

GREEN MANURE

One of the ways of adding humus to the soil is by means of "green manure." This consists of growing plants of any kind, which should be dug in long before they come to maturity. Unfortunately, green manures cannot be relied on to produce as good results as farmyard manure, as they do not add phosphates or potash. They are also slow in action, and it may take, for instance, from the autumn to the spring before the green manures have rotted down into a condition suitable for plants to grow in.

Most " green manures " like rye and mustard merely give back to the soil the food taken up during growth, but when members of the legume family are used—clovers, peas, vetches, lupins, and so on—a good deal of nitrogen is collected from the air and is added to the soil. It is not a bad plan for the gardener to sow all the seeds he had over at the end of the season on a patch of land to act as " green manure."

NIGHT SOIL

One is often asked as to the value of human excreta as a manure. The answer is that it is similar in value to that of animals, though the liquid portion is the most valuable. Now that earth-closets are almost extinct, sewers often terminate in sumps, and from these cesspools the liquid naturally drains away. The solid material that is left is of little value as a manure, as all the soluble plant foods have been washed out. Where the liquid does not drain away the value of the material depends on the amount of water it contains. Its value is, however, generally less than the expense entailed in removing it and applying it to the land.

It is to be hoped that town councils will compost sewerage wastes correctly in order to be able to supply gardeners in the districts with sufficient humus.

GUANO

Guanos are sometimes used, though they are rather expensive and are rich in plant foods. Peruvian guano, for instance, decays rapidly, and yields a continuous supply of nitrogen throughout the season. Meat and bone guanos are, however, much used, being made from slaughter-house refuse, condemned meat, and waste carcasses. This is generally applied at from 4 to 6 ozs. per sq. yd. a few weeks before sowing seed or planting out.

HOOF AND HORN

This is a very slow-acting manure which contains nitrogen and phosphates, but no potash. It should be applied in the same way as meat and bone meal.

FISH MANURE

This is quite a popular manure, and is offered by manufacturers more or less free from objectionable odour. It is made from waste fish and fish residues, and, if the makers have removed the oil, it is quite quick-acting. Without any additions it is rich in nitrogen and phosphates, but contains no potash. Some manufacturers do, however, add potash during the process of drying and packing, and it then forms a complete manure. It is usually applied at 2 to 4 ozs. to the sq. yd., as in the case of meat and bone meal.

SPENT HOPS

Spent hops are the residue left behind during the manufacture of beer, and form quite a good substitute for farmyard manure, providing chemical plant foods are added as well. Hops contain no phosphates or potash and only a little nitrogen, but plants seem to root well in the organic medium they provide. They may be dug in in the autumn or spring, or used as a top-dressing along rows of peas and beans during the summer. When dug in they should be used at the rate of 1 lb. to the sq. yd.

SHODDY

Wool shoddy is more valuable than cotton shoddy and it

may be used where obtainable. It is a waste product of the woollen trade, and of the important plant foods contains only nitrogen. To be really valuable it should be free from oil. Shoddy takes a long time to rot down, and should always be dug in in the autumn. It is a suitable manure on heavy soils, and acts as a sponge on light land. It is slow in action, and may take many years to rot down properly. It can be applied at 1 lb. per sq. yd.

SEAWEED

Those who garden near the sea will find seaweed a very practical substitute for organic manure. It is low in phosphate content, but apart from this it is almost as valuable as farm-yard manure, especially when rotted down. It should be applied at the same rate as dung, and may be dug in in the autumn, or used as a top-dressing in the spring.

SOOT

Soot is a nitrogenous manure which is often used in order to help to lighten heavy soils. It also darkens sandy soils and thus enables them to absorb and retain heat better. It is more generally used as a top-dressing in the spring than for digging in in the autumn. It may be applied at 5 ozs. to the sq. yd.

OTHER SUBSTANCES

Occasionally other substitutes for farmyard manure are offered, such as malt culms, greaves (a low grade meat guano), and horticultural peat.

ARTIFICIAL MANURES

Once the gardener has realised that for the successful culture of vegetables the incorporation of plenty of organic material is necessary, he may supplement such manures by the addition of artificial fertilisers.

Artificial Fertilisers may be regarded as " Tonics." The main thing is to dig in ample organic matter each year—and then if necessary add the special tonics according to the needs of the soil or plants.

There are many gardeners who find that they can grow

first-class crops without artificial fertilisers once they have " built up " the humus content of their soils.

Artificial fertilisers, however, should never be used alone.

Remember however, that fertilisers with an organic base such as Fish Manure and Poultry manure do help increase the organic content of soil.

As far as is known at the present time, the three plant foods normally deficient in any soil are nitrogen, phosphates, and potash. Each has its part to play in the building up of the vegetable, though some plants need more of one class of food than another. For instance, cabbages require more nitrogen, while peas need more phosphates.

It is useless to apply one of the substances in the hope that it will make up for a deficiency in the other. These three plant foods should be present in the right proportions if perfect growth is to be obtained. Each of these three groups of food has its own functions and it will be as well to explain these here.

NITROGEN

Nitrogen has to do with the building up of the stems and green leaves of the plant. Nitrogen-starved vegetables are light green in colour and generally small in size. The application of nitrogen will darken leaves and make them larger and more vigorous. When, however, too much nitrogen is given, all the energies of the plant seem to be directed towards the production of leaves and rank shoots, and as a result fruitfulness may be impaired.

If a plant is " soft " owing to overdoses of nitrogen, insects will feed ravenously on the lush growth and the plant will be made liable to fungus diseases. Too much nitrogen defers ripening.

The most commonly used nitrogen fertilisers are sulphate of ammonia, nitrate of soda, calcium cyanamide, and nitrochalk.

Sulphate of Ammonia. Sulphate of ammonia is used more than any other nitrogenous fertiliser to-day. It is not readily washed away in the soil and so is much in demand in areas where the rainfall is heavy. It contains 21 per cent nitrogen, and is generally cheaper per unit than other nitrogenous manure. It can be mixed with superphosphate and sulphate of potash, and, because it releases its nitrogen steadily, may be applied in a single dressing in the spring. It is not, however, usually used as a top-dressing.

Nitrate of Soda. Nitrate of soda provides nitrogen which is immediately available to plants. It is, therefore, very quick-acting, and can be used any time of the season to hasten growth, especially after a cold spell. It should be used in small doses, say at ½ oz. to 1 oz. per yd. run, or 1 lb. to 40 sq. yds. It contains generally 15.6 per cent nitrogen and is useful under sour soil conditions, as it is not acid. It must not be mixed with superphosphate or sulphate of potash.

Calcium Cyanamide. Calcium cyanamide is a black soot-like substance which is somewhat corrosive. It should not be used on growing crops, but should be applied at least ten days before sowing seeds. It is usually equal to sulphate of ammonia in nitrogen content, but has the advantage of containing calcium, or " lime," also. It darkens the soil and so makes it warmer, and, of course, is not acid. It is useful to use on the compost heap to help to rot down woody material and green leaves, and has been found to give a certain amount of control to the club root disease. It is generally applied at the rate of 2 ozs. to the sq. yd.

Nitrochalk. Nitrochalk contains about the same amount of nitrogen as nitrate of soda. Like calcium cyanamide, it contains lime, but it has the advantage of being in a granular form and so can be applied to growing crops. It is quick-acting and has proved a very useful fertiliser on acid soils. It has been much used on members of the cabbage family in order to give them a fillip.

PHOSPHATES

The application of phosphates, or phosphorus compounds, to the soil has an effect on root growth. This increase in root production has, of course, an effect on the production of leaves later on. Phosphatic manures are especially needed by root crops. Crops grown on soils deficient in phosphates may ripen ten days or so later than crops grown on soil containing phosphates. Phosphates seem to help to produce the steady, firm, continuous growth that is most valuable in times of heavy insect attack or during a drought.

Phosphates may be applied as superphosphate, steamed bone flour, bone meal, mineral phosphates, and basic slag.

Superphosphate. Superphosphate may be used by the plant immediately, as it is soluble. It does not, however, wash out easily from the soil, and so may be applied before sowing the seed or putting out plants. If applied as a top-dressing, it may burn the leaves of a growing crop. It can be mixed with sulphate of ammonia, and is a greyish, slightly sticky powder. It may be applied at 1 oz. per sq. yd.

Steamed Bone Flour. Steamed bone flour is a slow-acting manure. It is used for plants such as peas and beans that need a steady supply of phosphates throughout the season. It is generally used at 2 ozs. to the sq. yd.

Bone Meal. Bone meals when sold contain the gelatine which the steamed bone flour does not. They are, therefore, even slower in action than the above manure, and cannot be expected to give such good results.

Mineral Phosphates. Mineral phosphates are not much used by vegetable growers, as superphosphate is preferable, except on permanent borders.

Basic Slag. Basic slag is sometimes applied early in the winter at the rate of 4–6 ozs. to the sq. yd. It will then be of use the following spring. Its best use is probably for soils rich in humus, like the peats, and for very heavy clays. It contains a certain amount of lime.

POTASH

When farmyard manure was easily obtainable, the application of potassic manures was not so important, for a ton of farmyard manure contains 15 lbs. of potash, which is equivalent to-day to about 30 lbs. of sulphate of potash. Potash plays an important part in the production of firm, well-flavoured vegetables. It is needed by all crops, but particularly by the peas and beans. It will help to produce pods of a better

Spraying brussels sprouts with Liquid Derris to control the Blue Bug or Aphis. You have to spray the underneath of of the leaf as well as the upper surface.

The Author looks at his rhubarb forcing pots to see how the plants are getting on. Rhubarb forced in this way is very good indeed.

colour and of greater weight. Plants grown with sufficient potash have firm leaves which are resistant to disease. A healthier, better plant with strong fibre results from potash applications. The lighter soils are normally deficient in this plant food.

The chief potassic fertilisers are sulphate of potash, muriate of potash, kainit, and included in this heading will be placed wood ashes.

Sulphate of Potash. Sulphate of potash may seem an expensive fertiliser, but when valued on its content of potash it will be found to be no dearer than other potassic fertilisers. It is probably the safest artificial manure to use where good quality is required. It can be mixed with sulphate of ammonia and superphosphate. It is generally applied in the spring, and it is not easily washed away from the soil. A good dressing is 1 oz. to the sq. yd.

Muriate of Potash. Muriate of Potash has a similar taste to ordinary common salt. It has an irritating action on the roots of growing plants and may do damage. It is not to be recommended for the vegetable garden.

Kainit. Kainit is the cheapest form of potash sold. It is more impure than muriate of potash and contains many other salts such as Epsom salts and chloride of magnesia. It is used for crops like asparagus, beetroot, and celery because of the salt it contains, but should not be used on the heavy and silty soils, as it tends to make them set hard like cement. Applied to these crops, it is used at 2 to 3 ozs. per sq. yd.

Wood Ashes. Wood ashes are included under this heading, although they are not truly an artificial manure. They contain a very small percentage of potash, and are only one-twelfth as valuable as sulphate of potash. Their value mainly lies in the improvement of soil texture, and as bonfire ashes have to be used they provide a cheap form of manure.

N.B. Mr. J. Featherstone, M.Sc., the Lecturer in Chemistry at the Cheshire School of Agriculture, who has kindly gone through this chapter for me, examined many forms of coal ashes sent in by listeners as the result of my broadcast talks, and he found them to be definitely dangerous, chiefly because

B

of the sulphur compounds they contain. I personally have known soils that have been ruined by the use of coal ashes.

DUAL-PURPOSE PLANT FOODS

There are artificials on the market at the moment that contain more than one plant food. One would instance Chilean potash nitrate, nitrate of potash, and phosphate of potash.

Chilean Potash Nitrate. Chilean potash nitrate is similar to nitrate of soda, but contains 15 per cent of potash as well as 15 per cent of nitrogen. It is dearer than nitrate of soda, but is very useful to use on plants that need these two plant foods immediately. Applied, for instance, to plants like cabbages on light soils, this manure will help to produce not only a greater bulk of leaves, but a darker and better-hearted cabbage as a whole. It is usually used at the same rate as nitrate of soda.

Nitrate of Potash. Nitrate of potash contains nitrogen and potash also, but it is an expensive manure to use. When vegetables are being grown for exhibition, it is sometimes purchased and applied in very small quantities.

Phosphate of Potash. Phosphate of potash is highly concentrated and expensive. It is seldom used on crops grown out of doors.

SUITABLE MIXTURES FOR VARIOUS CROPS

It is possible to obtain fertilisers mixed in the correct proportions containing nitrogen, phosphates, and potash. These vary in price according to the plant foods they contain, and should always be bought on analysis. Those who wish to mix up their own manures should purchase sulphate of ammonia, superphosphate, and sulphate of potash, and vary the mixture according to the requirements of the plant.

For peas use :
    1 part sulphate of ammonia
    4 parts superphosphate
    2 parts sulphate of potash

For root crops use:
1 part sulphate of ammonia
5 parts superphosphate
1 part sulphate of potash

For the more permanent crops use:
1 part sulphate of ammonia
2 parts superphosphate
2 parts steamed bone flour
2 parts sulphate of potash

As a general manure apply:
1 part sulphate of ammonia
3 parts superphosphate
1 part sulphate of potash

On light soils and for salt-loving plants:
1 part sulphate of ammonia
3 parts superphosphate
2 parts kainit

For potatoes and onions use:
1 part sulphate of ammonia
2 parts superphosphate
2 parts sulphate of potash

Once these mixtures have been prepared they should usually be applied at 3 ozs. to the sq. yd.

N.B. The reason that these three artificials have been chosen is that they can be mixed with one another without any danger of harming the plants. Nitrate of soda should never be mixed with superphosphate, since the two react chemically and nitrogen may be lost. Beginners are advised to keep to the mixtures outlined and not to attempt special ideas of their own.

LIME

Lime is not only important in "sweetening" soil and preventing it from becoming acid, but in itself it plays its part as a plant food. The calcium in lime is valuable, and the basic part is also valuable in neutralising soil acids. On heavy soils, lime improves the texture and the workability. It is surprising how friable clays become after years of regular lime applications. Another function of lime is to help to release other plant foods ; it helps to decompose humus and organic compounds in the soil and releases potash to be used as plant food.

Lime should always be used for the cabbage and pea and bean family, but it is not so important for potatoes and roots. Regular applications of lime make it possible to keep down the club root disease.

If applied at 7 ozs. to the sq. yd. once every three years, to the break on which the cabbage family is grown, it should keep the soil in good condition.

Method of Application.   Lime should never be dug in, for it washes down into the soil very quickly. It should be sprinkled on to the surface of the ground, and will, of course, be forked or hoed in during the cultural operations.

Lime should not be mixed with the acid artificial manures already mentioned ; these should be forked in first of all and the lime applied as a top-dressing. Lime should not be mixed, either, with farmyard manure.

Kinds of Lime.   There are three main types of lime, the most important of which to the vegetable grower is perhaps hydrated lime.   This is convenient to handle, as it is generally sold in bags.   It is not so valuable, however as quicklime.

Quicklime, sometimes sold as lump lime or Buxton lime (this is sometimes ground into powder and sold as ground lime), has to be slacked down on the soil.   It is often difficult to obtain.

Chalk or Limestone, which is often sold as ground limestone, is half as valuable as quicklime, and must, therefore, be used at a heavier rate.   The usual rate of application is 7 ozs. to the sq. yd. of hydrated lime, and for ground lime 5 ozs. to the sq. yd.

CHAPTER III

THE PLANNING AND LAY-OUT OF THE VEGETABLE GARDEN

A garden has to have a plan as much as a house—even the vegetable garden !

1. Which is the warmest part of the garden?
2. How will a rotation fit in?
3. What kind of path is best in the vegetable garden?
4. What about the hedge?
5. Do you like flowers in the vegetable garden?
6. Fruit trees can often be a nuisance among vegetables.

THIS is obviously going to be one of the most difficult chapters to write, because it is impossible to visualise all readers' proposed vegetable gardens. Some of them will be long and narrow ; others wide and broad ; some of three-quarters of an acre and others just a rod. It will only be possible, then, to make some general observations, in the hope that these may be adapted to suit any garden that is going to be laid out.

It will be necessary to accept the fact that the garden will be either rectangular or square, though there are vegetable gardens planned by garden architects so that they are perfectly round, and in at least one case this circular kitchen garden is surrounded by a 12 ft. wall. Such a garden is difficult to work, and though as a design it may please the architect, it is a great nuisance to the gardener when he comes to arrange his rows and his rotations.

The garden should be so designed that the rows of vegetables may be arranged to run north and south. When the rows have to run east and west, far more shadows are thrown, and as a result the crops are not so early, and not, perhaps, so good. Those with small gardens appreciate short rows, because they can then arrange to have a greater variety. When the rows are of good length running north and south

PLANNING AND LAYOUT

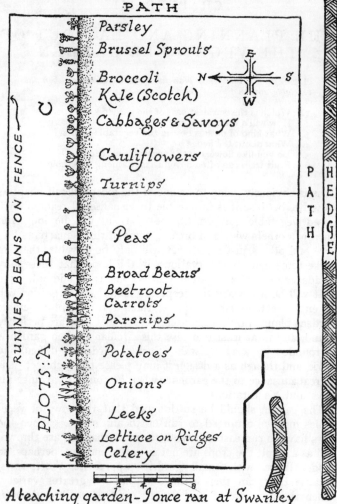

A teaching garden—I once ran at Swanley

A SIMPLE GARDEN PLAN

Unusual
Vegetables

Herbs

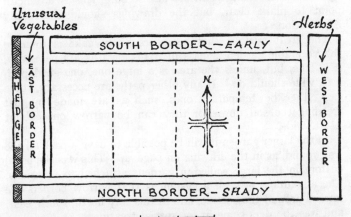

North border—shady plan with SOUTH BORDER—EARLY, EAST BORDER, WEST BORDER, HEDGE, NORTH BORDER—SHADY, N compass

SOUTH BORDER—EARLY

HEDGE

EAST BORDER

N

WEST BORDER

NORTH BORDER—SHADY

15 0 15 30 45

MAKING the MOST USE of YOUR SPACE

Soil
Manure

Leeks in Trenches
with Intercrops

Soil
Manure

in a small area, it means obviously that the numbers of rows
are perforce curtailed. Under such conditions it is a nuisance
to sow a quarter row of one variety and continue with a
quarter row of another variety and so on. This is a difficult
point to make clear, but the drawings should clarify my
explanation.

The great mistake that beginners often make is to have
the vegetable garden a mass of paths. Paths are necessary,
it is true, but, unless the area is a large one, one good path
4 ft. wide should do. If any other paths are necessary, these
can either be temporary ones, such as are made by just
treading the soil down, or they can be narrow ones about
2½ ft. wide.

In the larger garden it will be possible to have a path all the
way round, as in the drawing on page 39. This was the usual
custom in the large walled-in gardens attached to mansions.
The advantage of such a system is that narrow borders are
formed around the outside, and in this way north, south, east,
and west borders come in for special treatment.

The south border will be the warmest border of all, and is
generally used for the early crops. It tends to be on the dry
side, and so has to receive copious waterings. If there is a
fence or wall at the back of it, this is useful for growing dessert
plums, or even an apricot or peach. The east border is quite
suitable for permanent crops like seakale, rhubarb, and globe
artichokes. Such crops as the perennial spinach may be
grown there also. The north border, being the most shady
border of all, can be used for later crops—for marrows, for
kohlrabi, and so on. These narrow borders are useful because
it enables very short rows of special crops to be grown, and
those who are fond of the unusual vegetables (see Chapter XI)
will find the south and north borders just wide enough for the
few rows to be grown. The west border can be used for a
seed bed or for frames.

It is most useful, where rotations are to be carried out (see
Chapter IV), for the main part of this garden to be divided up
into three or four parts by means of a wire fence and posts,
on which fruit can be trained, apples on the cordon system,

for instance, or blackberries and loganberries. Those who do not care for fruit may use these semi-permanent erections for the growing of runner beans, marrows, or even tall varieties of peas. There is no need to have any line of demarcation in this way, but, human nature being what it is, such divisions do help the gardener to follow out a definite rotation. In the smaller garden the path may just go down one side, as in drawing. In this case the seed-beds had to be in between the rows of other vegetables, and fitted in as space allowed. It was only possible to cater for a three-course rotation, and a very narrow pathway was allowed for on the east side. The drawing shown is an actual garden 58 ft. long and 42 ft. wide, which was used by the writer as a demonstration garden for a schoolmasters' course. It was chosen as being quite typical of the small vegetable garden that might be made at the bottom of the lawn ; the hedge in the plan divided the flower-garden from the vegetables.

With regard to the paths themselves, these may be made with cinders, gravel, crazy paving, or concrete. Somehow with vegetables the crazy paving or flag path is not quite in keeping, and the gravel or concrete path is more lasting and will stand the constant barrowing that has perforce to be done. If the gravel path can be tarred or covered with one of the more modern bitumen compounds, so much the better, for it is easier to keep clean and there is less danger of taking portions of the path on one's feet on to the garden. This is one of the greatest disadvantages of the cinder path.

Whatever paths are made, they should have a good foundation. It must be porous, so that excess moisture can get away, and this porosity can be achieved by the use of clinkers, old iron, flints, and similar material, buried 3 ft. down. If the pathway can be excavated to this depth, then all kinds of waste material can be buried. This can be covered with larger stones, and finally the gravel can be put into position. A 2 in. layer of gravel is enough, and a ton of gravel will cover 18 sq. yds.

The concrete path is perhaps the cleanest and most durable of all. It should have the same solid foundation on to which the

B*

concrete may be laid. Following are a few essential instructions on the putting down of concrete.

Remove the turf or soil and then consolidate the ground by rolling. Put down some strong pieces of wood 2 ins. in depth and drive a few pegs in to keep this wood in position (see photograph). These strips of wood help to keep the concrete in position while the path is being made.

On clean wood or stone floor mix up the cement, using two buckets of sand, one bucket of cement, and three buckets of shingle. Mix the cement and sand first by turning over and over with the shovel, then add the shingle and repeat the process. After this add a little water from time to time, and for this quantity of material not more than three-quarters of a bucketful of water will be required.

Damp the surface of the soil where the concrete is to be put before placing into position, but if the soil is sodden spread some newspapers on the top and place the concrete on them. Do not put down too much concrete at a time. Level off the concrete by working a piece of wood forward over the surface, the two sides of the wood resting on the wooden edges.

Try and prevent new concrete from drying out too quickly, so cover up the path, when laid, with damp sacks.

One bag of Portland cement, $3\frac{3}{4}$ cubic ft. of shingle, and $2\frac{1}{2}$ cubic feet of sand will make enough concrete to lay a path 2 ft. wide, 2 ins. thick, and 15 ft. long. See that the concrete is put into its position within thirty minutes of mixing. Always use clean materials.

Apart from the fruit-trees that are used to divide the main part of a large vegetable garden into its plots, it is unwise to plant fruit-trees where vegetables are to grow. The trees have to be sprayed from time to time, and the spray damages the crops below. Further, the trees provide shade and their roots rob the ground. There is also the problem of manuring, for whereas vegetables need plenty of organic manure, dessert apples, for instance, require a minimum of nitrogen.

Again, it seems hardly necessary to attempt to disguise the kitchen garden by planting a herbaceous border right through the middle of it. Let the kitchen garden be the kitchen garden, and not a general muddle ! It is far easier to grow the best crops of the highest food value if they are on their own and can be given the conditions they require.

By all means let the situation be an open one, and do not hedge it about with tall trees. Quite a dwarf hedge, say of *Lonicera nitida*, will make an excellent division between it and the flower-garden. These remarks do not apply, of course, to the large walled-in garden, but few to-day can afford such a luxury. There is nothing ugly in vegetables, especially when well grown. The necessity for keeping the lines straight when sowing and planting vegetable crops, and the almost soldier-like rows and distances adopted, do give an air of utility, but this does not mean to say that it is anything to be ashamed of.

The allotment may be planned in a similar way to the small garden that the schoolmasters used, though allotments, generally have paths on either side. The size and length of an allotment is not settled by the owner, and so the planning must conform with the general outline.

Again, all that can be said is to keep the paths down to a minimum and to make the plan a useful one for the production of the best crops possible.

CHAPTER IV

ROTATIONS AND CROPPING

You ask me questions on this important subject and I answer in detail telling you about :—

1. The possible chance of land deteriorating.
2. How a rotation helps to keep down pests and diseases.
3. Why a rotation saves time and labour.
4. A good three-course rotation.

IN planning out the garden in the previous chapter, mention has to be made of rotations. The word rotation is one which is not easily understood, and nor, evidently, is the need for rotations, for in one's experience in various counties of England, either as the county adviser or as garden editor to the B.B.C., one has found again and again that crops are ravaged by diseases largely because rotational principles are entirely neglected.

In the garden it can truthfully be said that a rotation is a system by which vegetables of the same character do not follow one another on the same piece of ground year after year. The use of the words " vegetables of the same character " is important, and allows for crops not necessarily related to be grown side by side for some other reason than their affinity. For instance, one can classify the deep-rooting crops together, or the shallow-rooting crops. The vegetables like the peas and beans, that enrich the soil with nitrogen, can all go into one group. Each of these groups may need a particular type of cultivation ; each may require certain manures. Thus by keeping vegetables of the same character together it is possible to treat them largely as one.

This is the first step towards rotation—the classification by one method or another of the crops to be grown into groups, and seeing that the group is grown in one particular part. The next thing is to see that that group does not remain on

44

the same plot of land year after year. Take the pea and bean family, for instance ; they have the power to add nitrogen to the soil ; they do not necessarily need this nitrogen themselves ; sensible gardeners therefore grow their peas and beans in different parts of the garden every year, so that each part in its turn may be enriched at no cost to themselves.

There are many reasons why rotation should be carried out. Land which gets the same treatment year after year tends to deteriorate. Crops, for instance, that only need shallow cultivation would only receive shallow cultivation, and thus the land they were grown in year after year would never be cultivated deeply. Rotation prevents the exhaustion of a particular plant food in the soil. A particular crop may take from the soil large quantities of certain plant foods, and so the growing of this crop, or group of crops, on one plot of land may tend to produce the impoverishment of the soil in some directions.

Then, again, one crop can leave the land in a better condition than another. The growing of celery in trenches, for instance, ensures deep cultivation, and thus provides excellent soil for crops that are to come after. To return to the peas and beans, these leave nitrogen of which the cabbage family can make much use, and so better crops result.

It is possible, too, by means of rotations to keep down pests and diseases. The obvious example is club root. When members of the cabbage family are grown for years on the same piece of land, the club root disease tends to increase year after year, until, as is the case of many allotments in England, cabbages are practically impossible to grow. If rotations had been carried out, the cabbage crop would have never been on one plot of land more than one year in four, and this would have given a chance of eradicating the disease. Pests too, like carrot fly, find it far easier to damage a crop, if the carrot seeds are sown directly on top of the place where the chrysalids are buried after the previous year's attack.

It is said that some plants excrete what are known as toxins or " poisons." These toxins accumulate after a time when plants are grown on the same land continuously, and are

A TYPICAL 3 COURSE ROTATION

	Year 1	Year 2	Year 3
Plot A	Potatoes	Roots	Brassicas
" B	Roots	Brassicas	Potatoes
" C	Brassicas	Potatoes	Roots

FOUR COURSE ROTATION

	Year 1	Year 2	Year 3	Year 4
Plot A	Potatoes	Peas & Beans	Brassicas	Roots
" B	Peas & Beans	Brassicas	Roots	Potatoes
" C	Brassicas	Roots	Potatoes	Peas & Beans
" D	Roots	Potatoes	Peas & Beans	Brassicas

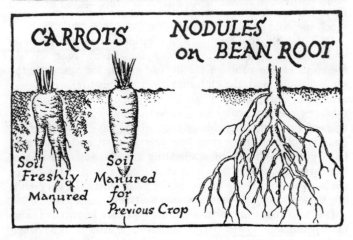

CARROTS   NODULES on BEAN ROOT

Soil Freshly Manured   Soil Manured for Previous Crop

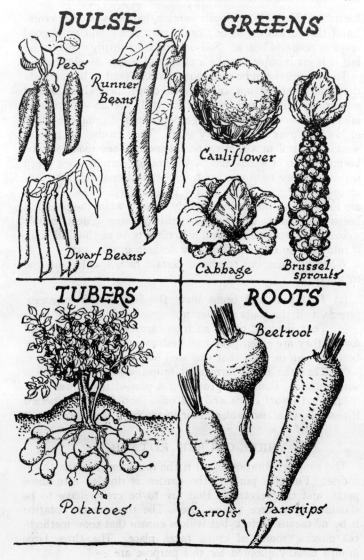

PULSE
Peas

Runner Beans

Dwarf Beans

GREENS
Cauliflower

Cabbage

Brussel sprouts

TUBERS
Potatoes

ROOTS
Beetroot

Carrots

Parsnips

harmful. They are, curiously enough, harmless to other crops. Land that is known to be "cauliflower sick" will grow good crops of peas and beans. Soil sickness is not easily explainable, but it is inadvisable to take a chance of toxins developing.

To sum up, it can be said that rotations (and to be complete they are rotations not only of the crops themselves, but of manuring, tilling, and working as well) are an economy in labour, because they save the gardener from digging the whole of his land over deeply every year. They ensure the regular working of soil in a systematic manner. They make for the keeping down of weeds and they allow for periods when green manuring may be carried out. Any rotational scheme gives an opportunity for liming, as the break on which the cabbages are to be grown will be limed fairly heavily, while the peas and beans will have, say just a light dressing. Most people welcome any scheme that will help them to be methodical, and, if rotations do nothing else, they do help in this way.

When planning out rotations, certain facts should be borne in mind :

(1) That peas and beans leave the land rich in nitrogen, especially if the roots are left in.

(2) That the root crops, such as carrots and beetroot, will fork if they are given plenty of fresh manure, and so they are better grown on land that was well manured the year before.

(3) That the more permanent crops, which may interfere with rotation, should be grown on a plot of their own.

(4) That dwarf crops and tall ones should be interspersed if possible, to allow light and air to reach all the crops.

THREE-COURSE ROTATION

The simplest rotation of all is the one known as the three-course. For this purpose the garden is divided into three parts, and the vegetables that are to be grown have to be classified into three groups also. The three-course rotation is by no means perfect, but it does ensure that some methodical moving round of crops takes place. The three large groups usually adopted for this purpose are :—

(1) The cabbage family, which will include the Brussels sprouts, cauliflowers, etc.

(2) The root crops.

(3) The group consisting mainly of potatoes.

It is very difficult indeed to get three large groups, but it will be seen that deep-rooting crops do alternate with the shallow-rooting ones ; for fear of club root, turnips should be classified with the cabbage family.

It is difficult in such a rotation to know exactly how to cater for celery and leeks, but these may be fitted in as on page 38, or it is possible to use these as the dividing-lines between the larger crops.

FOUR-COURSE ROTATION

The four-course rotation is the one usually adopted, and it is comparatively easy to divide all the crops up into four large groups.

Group 1. Early potatoes, second early potatoes, and perhaps, if necessary, the main crop, though these are often grown on their own.

Group 2. The pea and bean family : runner beans, broad beans, French beans, and peas ; and here, if necessary, the celery, leeks, onions, and shallots may be included. (Those who need few potatoes should grow celery, leeks, and onions on the potato break.)

Group 3. The root crops : parsnips, carrots, beetroot, salsify, and scorzonera.

Group 4. The Brassica family, i.e. cabbages, cauliflowers, Brussels sprouts, kale, kohlrabi, turnips, and swedes.

It will be noticed that other crops have not been included— lettuce and spinach, for instance—but these may be grown as intercrops or catch-crops wherever possible without interfering with the main scheme. The chives and the parsley can make edgings, and the permanent crops can be planted together on their own. The plans that follow should explain how the rotations are worked. It will be seen that in the case of the three-course the main scheme is potatoes, then roots, then Brassicas ; while in the four-course the idea is that potatoes should be followed by peas, then by Brassicas, and finally by the roots. Alternative plans are possible, so that it will be seen that there are no hard and fast rules in this connection.

CHAPTER V

CLASSIFICATION OF VEGETABLES

This is not perhaps one of the most interesting chapters, but a necessary one.

Crops can be classified in various ways :—

1. Natural Orders.
2. By the part of the crop which is eaten.
3. Annual *versus* permanent crops.

VEGETABLES can be classified in all kinds of ways : according to their time of cropping, according to their times of sowing, by their natural orders, by the way their roots grow, or by the way they bear the edible portion.

For instance, to take the first case—the time of cropping : various vegetables are known by the prefix " spring." This means to say that the crop concerned comes into use in the spring-time. It is well worth while to note this, because very often students fall into the error of imagining that a spring cabbage is a cabbage whose seed has to be sown in the spring, when of course it is a cabbage that is cut and used in the spring.

It would be possible to classify crops into groups according to the approximate times or dates on which they were sown. Obviously the two big groups in this case would be the spring sown and the autumn sown vegetables, while there might be another group known as the summer sowing varieties. There seems little advantage in such arbitrary classifications, and their only convenience is to remind the beginner when the sowings should take place.

All known plants are, however, classified by botanists into what are called natural orders. Natural orders are divided

LEAFSTALK and STEM CROPS

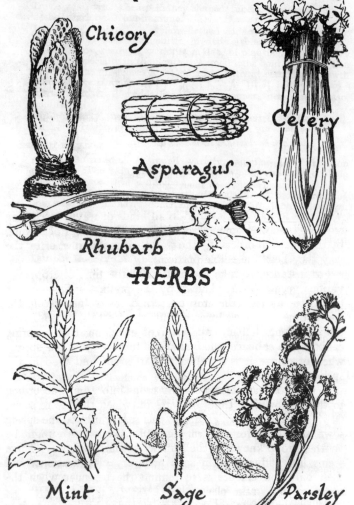

Chicory

Celery

Asparagus

Rhubarb

HERBS

Mint   Sage   Parsley

BULBS

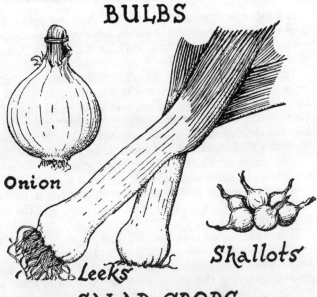

Onion

Leeks

Shallots

SALAD CROPS

Corn Salad

Mustard & Cress

Lettuce

Endive

into smaller groups, or genera, while these are again divided into species. Some natural orders have many species, while others only have one or two. Within the species themselves there may be varieties.

There is an advantage in knowing something about natural orders, because in this way one can have a very rough guess as to how the vegetables themselves should be grown and what diseases and pests they are likely to be subject to. Take the big family Cruciferæ which contains the kales, cabbages, sprouts, radish, mustard and cress, and so on—all this family is liable to be attacked by the club root disease. Therefore if one wishes to know whether such and such a plant is liable to be attacked by club root or not, then all that has to be done is to find out to which natural order it belongs, and the matter is soon decided.

It is well known that bacteria live on the roots of some vegetables, in symbiosis. This means to say that these special bacteria have the power of abstracting the nitrogen from the air and attaching this to the roots in the form of small white nodules. They do this without harming the roots at all. These roots, then, are rich in nitrogenous foods, and should be left behind for the crop that is to follow after. Which plants, then, have the power of enriching the soil in this way ? The members of the Leguminosæ family.

There are other reasons also which make it quite advisable for even the beginner to know into which natural orders fall the vegetables which he is going to grow. These reasons are not always self-evident, but they will become self-evident as experience increases.

There are actually ninety-six natural orders, but only ten of them affect the vegetable grower. They are as follows in alphabetical order :

Chenopodiaceæ.

Beetroot, spinach.

Compositæ.

Artichoke (globe and Jerusalem), chicory, endive, lettuce, salsify, scorzonera.

Cruciferæ.

Broccoli, Brussels sprouts, cabbage, cauliflower, kale, mustard and cress, horse-radish, radish, seakale, swede, turnip, water-cress, kohlrabi.

Curcurbitaceæ.

Cucumber, vegetable marrow, squash, pumpkin.

Labiatæ.

Balm, basil, marjoram, mint, pennyroyal, thyme, sage.

Leguminosæ.

Beans (broad, French, and runner), peas.

Liliaceæ.

Asparagus, chives, leek, onion, shallot.

Polygonaceæ.

Rhubarb.

Solanaceæ.

Eggplant, potato, tomato.

Umbelliferæ.

Carrot, celery, fennel, parsley, parsnip.

The last two methods of classification concern the way the roots grow or the place where the edible portion is produced. This is the kind of classification that most people find very easy to remember, and which always seems self-evident. Such a classification is always useful when planning a rotation, and it will be seen that in Chapter IV most of the rotations are conceived from such a simple grouping. The classifications may be grouped together if necessary, and very often, for instance, the tubers are grown with the bulbs because they both need heavy manuring and constant cultivation.

A convenient method of classifying the commoner grown vegetables is as follows :—

Bulbs.   Leeks, onions, shallots

Greens.   Broccoli, Brussels sprouts, cabbage, kale, savoys.

Herbs.	Fennel, marjoram, mint, parsley, sage, thyme.
Pulse.	Broad beans, French beans, runner beans, peas.
Root Crops.	Beetroot, carrot, parsnip, swedes, turnips, salsify, scorzonera.
Salad Crops.	Corn salad, endive, lettuce, mustard and cress.
Leafstalk and Stem Crops.	Asparagus, chicory, celery, rhubarb, seakale.
Tubers.	Artichokes (Jerusalem), potatoes.

It will be noticed that even these classifications are not complete, because many of the salads and more unusual vegetables are not mentioned. So many of the salads are temporary crops that they hardly effect rotation, while only a few of the unusual vegetables will be grown, and probably not more than a short row even then, in, say, the west border.

It is often convenient to have a classification of permanent crops, and if this is done rhubarb and asparagus naturally come in tògether. Though the Jerusalem artichoke has been grouped with the potatoes, it is seldom that these appear on the same plot of land, because, where the potato likes rich land, the Jerusalem artichoke will grow in any odd corner and needs no special manuring.

CHAPTER VI

THE USE OF FRAMES AND CLOCHES

More cloches and frames are used to-day than ever before.
Help is given in connection with :—

1. The making of the hot-bed.
2. The use of the cold frame.
3. The Dutch light *versus* the English light.
4. The continuous use of the continuous cloche.
5. The vegetables that can be grown under these glass protectors.

THE vegetable-grower, even though he may have quite a small garden at his disposal, should seriously consider the use of frames and cloches. A frame is extraordinarily useful in raising plants for putting out into their permanent position later on, for helping other plants to over-winter so that much earlier crops result in the spring, or for growing vegetables like cucumbers, which do not get much of a chance to produce heavy crops in the open.

The frame may be a permanent brick-built one or can be quite a temporary structure with wooden sides. It may be quite a cold frame or one which is heated by means of hot-water pipes, or even to-day by electricity. The frame may be a " hot " one, and for this purpose a special manure hot-bed may be made to produce the heat required.

Cloches, too, are invaluable in giving plants protection during the colder months of the year and in the colder parts of England. After all, in England we usually have only seven good growing months in the normal way, but with cloches one can keep plants growing over a far longer period.

It will be impossible in this chapter to mention all the uses to which frames and cloches may be put. From time to time, however, throughout the book suggestions will appear as to when seeds may be sown in frames or when plants may be protected by them. Similarly, the keen vegetable-grower will find all kinds of uses for the cloches once they are in his possession. They can be moved from crop to crop, and as a result the vegetables will come into use much earlier. It is possible for cloches to be in use all the year round.

THE HOT-BED

The hot-bed is very useful for producing vegetables at a time of the year when they are rather scarce. It is always best to use horse manure, and when a quantity has been obtained it should be stacked until required. A hot-bed is usually made up in January.

When required, the manure is turned several times at intervals of two or three days, and this allows the steam and ammonia gas to escape. When turning, the manure must be thoroughly mixed and all the hard lumps broken up. In the case of fresh manure, it is sometimes necessary to water the heap to prevent it from burning. If old and new dung can be mixed together during the turning process, so much the better. In ten days or a fortnight's time the manure should be ready to put into the frame.

Sufficient should be placed into position so that when it is trodden down it is at least 8 ins. thich. It may then be covered with soil 4 to 6 ins. deep. If this soil can consist largely of well-rotted leaves put through an eighth-inch sieve, or old sifted hot-bed manure, so much the better. In the French garden, old sifted hot-beds are used entirely as soil in which to grow the plants. The glass light may then be put into position and the soil will commence to heat. It is always better to have a sunken hot-bed such as has been described than a raised hot-bed, as tested by some growers. A sunken hot-bed gives a more steady and lasting heat.

In such a frame various vegetables may be grown ; for instance, carrots, the seed being sown broadcast and the most suitable variety being *Demi-longue à forcer*. Lettuce can be grown at the same time as the carrots, if desired, the variety to use here being *Gotte à forcer*. The plants that are put in, say, the third week in January at 9 ins. square should be raised by sowing the lettuce seed outside during the first week in October. These lettuces are kept from being damaged by the weather by being pricked out under cloches at the end of October.

When the grower becomes expert he will find that it is possible to sow turnips in the same frame at the beginning of April, using *Demi-longue à forcer*. Two seeds are put in 10 ins. apart between the rows of lettuce. There are thus three crops growing in the one frame.

The lettuce will soon be cut, and then the lights may be taken off and the turnips and carrots used as desired. This is really a modified form of what is called French gardening.

The hot-bed can, of course, be used for other purposes than this. It will grow good crops of cucumbers if it is made up later in the season. It can be used to raise plants like maize and egg plants where a greenhouse is not available. It can be used to raise onions, leeks, and celery plants which need sowing early in the year.

THE COLD-FRAME

The cold frame is similar to the hot-bed frame except that there is, of course, no bottom heat. It is useful for protecting autumn-sown seeds. Thousands of cauliflowers are kept in this country throughout the winter for putting out in the spring. Parsley can be covered, and so can winter spinach or late endive. The frame comes in useful too, for hardening off plants that have been raised in a glasshouse or in a hot-bed. The grower may have a small greenhouse and wish to clear it partially for raising another crop. It is then that the cold frame comes in useful, as many of the plants can be accommodated there. It acts, therefore, as a go-between between the greenhouse or the hot-bed and the open air.

Many crops can be grown earlier even in a cold frame. Lettuces, radishes, carrots, peas, and beans can all be produced earlier with the help of such a frame.

There is no need for this to be elaborately built. There are many frames on the market to-day that consist only of a bottomless box on which a glass light is placed. Temporary

FRAMES and CLOCHES

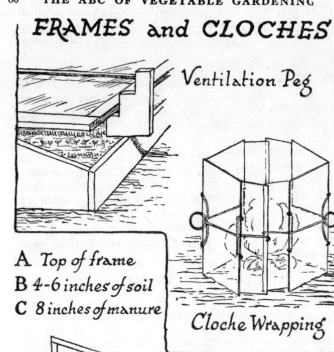

Ventilation Peg

A Top of frame
B 4-6 inches of soil
C 8 inches of manure

Cloche Wrapping

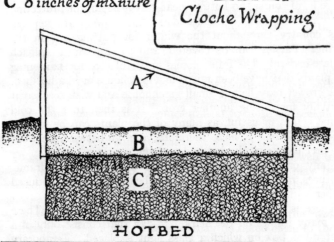

HOTBED

FRAMES and CLOCHES

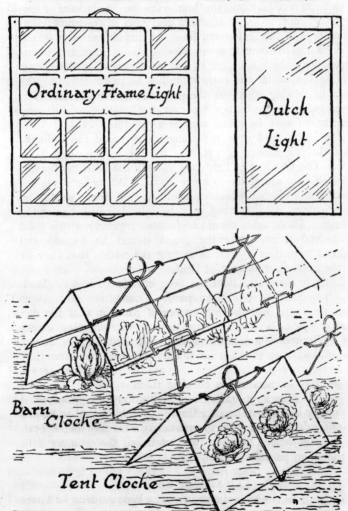

Ordinary Frame Light

Dutch Light

Barn Cloche

Tent Cloche

frames can always be made by the use of a few boards back and front on which a light may rest.   The back of the frame may be 12 ins. high and the front 9 ins., or, in the case of low-growing crops, 10 ins. at the back and 7 ins. at the front.   The advantage of the temporary frame of this character is that it may be moved about to cover growing plants, to protect plants throughout the winter, or to put over crops for the spring. During the winter the cold frame has to be covered up with mats or sacking whenever there is any danger of frost.   The crops grown in the frames, however, need not be coddled, and ventilation may be given whenever possible.

The lights used over the frames may be of the ordinary English type, measuring 4 ft. by 4 ft., 6 ft. by 4 ft., or 7 ft. by 5 ft.   The two former lights are usually the most convenient because they are easier to move about.   Whatever lights are used, the gardener should remember that these should be standardised, so that they may be interchangeable over the frames.   These lights should be painted regularly with a good white-lead paint, while the panes should be washed and cleaned from time to time so as to make certain that they let in the maximum amount of light.

Latterly the Dutch light has been introduced into England, which consists of one large pane.   These have advantages over the lights with large numbers of panes in that the dirt that creeps in between the overlapping panes of glass makes for a tremendous amount of shade.   The Dutch lights are not paned, and when they are laid side by side over the frames they fit so tightly together because they are not paned that there is no seepage of moisture in between them.

The woodwork of frames and lights may be preserved if necessary by a substance like Cuprinol.   This is said to have a less harmful effect on plant growth than gas tar or Stockholm tar.

The comparison between the Dutch and the ordinary light is shown on page 61.

CLOCHES

Continuous cloches are now in use by keen gardeners all over the country.   As a matter of fact they are very popular in

U.S.A. also, where they are called " miniature greenhouses."
There are three main types of Continuous Cloches in use—the
Tent, see figure 1, the Barn, see figure 2, and the Tomato T,
see figure 3.   As a matter of fact there are various sizes to be
had in both the Tent and Barn but generally speaking the Low
Barn pattern is in the greatest demand for the general run of
crops, and the Tomato T for tomatoes and taller crops like
broad beans and peas.

The word " continuous " used with cloches is intended to
demonstrate the importance of putting the cloches up in a
continuous row to get the maximum effect, and just as you
would not have a greenhouse without ends so is it important
not to have a continuous cloche row without ends ; the closing
of the ends is done with a sheet of glass with a bamboo or wire
stake driven in to keep the end pane firmly in position, the top
of which can easily be tied to the top of the nearest cloche.

Cloches when put into position a fortnight before seed
sowing warm the ground and so ensure a sufficiently high soil
temperature to promote rapid germination.   They also prevent
the soil from becoming sodden due to heavy rain, and thus
enable the gardener to get his seed sowing done just when he
wants to.   It is such a nuisance to make up your mind to sow
a particular crop on a Saturday afternoon and then to find
that owing to a heavy rain on the Friday the condition of
the soil makes it impossible to do so.

Cloches also prevent land from becoming frozen ; by their
warming effect they also enable seed to be sown many weeks
earlier in the open.   Cloches prevent the wind from beating on
the leaves of plants, so preventing excessive transpiration and
actual physical damage.   Cloches trap the sun's rays and
seem to bottle them up for the plants but, of course, they
cannot manufacture sunshine.   Crops under cloches mature
more quickly and because they are not so long on the ground
a larger number of crops can be taken from a particular strip
of land in the season.   Cloches are self-ventilating.   They
are not like frames that have to be attended to regularly.
Their construction ensures the right ventilation day in and
day out.

It has been suggested that cloches keep the rain off plants but this isn't so.   What happens is that the rain does not, of course, actually fall on the leaves of the plants themselves and cause them to be mud splashed (an important point with spinach and lettuce) but it does reach the roots by penetrating the ground on either side of the cloches and so seeping in well underneath.   It is important, however, to prepare the ground properly before the cloches are put into position and to see that ample well rotted compost is buried a spade's depth (I use a good bucketful to the sq. yd.) and that damp horticultural peat is worked into the top 2 or 3 inches at $\frac{1}{2}$ a pailful to the square yard.

Some crops like lettuces, for instance, can be grown under cloches from start to finish.   Other crops are just started under continuous cloches and are then uncovered and are allowed to grow in the open.   It is possible in addition to start peas off under a Tent cloche and then substitute for this Barn cloches when the plants have grown taller and finally to cover with T cloches to give the extra height.   Continuous cloches are so made that they can easily be moved about and stacked by up-ending them when they fit neatly one into the other, and thus take up the least amount of room.   There is never any need to take cloches to pieces and in fact the gardener who plans carefully will have the majority of his cloches in use all the time.

USING THE CONTINUOUS CLOCHES

It would be impossible in a book of this size to deal with all the ways in which continuous cloches may be used over vegetables and those who are desirous of the fullest information on the subject should consult the book " The A.B.C. of Continuous Cloches " by the same author.

It is obvious that cloches are invaluable in the winter and early spring for they enable the plants to go on growing in what would otherwise be adverse circumstances.   They are also ideal in the north and colder districts and they can turn the north as it were, into the warmer south ; they are particularly useful near industrial towns and cities for they keep the

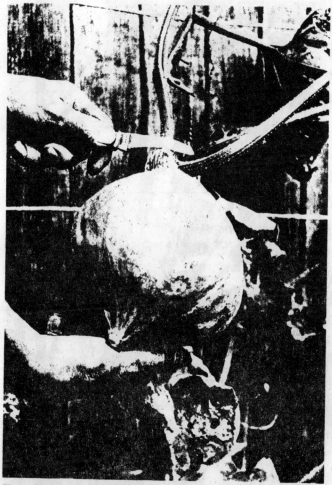

This is a Hubbard Squash—a delicious vegetable. The Author grows his trained up a fence. You will see the supporting wires.

Here are the haricot beans threshed out in the late autumn. They will now be stored away in jam jars for use in the winter.

soot and fumes off the plants. They are excellent for raising plants. For instance Brussels sprouts can be sown at the end of January and tomatoes in March, whereas in the normal way this would be impossible out of doors.

Cloches also enable the gardener to ripen his crops off properly in the late summer and autumn and may make all the difference between success and failure. For instance, if outdoor tomatoes are covered with cloches from the beginning of October onwards the remaining trusses of fruits ripen perfectly. Even if it means cutting the tomatoes down from their stakes or wires and laying the plants down on straw, so that the cloches can do the covering. Cloches will also ripen off onions splendidly. They will ripen off the haricot beans and so on.

However it will be simpler to take each vegetable separately and just make a few suggestions as to how cloches can best be used in connection with them.

Asparagus. Asparagus rows may be covered with cloches in January with the result that good sticks may be cut in March.

Beans, French. Can be sown under cloches Mid March for harvesting in June or the July and August sowings may be covered with cloches in October and thus the season lengthened.

Beans, Broad. Sowings can be made in January for harvesting in June. Sowings made in November may enable crops to be picked even a little earlier than this.

Beans, Runner. Under cloches a sowing may be made in the middle of March for harvesting in the middle of July.

Beans, Haricot. Under cloches the seeds should be sown at the end of March for harvesting late in August. The cloches in position from March are removed at the end of June until the second week of August and go back again for pod ripening.

Beetroot. First sowings are generally made at the end of February for harvesting at the beginning of June. Subsequent sowings may be made as desired, while a sowing

C

in August is usually made in the open for covering with cloches at the end of September in order to provide roots for pulling in November.

Broccoli. Tall Barn or Tomato cloches are excellent for protecting broccoli in the winter, especially if the plants are bent over towards the north.

Brussels Sprouts. Sow under cloches at the end of January to give this crop a long season of growth, which it needs.

Cabbage, Spring. Covering with cloches during the winter ensures a very early cut of excellent hearts. A sowing made under cloches at the end of January extends the season.

Carrots. The first sowings under cloches in January will be harvested in May. The last sowings made in August in the open will be covered with cloches in September and harvested in October and November.

Cauliflowers. The first sowings may be made in January and February under cloches for harvesting in July and August, while sowings made in September and October under cloches enable the plants to be put out in March for cutting in June.

Celery. The plants can be raised by sowings made under cloches in the middle of February. Early in the winter Barn cloches may be used over the celery rows to keep off frost and prevent the rain seeping down into the centre of the plants and spoiling the crop.

Cucumbers. Sowings of a good variety like Conqueror made under cloches in April enable first-class cues to be cut in August. Cloches are in use for covering from April to June.

Endive. The cloches are here mostly used for blanching purposes. They are whitewashed on the inside and go over the endive where they are growing. After 3 weeks this salad crop is properly blanched and ready for the table.

Leeks. First-class plants can be raised by sowing under cloches early in February.

Lettuces. Continuous cloches enable lettuces to be produced in the open almost all the year round.   There is no crop that does better under cloches.   Sow a variety like Holborn Standard in January for harvesting early in April. Sow a variety like May King in February for cutting in May. Sow Continuity in March for cutting in June.   Sow Webb's Wonderful in April and in May for cutting in July and August. For winter use sow in mid August, All the Year Round for harvesting in November and December and sow the variety May King under cloches in October for cutting in February and March.

Marrows. The seeds are sown out of doors where the plants are to grow in April.   The ends of the cloches should be closed.   Sowing can either be done in situ under cloches or a number of plants can be raised under cloches for putting out after the middle of May without cloche coverage.

Onions. Excellent onion plants can be raised by sowing under cloches in January.   These can be planted out in the spring.   The July sowings out of doors may be covered up with cloches during the winter and thus give the ideal protection with salad types like White Lisbon or bulbing types like Giant Rocca or Up to Date.   Cloches can be used for all types of onions in the autumn for ripening off purposes.

Parsley. Continuous Cloches enable parsley to be picked all the winter for they give just the protection the plants need.   Sowings may be made under cloches early in March.

Peas. The first sowings of peas under cloches may be made in January for harvesting in mid May.   Sowings may also be made in November for early May harvesting.   Continuous cloches save pea guards and prevent the plants from being beaten down by wind or rain.

Radish. Radishes may be sown under cloches almost any time from January onwards.

Spinach. Cloches give the ideal protection to spinach in the winter and as a result New Zealand spinach can be kept growing till Christmas time.   First sowings of Prickly Spinach may be made in January while similar sowings made in September may be overwintered under cloches.

Sweet Corn. Sow Sweet Corn under cloches in April and so harvest the cobs of a variety like John Innes in July.

Tomatoes. Sow a good variety like Hundredfold under cloches in March and harvest in July and August.   The plants can be raised under cloches instead of being raised in a greenhouse.

Turnips. First sowings are made under cloches in the middle of March for harvesting in May.   An excellent variety for this purpose is Sutton's Gem.   Winter turnips sown in July may be protected by cloches from October onwards.

CHAPTER VII

SEED SOWING AND TRANSPLANTING

The seed has to be bought and it is often expensive, so readers are told about :—

1. Good seed *versus* poor seed.
2. The making of the seed-bed.
3. How to sow the seed economically.
4. How to make dark-coloured seeds easily visible.
5. What thinning really means.
6. The advantage and disadvantage of a dibber.

THE Government have done much to ensure that the vegetable seeds which are supplied by all seedsmen in this country to-day have sufficiently high germination. Under the Seeds Act of 1920, all seeds named under the above Act have to be tested in accordance with the provisions of the Act.

This means to say, for instance, that the germination of peas must be up to 70 per cent, and dwarf or broad beans 75 per cent. The lowest percentage required is that of parsnips at 45 per cent. The following table gives the percentage germination required, and this is given so that readers may know whether seeds should be sown quite thinly or fairly thickly.

	PER CENT
Beans, dwarf and broad	75
Beans, runner	60
Beetroot	50
Broccoli	60
Brussels sprouts	70
Cabbage	70
Carrot	50
Cauliflower	60
Kale	70
Kohlrabi	70

PER CENT

Onion	68
Parsnip	45
Peas . . . '	70
Swede	75
Turnip	75

It will be seen that, generally speaking, the germination required by law is very high, and so all seed sowing can be done thinly without any fear of poor results. It must be remembered, though, that the germination tests are made under ideal conditions in the laboratory, and so if the ground is wet or sodden, or the soil is dried up, the same germination results cannot be expected.

GOOD SEED

As has been seen, there is a law which prevents vegetable seeds of poor germination from being sold, but there is no law which stops a seedsman from selling a poor variety, or a type which is not suited to certain conditions. For this reason the utmost care has been taken in selecting varieties that are known to be of good flavour and to crop heavily. Unfortunately, there are far too many varieties on the market to-day, and many of them are synonymous. For this reason, as far as possible the name originally given to the variety is used, and this should be obtained from the seedsman who has specialised in its production.

It is well worth while taking the greatest care in selecting a seedsman for the supply of vegetable seeds. The author will be glad to help those who have difficulties in obtaining the varieties he recommends. Generally speaking, it is a good thing to obtain the seed from a firm that has been established for a good many years and has a good reputation. Such firms usually have varieties of assured strains and of high vitality also. Only those who have been regularly to the official trials know to the full extent the possibilities of poor crops as the result of poor strains of seed.

Some seeds last longer than others, but to get the best results it is safer to obtain the new seed from the seedsman every year. Celery seed, for instance, may be kept for several years with success, but it will perhaps be more economical to purchase exactly the seed that is required in the particular year than to buy larger quantities and hope to save the seed over a long period.

THE SEED-BED

One of the first things the beginner has to learn is to prepare a seed-bed. A properly prepared bed of this kind should contain the three requirements for successful germination, i.e. air, warmth, and moisture. In order to produce these conditions a good deal of forking and raking has to be done.

The bed, too, must be prepared in such a way that all the particles of soil are in a fine condition. It is generally stated that, after the bed has been prepared, each particle should be no larger than a grain of wheat. If the land is left rough then the small seeds may fall into the crevices thus formed, or large portions of the unpulverised soil may bury them.

It is usually more difficult to get heavy soil into the seed-bed condition than it is light soil, and for this reason the heavier clays should be prepared some time beforehand. Land that has to be used for seed-beds under such conditions may then be left in a rough condition throughout the winter (see paragraph on ridging, pp. 16 and 17), so that the action of the weather and the frost will help to produce a kind of tilth which no amount of personal labour can achieve. In the case of the lighter soils, regular cultivation and hoeing should be done deliberately and systematically ; it will be found that seeds will grow better than in soil which has been left undisturbed for some time.

Some seed-beds may be improved by the addition of, in the case of heavy soils, sand, and, in the case of light soils, finely ground peat or well-sifted exhausted manure. In the former case the sand is used to help aerate the soil, and in the case of the latter to help retain moisture and to give a good medium into which the roots may grow.

A DRILL BEING MADE with a HOE

To ensure straight lines
Keep the right foot on the line
and the blade of the hoe against
the line

View
end-on

SOWING and TRANSPLANTING

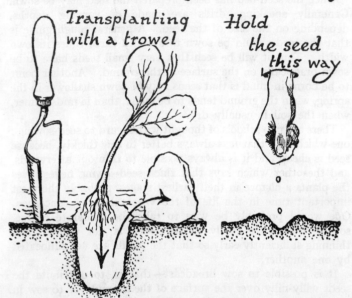

Transplanting with a trowel

Hold the seed this way

HOW A DIBBER SHOULD BE USED

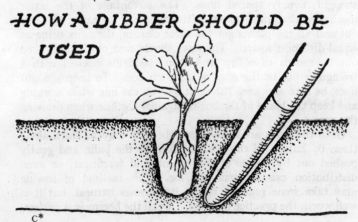

C*

THE SOWING OF THE SEED

Once the seed-bed has been prepared the seed may be sown. Generally speaking, drills are made of varying depths, depending on the size of the seed. A general rough guide is that the seed should be sown to a depth three times its own width. Thus it will be seen that very small seeds have to be sown practically on the surface of the ground. Another point to be borne in mind is that seeds may be sown shallower in the spring, when the ground tends to be moist, than in midsummer, when the soil is usually dry.

There are two schools of thought with regard to seed-sowing : one which says that it is always better to sow thickly, because seed is cheap and it is always possible to thin out afterwards, and the other which says that thick seed-sowing never gives the plants a chance in their earliest stages, probably the most important time in the life of the vegetable crop concerned. One would probably be wise to take the moderate course, sowing sufficiently thinly so that seed is not wasted, and thinning sufficiently early so that the plants are not suffocated by one another.

It is possible to sow broadcast—that is, to distribute the seeds willy-nilly over the surface of the ground—or to sow in straight, evenly spaced lines. The advantage of the latter method is that subsequent cultivations are far easier to carry out and all the plants get the same chance, the rows being at equal distances apart. The rows should first of all be marked out by means of a line and then the drills opened with a triangular hoe or the edge of a Dutch hoe. To keep straight lines, be sure and keep the right foot on the line while working and keep the blade of the hoe up against the line when drawing the row.

Once the drills are opened out the seed may be sown along them by hand. If the seed is taken in the palm and gently pushed out by means of the thumb and forefinger, an even distribution can be arranged for. This method of sowing may take some practice before it becomes natural, but it is well worth the practice entailed. Until the beginner is perfect, the seeds may be placed in the palm of one hand and sprinkled carefully, as one would sprinkle salt, with the thumb and forefinger of the other.

With dark-coloured seeds it is a good plan to mix them with a little hydrated lime first of all, so that the seeds may easily be seen when they reach the soil. In this way the evenness of the sowing can be more readily gauged.

Once the seed is in position it may be covered up either by raking the soil over, using a rake in a backwards and forwards motion and in a straight line to prevent the seeds in the drill from being distributed outside them, or if the seeds are very small, they may be covered by sifting a little soil over the rows.

On light land it is generally a good plan to tread the rows down or to beat them lightly with the back of the spade. This induces the moisture to rise to the surface and so helps in the early germination of the seed. Once, however, the little plants are through, hoeing should be done in between the rows so as to prevent the rest of the moisture from evaporating into the atmosphere. Actually, if the rows are well marked by means of pegs, hoeing may be done before germination takes place, and this will allow moisture to rise to the actual place of germination and not up into space between the rows.

In some cases, as has been explained in Chapter VI, rows may be covered with cloches during the autumn or winter months of the year. When sowings are made during the hot summer, a little shade may be given by a temporary structure of sacking or trellis. During very dry periods watering may be carried out, and during wet periods a certain amount of protection is often necessary.

STATION SOWING

A new method of sowing known as " station " sowing has much to recommend it. Instead of sprinkling the seeds along the drill, and then thinning the plants out later, 3 seeds are sown at " stations " so many inches apart along the drill, the distance differing according to the type of vegetable. With beetroot that have to be thinned to 8 inches apart, 3 seeds should be sown at every 8 inches. With carrot that are normally thinned to 6 inches apart, 3 seeds are sown every 6 inches and so on. In order, however, to provide an inter-crop of the same vegetable which may be pulled when half-grown, the usual plan is to sow at half stations, then thin down to one plant per station if each seed grows, and finally thin out every other plant when half grown, in order to leave the main " plant " at the right distance. For example, if the beetroot are to be at 8 inches apart, station sowing would be done to 4 inches, (i.e. 3 seeds at every 4 inches) and every other beetroot would be pulled out when the size of a golf ball so as to leave the remaining roots at the right distance, i.e. 8 inches. These golf ball sized roots are delicious when cooked and prove a welcome change.

The same rule can be applied to other crops.

Some seeds, particularly parsnips are apt to germinate slowly, and the result is it is difficult to see exactly where the rows are. This difficulty is accentuated, naturally, in the case of long rows. For this reason it is customary to mix radish seed with the particular seed it is desired to sow. The radishes germinate quickly and show the actual line of the row, and in addition, the radishes prove a welcome catch-crop, and are pulled, and out of the way, long before the main crop needs the room. It is said that this is a good method of ensuring thin sowing.

THINNING

As has already been suggested, thinning should always be carried out as soon as it is possible to handle the seedlings. They should always be thinned with care and the best plants left in position ; the weakest, and any which seem to show peculiarities, should be removed. When thinning is done early in this way, the root systems have hardly had time to become established, and so the little plants come away easily and do not disturb their neighbours so much as if they were left in until a week or so later.

After thinning, the soil along the rows must be firmed and then the soil given a good hoeing. During very dry periods a good watering with a fine rose may be necessary also, and the hoeing, of course, should be done after this.

It is customary to thin rows at two periods. In the first case the thinning is done to, say, half the distances ultimately intended to leave for the crop, and in the second case to remove every other plant. The advantage of this method is that, in certain cases like carrots and onions, fresh young plants are produced which do not interfere with the permanent crop, and so a type of catch-crop is made available. The pulling of the choice young roots naturally adds to the profit of the land concerned This final thinning must never be delayed or otherwise the main crop will be harmed.

In many cases the seedlings produced in the seed-beds may be transplanted into other beds to grow on. This is often done in the case of lettuces, cabbages, endive, and the like, while even such root crops as beetroots and carrots may be transplanted in the earlier stages successfully.

PLANTING OUT

Once good plants have been produced, it is a pity to ruin them by careless planting out. This does not mean to say that the seedlings should be allowed to get too thick in the seed-bed before they are moved. Again, plants raised in frames or glasshouses must never be put out into the open until they are sufficiently hardened off.

The land into which the plants are to be set should be prepared some time beforehand, and then, just before planting out, given a good raking or forking over. As in the case of seeds, the roots of the plants will appreciate soil that has been freshly stirred.

If transplanting can be carried out during a showery period, so much the better. If not, then a good watering may be given afterwards or the hole may be filled up with water as the plant is being put into position. Some people make up a mud puddle in a bucket and swish the roots of the plant round in this before they put them into the soil. For land that is subject to club root it will be necessary to put a solution of mercuric chloride into the hole first of all when planting brassicæ (see Chapter XIII).

To make certain that the plants will come out of the seed-bed without injuring the roots it is a good scheme to give the seed-bed where they are growing a thorough soaking of water the day before. In this way the plants themselves are fresh and the leaves are stiff, while the roots come away easily and do not break so much as they would if the soil were dry. The soil should be forked well to loosen it in between the little seedling rows and then it will be found that the plants will come out easily. Once out of the ground, the plants should be put in water or kept in the shade until they can be put into their permanent position; the sooner they are planted the better.

In the case of large plants, where it is obviously impossible to get them up without injuring the roots somewhat, it is a good plan to shorten the leaves so as to balance up the root and leaf system. This is very useful in the case of cabbages and cauliflowers and is often done with onions and leeks as well.

Many people use a dibber satisfactorily for making the hole for the seedling plant. Dibbers are quite all right providing the plants are small and the root system has not developed considerably. With larger plants a somewhat flattened trowel is advisable, as this can make a large hole into which the roots may be spread.

When using a dibber, a hole should be made sufficiently large to take the plant, and the roots lowered into the hole, making certain that they are not turned upwards. The plant should go down so that the bottom seed-leaf rests on the surface of the soil, then the dibber is inserted diagonally at the side of the plant and the soil levered towards the bottom of the root. In this way the roots are planted firmly. There is no need to fill up this second hole made by the dibber, and it provides quite a useful channel for watering.

EARLIER TRANSPLANTING

Beginners are often puzzled by the use of the term " pricking out." This really means the transplanting of the little seedlings once, or perhaps twice, in their very early stages. Lettuces are often pricked out as soon as the seed-leaves are large enough to handle. Very small holes have to be made with a pencil, and it needs a good deal of practice to get these tiny seedlings established in their new position. Such pricking out does ensure that practically every seedling raised comes to profitable maturity, and many market gardeners claim that early and frequent transplanting not only improves the quality, but hastens the maturity also.

CHAPTER VIII

THE CULTURE OF THE VARIOUS VEGETABLES

This is a long chapter and deals with the growing of all the ordinary vegetables.
They are listed in alphabetical order for the convenience of readers. My secretary says these are the most interesting points :—

1. That asparagus can be grown in practically all gardens, and that there are male and female plants.
2. That a nurse crop may be used for French beans.
3. That the French haricot vert is a possibility.
4. That there is a beetroot which is free from white rings.
5. The tip about how to cook seakale beet.
6. That there is a broccoli that produces a very large number of white curds on one plant.
7. That there is self-bleaching celery that can be grown on the flat.
8. That the Emperor Nero was fond of leeks and said they helped to clear his voice.
9. That mushrooms can be grown in all kinds of places.
10. That the old idea that the radish was hot and so brought about indigestion does not hold good to-day.
11. That the New Zealand spinach " creates its own mulch."

ARTICHOKE, GLOBE

THIS is one of the permanent crops which is said to have been introduced into England about 1548. It is grown for the sake of the large flower-heads it produces, as it is these that are used as the vegetable. It is not as popular in this country as it is on the Continent.

Soil. This crop seems to do best in a deep, rich, moist soil, and better heads are produced if the plants are grown in a sunny situation. Should the land be heavy, it may be improved by the use of wood ashes and sand, and the soil where the artichokes are to be planted should be ridge dug in the autumn so that the frost and cold winds may do the necessary pulverisation. Artichokes may die out on wet soils during severe weather if they are not protected or if the soil is not lightened in some way. It is in the summer that the artichokes need moisture and not in the winter.

Manuring. Before planting, farmyard manure or compost should be applied to the ground at the rate of one good barrow-load per 12 sq. yards. In addition, the following artificials should be applied per square yard : 1 oz. sulphate of potash and 2 ozs. superphosphate. In the spring, when the plants are growing, nitrate of soda may be used at $\frac{3}{4}$ oz. to the sq. yard.

Every year a certain amount of manure may be forked in between the rows during the spring, and a similar quantity of artificial manure, as mentioned above, given in addition.

Propagation. It is possible to raise plants from seed, though in this way one cannot rely on the best varieties coming true to type. If seed has to be sown, it is a good plan to sow this thinly on a hot-bed in February, and, directly the seedlings are large enough to handle, to pot them up into 3 ins. pots and grow them on in a cold frame. They may then gradually be hardened off until they are planted out into their permanent position the second week in April.

It is better to propagate by means of suckers, which should be taken off from the old plants with a sharp knife when they are about 9 ins. high. Each sucker should have a portion of root attached to it, and it is a good plan to do this during November and then to pot up each sucker, standing the pots in a cold frame for the winter. The plants are then ready to put out at the same time as the seedlings.

It is possible also to remove the suckers in April so as to plant them out immediately in rows 4 ft. apart, the plants themselves being 3 ft. apart in the rows. The suckers are put in 4 in. deep and the land then trodden firmly and watered well. It may be necessary during a hot spring to give a certain amount of shade until the plants are well established.

Slugs often attack globe artichokes, and for this reason a little circle of finely sifted coal ashes is sometimes put around each plant. In May, should the weather be dry, a mulching with straw may be given, together with occasional waterings. Flowers should never be allowed to develop the first year.

General Cultivation. Regular hoeing and weeding should be carried out, and when this is being done the plants may be disbudded. The lateral heads should be removed when they are about the size of an egg. The advantage of leaving the laterals until this stage is that they can be fried or can be eaten raw.

In the autumn, after all the heads have been cut, the stems may be cut down, together with large leaves. The central smaller leaves should not be touched, as these will protect the crown.

In districts where severe frosts may be expected, the soil may be drawn up to the plants and a little dry straw thrown over them. In the spring this litter should be removed and the earth drawn back level again. It is never a good plan to leave a plantation of artichokes down longer than five years.

Harvesting. The flowering heads should be cut while they are still young and tender and just before they are fully developed. If they are left on the plant too long they become coarse. They are usually cut with a stem 6 ins. long or so, and this is then stood in water under cover until required. The main heads are always the best, and if the laterals are not removed in the early stages they produce a second crop.

Varieties

One of the best varieties is **Camus de grande Bretagne,** though the large **Green Globe** is much liked because it is devoid of prickles.

N.B. It is possible to use what are known as chards. These are the summer growths of the artichokes which are blanched. In this case selected plants are cut back in July to within 6 ins. above the ground and a thorough flooding is given. This flooding should be repeated every week except during rainy periods, and at the end of September many side-growths will have developed. These should be blanched by first of all placing straw around them and then earthing them up like celery. The blanching takes six weeks. These chards are then cooked in the same way as cardoons.

ARTICHOKE, JERUSALEM

This is a far more popular vegetable than the globe artichoke, and is the only near relation of the sunflower used in Great Britain for human consumption. The vegetable was introduced into this country about 1617. It is a hardy herbaceous perennial, but is usually replanted every year.

Soil. The Jerusalem artichoke will grow in almost any soil, and will produce heavy crops under very indifferent treatment, therefore it can always be tried on land which has proved unsuitable for any other crop.

It will produce the finest samples when grown in an open situation in a deep friable loam and when liberally manured like potatoes. It does not care for excess of moisture.

Preparation of Soil. The land is bastard trenched in the autumn, adding any farmyard manure or compost that can be spared. The land is left rough during the winter, and then in the spring the soil is forked down level.

Manuring. In addition to organic manure, 2 ozs. of sulphate of potash and 3 ozs. of superphosphate should be forked into the top 6 ins. a fortnight or so before planting.

Propagation. The plant is propagated by means of tubers saved from the previous year's crop. The tubers used should be about the size of a pullet's egg. Where the tubers are larger they may be cut, providing there are three eyes to each tuber.

Planting. Rows should be made 2 ft. 6 ins. apart and the tubers put in 12 ins. apart in the rows and 6 ins. deep.

General Cultivation. Directly the plants are through the ground hoeing should be carried out regularly, and when the young growths are well above the soil the rows may be earthed up in the same way as potatoes. Towards the end of November the stems may be cut down to within 1 ft. of the ground.

Harvesting. It is possible to lift the whole crop up at one time and to store the tubers in sand, or to lift a few roots up as they are required. When lifting with a fork, care should be taken not to damage the artichokes, and any medium-sized or small tubers should be selected for planting the following season. The largest tubers not required for further replanting may be stored in sand or put into a clamp (see Potatoes).

Varieties

New White has a more delicate flavour than the old-fashioned purple variety. It is of a better shape also.

ASPARAGUS

For some reason or another asparagus is looked upon as a luxury, and this makes the ordinary man-in-the-street frightened of growing it. An asparagus bed is comparatively easy to lay down and costs little to maintain, and there is no reason at all why all gardens should not contain a row if the householder so desires.

Soil. Commercial growers have shown that it is possible to grow this crop successfully in almost any soil if good drainage is provided.

Manuring. There is need for generous manuring, and if possible farmyard manure or a good organic substitute like compost should be applied every year. This may be applied in the autumn, after the asparagus foliage has been cut down and burnt. In addition, artificial manures may be used—say 2 ozs. of superphosphate and 4 ozs. of kain'. per sq. yard. Nitrate of soda may be given in the spring at the rate of 1 oz. to the sq. yard directly growth becomes active. This is quite useful, especially during the first few years.

Salt is often recommended, and on light soils it certainly is useful. Too much salt, however is apt to make the bed cold, and at any rate it should never be used until the bed has established itself. On sandy soils, when salt is applied it should be put on in the north near the end of April and in the south towards the middle of April at the rate of, say, 1 oz. to the sq. yard. Another dressing may be given three weeks later at the same rate, if desired.

(a) Calcium cyanamide if used at 2 ozs. to the sq. yd. all over the rows in the spring just after the weeds have started to show, will give complete control of chickweed and drastic scorching of other weeds. In some seasons such a dressing will give complete weed control throughout the length of the cutting season.

Preparation of Soil. If it proves possible, the land where asparagus is to be grown should be bastard trenched to the depth of 3 ft. in the autumn, and during this process, should the land be on the heavy side, sand or bu.nt earth may be incorporated. If half-rotten stable manure can be used, buried about 2 ft. deep at the rate of 7 cwt. per square pole, so much the better.

Propagation. It is possible to raise plants by sowing seed, but this operation is generally left to the seedsman or nurseryman. Those who wish to get quick returns—and most people do—should purchase three-year-old plants ; it is really better to plant one-year-old plants, though this means waiting three or more years before a crop can be cut.

If it is desired to raise plants, the seed may be sown very thinly in drills 1 in. deep and 1 ft. apart. As the seed germinates slowly, it is usual to sow a few radish seeds with it. These show the rows and enable cultivation to be carried out very early. Young seedlings should be hoed regularly, and in dry periods watered copiously.

Planting. It much depends on the type of bed how planting is carried out. In the olden days it was customary to have raised beds, but many gardeners to-day prefer the flat bed if the drainage is perfect. In some cases the beds are 3 ft. wide, and in large gardens a series of such beds is made with a temporary pathway 2 ft. wide between them. In other cases single rows are planted 4 ft. apart, the plants being put in 2 ft. apart. There are many schemes of asparagus planting, some preferring rows 3 ft. apart and the plants 18 ins. in the rows, others who like double rows 4 ft. apart and 18 ins. between the rows and 18 ins. between the plants.

On the 3 ft. bed two rows of plants are planted 9 ins. in from the edges of either side. If one-year-old plants are used, they should be examined to see whether they have three or four good strong buds at the crown. Two- or three-year-old plants will naturally look stronger. It should be possible to get the plants into position early in April, and if planting can be done on a mild day, so much the better. It is usual to take out a trench 9 ins. wide and 9 ins. deep and to spread the spidery-looking roots of the asparagus out evenly in this trench. If the plant is set upon a little mound of soil, it will be found easier to get the roots into position and it will ensure that the crown (or the growing bud part) of the plant is about 4 ins. below the soil level after covering in.

The roots of the young plant should never be exposed to the dry winds or to the sun, but should be planted as soon as possible. If this is impossible, they should be covered with a damp sack and kept out of the sun's ray. When roots are bought they may travel well in damp moss, but little time should be taken in unpacking them and planting them when they arrive. For this reason it is a good plan to get the bed ready, so that when the parcel is delivered the plants can be unpacked and put in immediately.

Naturally two people can plant asparagus more quickly and expeditiously than one, one holding the plant in position and spreading out the roots and the other putting over the soil so that this can be trodden down carefully. As a rule the rows will be approximately 18 ins. apart and the plants themselves 18 ins. apart in the rows. In order to assist in the recognition of the rows during the early stages it is a good plan to put a fairly strong stake at either end.

It is possible to sow seeds in the permanent beds instead of raising plants and transplanting or even buying plants, and, if so, two seeds are usually dibbled in at intervals of 18 ins. along the rows. For those who do not mind waiting four years this is a satisfactory method.

General Cultivation. During the first year or two, if no crop can be taken, small crops are often grown between the rows. Radishes, lettuces, and onions are quite suitable for this purpose. These must be considered as catch-crops.

The beds should be watched, and, if blank spaces are found towards the middle of June, further plants may be obtained and planted immediately, making certain to water them in. Throughout the season hoeing may be carried out on either side of the rows or beds.

Experiments that have been carried out in America and in this country have shown that calcium cyanamide applied over the beds in the summer, when the weeds are growing, kills these satisfactorily and yet has no ill effect on the plants.

In the late autumn the foliage should be cut down close to

the ground. The female plants should never be allowed to let their berries ripen and drop on to the soil, or else unprofitable seedlings may appear. If the foliage can be burnt immediately it starts to turn brown, some pests and diseases may be controlled.

Owing to the fact that the stems are fragile and may snap off at the base, it is usual in windy situations to give the feathery growth some support when well grown. A bamboo or two at the ends of the rows and green twine run in between them will form an effective support.

There seems to be a slight difference of opinion among experts as to whether the rows or beds should be soiled-up in the winter or in the spring. Some prefer February, others late March, while in the case of heavy soils it is said that November is the best month, in order that the frost may act on this earthed-up soil and make it friable. As the crowns grow larger they naturally need more soil to cover them, and so the ridges along the rows become higher. Owing to the growth of the plants during the summer, the soil for these ridges may fall away, so that by the time the foliage is cut down again the ridges have practically disappeared.

Experiments have shown that male asparagus plants (the plants which do not bear any berries) give a 60-90 per cent higher yield than the female plants, therefore, try to rogue out the females and have beds or rows of males only.

Harvesting. As has already been suggested, cutting should not take place until the third year, and even then only two or three sticks should be cut from the plant. Every year cutting should cease by the end of June, and during the first two cutting years about the beginning of June. During the harvesting time the thinner shoots should be left to grow, only the thicker ones being cut. When cutting ceases, all the shoots are left.

It is easy to cut with a long, strong, narrow-pointed knife. This is plunged into the bed or ridge so as to sever the stick just above the crown without injuring it. Care should be taken not to injure other younger sticks that are coming through at the same time. On very light soils it is possible, after uncovering the " buds " somewhat, to snap the shoots off near to the crown instead of cutting them.   It is usual to cut when the brownish-green tips of the shoots are 3 or 4 ins. above the soil level.

Varieties

> **Early Argenteuil is** said to be the earliest, and under favourable conditions it may be cut from the beginning of April onwards.
>
> **Connover's Colossal,** originally an American variety, is later, having slender pointed buds which on exposure to the full light soon lose their reddish colour and become a lighter green than other kinds.
>
> **Mary Washington,** an American variety, is valued because it resists asparagus rust.
>
> **Martha Washington** is a later variety, very similar to Mary Washington.   Neither of these varieties seem to crop as heavily in England as they do in America.

BEAN, BROAD

Soil.   The broad bean is not particular as to soil, and will grow as readily on heavy land as on the lighter ones.

Preparation of Soil.   There is no special preparation needed other than the ordinary bastard trenching or digging that would be given to other crops.   In the case of the autumn sowings which follow previously well-manured crops, single digging only may be necessary.

Manuring.   The autumn-sown beans require no special manuring, but those sown in the spring may have a light dressing of farmyard manure or compost dug in three weeks or so before sowing the seed.   In addition, 3 ozs.' of fish manure and 1 oz. sulphate of potash per sq. yd. should be forked in.   Where farmyard manure or compost is not used, meat and bone meal may be applied at the same time at 5 ozs. to the sq. yard.   Superphosphate in this case may be omitted.

Sowing the Seed.   Seeds can be sown either in November outside or from early to mid-March.   Where a frame or cloches are available, sowings may be carried out in December and January, the young plants raised in frames put out into the permanent position during the second or third week of March.

It is always necessary to plant on a dry day, and when soil conditions are unfavourable it is better to delay sowing for a few days.

The Longpod types are usually sown in November and January and the Broad Windsors in March. The earlier sowings are more successful in the light soils and in the warmer climates, while the frames and March sowings have to be carried out under less favourable conditions. Even in the south, November sowings may not come through owing to the frost or wet weather.

The rows may be 2 ft. 6 ins. apart, the drills 5–6 ins. wide, and a double row of beans put into these drills staggered so that they are 6 ins. apart. The drills would be prepared 2–3 ins. deep. Dwarf varieties may be arranged in double rows 2 ft. apart, the two lines forming the double rows being 9 ins. apart and the plants 6 ins. apart in the rows. The double row is generally successful because it allows of a heavier yield per plot of land without impairing the efficiency of the plants.

It is a good plan to sow 12 to 14 beans in a group at the ends of the rows, as these may be planted out later on when 3 or 4 ins. high should any gaps appear.

General Cultivation. The soil should be kept clean between the rows with regular hoeing. A sharp look-out should be kept for the black aphis, and, directly this first appears, dusting or a spraying with derris should be given. It is not necessary to pinch out the tops except to encourage the early production of beans. Any side growths that are seen may be removed from time to time.

Directly the crop is over the tops should be cut down and the roots left in the ground and dug in. The tops can either be used in rotting down for manure or the stems can be dried, used as traps for earwigs or for making temporary mats. Leaving the plants in the ground after they have finished their productiveness only exhausts the soil.

Harvesting. The beans should be picked regularly, as this ensures a heavier crop ; it is better to pick rather on the young side than leave the pods to become old.

Varieties

These may be divided into three groups the Longpods, the Windsors, and the Small Pods.   Again the Longpods and Windsors may be divided into the white-seeded and green-seeded types and the small pods into the tall and dwarfs.

The Longpods are the hardier and give the heaviest yields.   They are also more attractive in appearance.   The Windsors have the finer flavour.   Further the green seeded varieties are more tender and delicious than the white seeded types.

LONGPODS :

Aquadulce, a very early tall-growing variety bearing enormous pods.

Seville Giant, Longpod, bears large, well-filled pods of good flavour.

WINDSORS :

Any good seedsmen's strain will do, i.e. **Early White-eyed Windsor.**

SMALLPODS:

Royal Dwarf Fan.   Grows 1 ft. high and is quick maturing.   If sown as late as July will give a crop the same year.

Beck's Dwarf Gem, similar to above.

Mazagan, a taller variety but usually a poor cropper.   Not worth growing.   Is liked on some very fertile soils.

BEAN, FRENCH, DWARF, OR KIDNEY

The French bean comes into cropping earlier, and can be sown earlier than its cousin, the runner bean.   It can be sown in pots under glass, in pots in frames, in the south border to get a crop early in the season, and in the main garden as late on as in June in order to get a picking towards the end of September.

Soil.   On the whole, this bean seems to prefer a light soil rather than a heavy one.   Being a legume, it will enrich the soil, and even on poor land which has been well prepared it can produce a heavy crop.   It seems to withstand drought almost better than any other vegetable crop.

Preparation of Soil.   The land is dug at least a spit deep and a moderate quantity of farmyard manure or compost added.   This digging will help to warm up the soil, and should be done in the autumn if possible.   In the spring the land where the French beans are to be grown may be cropped with lettuce, and these will give some protection to the young

plants as they come through. The lettuce should be cut as
the French beans grow.

Manuring. In addition to any organic manure which may
be dug in when the land is prepared, artificial manures may
be forked in when the land is being prepared for the " nurse "
crop. Superphosphate is applied at 1 oz. per sq. yd. and
sulphate of potash at $\frac{1}{2}$ oz. per sq. yd. Should the plants be
affected by a bad spell of weather after they come through,
potassic nitrate of soda may be applied along the rows at $\frac{1}{2}$ oz.
to the yard run ; this should be watered in. Lime is generally
necessary for all members of the pea and bean family, and may
be applied to the surface of the ground after the forking in of
the artificials at from 4 to 7 ozs. per sq. yd., depending on the
acidity of the soil.

Sowing the Seed. It is a good plan to provide for a
succession of pods by making sowings in various ways. For
instance, a sowing may be made in frames about the middle of
March in rows 1 ft. apart, the seed being placed 3 ins. apart in
the rows. When the plants are well through, they should be
thinned out to 6 ins. apart and the thinnings transplanted into
other frames if possible. There is no need to give any air until
the seed has germinated, but after this ventilation may be
given whenever possible. The plants must not be allowed
to get frozen, and so the frames should be covered up with
sacking or mats at night-time and during frosty periods in the
day. As the plants grow they may be given more and more
air, until by mid-May the lights can be removed during the
day-time. Under such conditions French beans need regular
watering, and if this is done, picking should commence after,
say, the 15th of June.

Another sowing may be made early in April in a cold frame,
and again this should be protected from frosts. Air may be
given when the seedlings are through, on all possible occasions,
and when hardened off they may be planted outside in a
sheltered border the second or third week of May. When
lifting and transplanting French beans, plenty of soil should
be kept around their roots. When in their new position,
they should be watered well and shaded. Such early crops

may need protection from frost even when outside, and growers should be prepared to put straw along the rows or to cover with continuous cloches until the end of the third week of May.

The first sowing outside in the normal way is usually done during the first week of May, or even earlier in the south-west. In this case the " nurse " crop will already be growing well, and drills should be made 2 ins. deep, 4 ins. wide, and from 2 to 3 ft. apart, depending on the variety.   In each little trench a double row is sown " staggered," so that the beans are 6 ins. apart in either direction.   Some growers prefer to sow twice as thickly as this, and then to thin out and transplant the seedlings either into the gaps or into further rows.   If this is not done, the same procedure as suggested for runner beans— i.e. the planting of a few extra seeds at the ends of the rows— should be carried out.

The last sowing is done the first week in July without the " nurse " crop, the rows being 2 ft. apart and the beans being spaced to 10 or 12 inches.   This spacing is usually carried out by thinning the plants sown at three times the thickness as soon as the rough leaves appear.   The soil for these later sowings is never specially prepared.   It is this sowing which can be covered with cloches in mid or late September.

General Cultivation.   Regular hoeing in between the rows and the drawing up of soil to the plants rather than away from them, especially when they are 3 to 4 ins. high.   The " nurse " crop must be cleared as soon as the plants are growing well, and the land where this crop has been growing forked over.

In the case of tall varieties on very rich soil, the plants may need supporting with bushy twigs, especially if the situation is somewhat exposed.   Slugs must be kept down by the bran and Metaldehyde method (see p. 282), as they will often ruin large numbers of plants in a night.

Harvesting.   *It is always better to pick French beans when they are young than to let them get old and coarse.*   Regular gathering will prevent the swelling of seeds in the pods ; this causes the plants to cease cropping.

Varieties

Undoubtedly the best French beans are more delicious than runners and can be made available over a longer period. They may be arbitrarily divided into two types, 1—dwarf and 2—Climbing.

Dwarfs

(a) *Extra Early for Forcing* in frames or under cloches.
Lightning, delicious pods, but not a very heavy cropper.
(b) *Early for the garden.*
The Prince. Undoubtedly the best early French bean to-day. Crops very heavily.
(c) *Main Crops.*
Here we have a number of varieties recommended by different seedsmen.
The Wonder, an excellent strain of the old Canadian Wonder which is first-class and under cloches, bears long pods and crops heavily.
Black Wonder, a similar type but slightly later.
Feltham Prolific. A dwarf variety, may be planted closer than others. A quick grower.
Superlative. A variety that does well in hot, dry weather and whose cropping lasts over an extended period.
Stringless Refugee. The variety insisted on by the canners, as it is, as the name suggests—stringless.
Similar varieties are known as Snap-podded beans.
The Mont D'Or, sometimes called the Waxpod bean and sometimes the Golden Butter bean. (Incidentally the latter is a bad name as it confuses it with the grocer's dried butter beans). This variety bears golden French beans.

Climbing Strains

There are climbing strains of French Beans which are grown in a similar manner to runner beans and for their culture, therefore, please see under " Runners." Normally, however, the climbing French beans are grown in the greenhouse in the winter and very early spring.

Varieties

Tender and True, usually recognised as the best climbing variety. Particularly good under glass.
Princess of Wales. Another. heavy cropping climbing type.

BEAN, RUNNER

Soil. Runner beans seem to grow well in practically all soils, but they do best where they can have an extensive root run.   It is, therefore an advantage to have a deep soil.

Preparation of Soil.   More care should be taken over the preparation of the soil for runner beans than for any other of the pod-bearing crops.   Trenches may be taken out 2 ft. wide and 2 ft. deep, and the bottoms of the trenches well forked up. Into each trench an 18 ins. thickness of well-rotted farmyard manure may be placed, and this can be covered with a 3 ins. thickness of soil.   If such trenches are prepared in the late winter or early spring, they may be left to settle down and further soil placed in the trench to bring it up to the level of the surrounding ground.

Such special preparations, however, apply mainly to those who are going in for the production of exhibition pods.   In the ordinary way the ground where the runner beans are to be grown should be bastard trenched and liberally manured.   If this can be done late in March or in early April, so much the better.

The trench method is quite an ideal one, and will take a double row of beans.

Manuring.   It is difficult to say how much farmyard manure or compost is necessary, as very large quantities may be used in the trenches.   One large barrow-load for instance may only do 6 ft. or so of trench.   Where farmyard manure is difficult to obtain, spent hops, compost or seaweed may be used.

Superphosphate should be added to the top 2 or 3 ins. of soil at the rate of $1\frac{1}{2}$ oz. per sq. yd. and sulphate of potash at $\frac{1}{2}$ oz., if these are applied when the trenches are being prepared, so much the better, but the application may be delayed until a week or so before the seed is sown.

Hydrated lime should be applied to the surface of the ground at the rate of 3 ozs. to the sq. yard.

Sowing.   Runner beans cannot be sown early (unless under continuous cloches), because they will not germinate unless the soil is warm.   For this reason it is not generally possible to sow until the second week of May.   Another sowing may be made towards the beginning of June.

The rows, when they are to grow up poles, should be 5 or

6 ft. apart, and the seeds should be sown 2 ins. deep. Where runner beans are to be grown on the flat, the rows may be 3½ to 4 ft. apart, the seed being sown 4½ ins. apart in the rows.

The seed is often put in in double rows 9 ins. apart. If the seeds are to be sown singly, 9 ins. apart in the drills, and the staggered or alternate method used, there is no need to thin afterwards.

Thinning. If the beans are sown thickly instead of being spaced out, then thinning has to be carried out when the beans are 2 ins. high. Space out 9 ins. apart.

Transplanting. If a number of runner beans are sown in a group at the end of the rows, then these may be transplanted, when they are 3 ins. or so, into any blank spaces that may appear in the rows at that time.

It is possible also to sow the seeds in boxes under glass to get earlier crops. Such sowing may be done in boxes at least 4½ ins. deep. It is often possible to obtain boxes from the grocer about 2 ft. long and 1 ft. wide. Such boxes are suitable for growing fifty plants. The seed may be sown in a light compost that has been placed in these boxes at the end of April, and the plants thus raised planted out early in June.

Staking. The poles, which are usually put into position just after sowing, or just before, may be 9 ins. apart. These poles generally cross at the top for the end, say 6 ins., and poles may be laid across the V's thus made. If the cross poles and the poles laid on lengthways are then lashed together, a very firm structure is produced.

If it is impossible to obtain a large number of stakes, strands of string may be used stretched from wire running along the ground and at the tops of the few poles available.

The use of wire netting is sometimes possible, and this has the advantage of being usable for several years.

Those with very small gardens will find it convenient to have a little group of sticks going to a point near a path or at the corners of a border. The runner beans can clamber up these and the effect is not only beautiful but practical. Those who think more of the ornamental side should grow those with the pretty bi-colour flowers.

General Cultivation. Runner beans that are grown on the flat should be kept topped from time to time. The tops of the plants are pinched out when they are 18 ins. high, and this pinching causes them to break. A further pinching may take place when the subsequent growths are 18 ins. long. After this the growths may be cut back from time to time either with a pair of shears or with a sharp " brushing " hook.

By whatever method the plants are grown, slugs and snails will be found a great nuisance, and so protection should be given by means of the Paris green method (see p. 282).

Hoeing should be carried out regularly, not only along the rows, but in between the plants also. When the plants are 4 ins. high, a little soil may be drawn up to them, and, in fact, all hoeing should be up to the rows rather than away from them.

Early in July a mulch of straw, rotted leaves, or lawn mowings may be put along the rows to keep in the moisture. This should be done after a very heavy watering, especially during a dry season. Runner beans must have moisture at their roots, and regular waterings will not only make for better pods, but will prolong the cropping period. In the evening the rows may be sprayed with water in order to help the flowers to set and to keep the pods tender.

Harvesting. The beans should be picked regularly, and in this way heavier crops will result. It should be possible to obtain pods 12 and 15 ins. in length fit for the table, though smaller pods are more delicious. Pods that have to be picked to prevent them from seeding may be kept fresh for several days if their stem ends are put in a saucer of water.

Varieties

Most seedsmen have their pet strains of runner beans and many concentrate on producing at least one variety with very long pods. It must be emphasised that the old-fashioned scarlet-runner has been superseded. The Painted Lady type do not give heavy enough yields either.

Planting Red Cabbages. Note the way the firming is done
with the handle of the trowel.

This is how you screw the tops off round beetroots before storing. You must grip with both hands.

The best varieties would seem to be :—

Princeps, an early dwarfish variety which crops 14 days earlier than any other type. The best kind for growing on the flat.

East Anglian Champion, a white seeded, white flowered kind, the favourite of the canning industry because it is so tender.

Prizewinner, a very large podded variety which is not coarse. Beans hang in large clusters.

BEAN, HARICOT

Unfortunately, the haricot bean or haricot vert, is seldom grown in this country, as it is easy to grow, and does well providing the soil is warm and well drained.

Soil Preparation. The preparation of the soil and method of seed sowing is the same as for French beans (see p. 91).

General Cultivation. To be a success, the seed of the haricot bean should be sown early, preferably at the beginning of April under cloches. This gives the plants an early start, and the pods mature late August or early September and so can be thoroughly ripened off under cloches. Those who haven't cloches will have to sow out of doors about the end of April. The whole plant is pulled up and dried, afterwards, being put into.a sack and beaten with a stick to thresh out the beans.

Varieties

Comtesse de Chambord. Tallish and rather spreading.
White Countess. An improved variety—definitely shorter.

BEAN (FLAGEOLET)

The beans of these types are eaten in the green stage like peas. The French are very fond of their haricot vert but they are almost unknown in this country. The sowing is done exactly as for Dwarf French beans. These are dwarf beans and do not need staking.

N.B.—Haricots vert are the green beans harvested like peas from green pods. They are eaten boiled when tender just like peas. They are sown and grown like ordinary French Beans.

Varieties

The two best varieties are :
Green Gem, a heavy cropper. Delicious.
Green Flageolet, somewhat taller. Extended season.

D

BEETROOT

Beetroots are generally grown too large, in consequence of which they tend to be coarse. They are usually considered only suitable to accompany cold meat as a kind of pickle and are used in salads. Latterly, however, they have become quite a fashionable vegetable when cooked, and served hot either mashed with butter or whole. They may be served as fritters also.

Soil. Probably the best soil for beetroot is that of a light loam which has a good depth. Clays can, however, be got into the right condition with a little care.

Preparation of Soil. It is not necessary to dig in large quantities of farmyard manure or compost for beetroot; it tends to cause the beetroot to fork. Rank soil is to be avoided. If the crop can follow one that has been well manured previously, all is well.

Deep digging should be carried out either in the autumn or early spring, and some time should elapse between that and the making of the seed-bed, so as to allow the soil to settle.

The long beetroots grow well on land that has carried celery or leeks the previous year.

Early in May the soil where the beetroot seed is to be sown may be forked over and then raked down finely.

Manuring. Though it is not usually necessary to add farmyard manure or compost to the land, seaweed may be used with advantage. This may be applied at the rate of a barrow-load to 10 sq. yds., and should be dug in deeply. The lighter soils may receive an application of salt at the rate of 2 ozs. to the sq. yd. when the plants are half grown.

A good fish manure may be applied at the rate of 4 ozs. to the sq. yd. ten days before sowing the seed, and be lightly forked in.

Sowing the seed. The seed should be sown either at the end of April or the beginning of May, depending on the district, in rows 15 ins. apart, the little drills being 1 in. deep. On the heavy clays, especially in the north, it may not be possible to sow until after May 15th.

Seeds may be sown thinly in the drills, but regular sowing is necessary. After sowing, the drills should be covered over and the surface of the bed should be left level.

Some of the smaller globe varieties grown as early crops may be sown in rows as close as 1 ft. apart. These earlier sowings are usually done on the south border at any time from the end of March to the middle of April, depending on the weather and the district. It is as well to protect these earlier sowings with fish netting, as birds are most partial to the seedlings. A late spring frost will damage them also. In this instance the seeds are only sown $1\frac{1}{2}$ in. deep.

Further sowings of the early globe varieties may be made in July, so as to obtain delicious little roots in the autumn and winter. Sowing is done as advised in the previous paragraph. Broadcast sowings are also possible, providing these are done thinly.

Thinning. The rows are usually thinned so that the plants are 8 ins. apart. This is done at two periods, in the first place when the plants are 3 ins. high to half the distance, and then, when they are the size of golf-balls, to the full distance. In this way the later thinnings may be used in the house.

For the early crops in the south border it is only necessary to thin to 9 ins. in the rows, and this holds good for the late July sowings also.

Transplanting. It is possible to transplant the young beetroot seedlings if necessary. Sometimes gaps occur in rows for no apparent reason, and these may be filled in at the first thinning. When transplanting is carried out, a good watering should be given every day during dry weather until the plants are well established.

General Cultivation. Regular hoeings are as necessary for beetroot as for any other crop, but these have to be more carefully done. The roots should never be damaged by the hoe, as if they bleed the colour is lost. There is no need to bring the soil up to the rows.

Apart from the watering of the thinnngs, it is usually waste of time to water the crops. Beetroots are fairly easy to grow providing the initial cultivation is well done.

Harvesting. Beetroots may be left in the ground until they are needed in the winter providing they are covered with straw, bracken or continuous cloches during severe frosts. It is generally safer to lift the roots and to store them in a clamp, as for potatoes. The tops should be cut off before storing, but this should never be done too near to the crown or bleeding may take place. Beetroots may be stored in sand or dry earth in a shed, and if this has to be done they should be dug up before the middle of October. They will keep, if well stored, until the following June.

The long beetroots may have the end of the tapering root removed without much harm being done. Apart from this, beetroots should always be handled carefully as they suffer from rough treatment.

Varieties

There are three main types of beet (a) the round or Globe, (b) the Intermediate, or (c) the Long.

ROUND OR GLOBE :

Empire Globe, a variety which bears beautiful globe-shaped beets which when cut through will be found to be of a dark crimson colour and free from white rings.

Detroit, the canners' favourite. A very dark red strain. Small roots.

Egyptian Turnip-rooted. The best variety for shallow soils.

Model Globe. Said to be the earliest strain of all. Has very few leaves. Does particularly well under cloches.

INTERMEDIATE :

A type of beet which ought to be more grown. Has all the advantages of the long beet, with its flavour, but is not too large to go into the pot for cooking.

Obelisk. The best-known Intermediate. Delicious. Of " tankard " shape.

LONG SHAPED :

Cheltenham Green Top, the most popular variety, giving roots of excellent colour.

Dell's Crimson. Excellent flavour. Medium sized roots. Good form.

Bell's Non-bleeding. Retains its colour, even when cut into slices before cooking. Does not bleed when broken or bruised.

Frames. It is possible to grow beetroot in frames or under cloches providing a globe variety is used. Two sowings may be made, one during the middle of February and one in March. A hot-bed should be made for the purpose in open, and the seeds sown in rows 9 ins. apart. Under cloches no hot-bed is necessary. When the plants are through, they should be thinned out to 6 ins. apart.

Delicious young beets are thus produced at a time of the year when the only other beetroots available are the larger roots that have been in store ·for some time. Beetroot in frames need only be grown for the epicures.

BEET, SEAKALE

The seakale beet—or seakale spinach, as it is erroneously called—is grown for the thick white stems it produces and for the large green leaves growing at the ends of these stems, which are delicious when used as spinach.

Soil. All soils seem to suit this vegetable, from the very light to the very heavy.

Preparation of Soil. Deep digging and cultivation are necessary if heavy crops of long thick white stems are desired. This crop should not be treated in the same way as beetroot, because it will appreciate heavy manuring, and waterings from time to time with liquid manure.

Sowing the Seed. Seed should be sown late in April or early in May in drills 15 ins. apart. Despite thin sowing, it will be necessary to thin so as to space the plants out to 12 ins. apart in the rows.

Harvesting. The leaves and stems should be pulled regularly and not cut. In this way further stems and leaves are produced, a thing, curiously enough, which does not happen when the stalks are just cut and the remaining portion left to rot on the plant.

N.B. Housewives are advised to put a teaspoonful of lemon-juice into the water in which the stalks are boiling, so as to preserve the brilliant white colour.

This is a very delicious vegetable which should be more widely grown.

BORECOLE (*see* KALE p. 131)

CULTURE of VARIOUS VEGETABLES

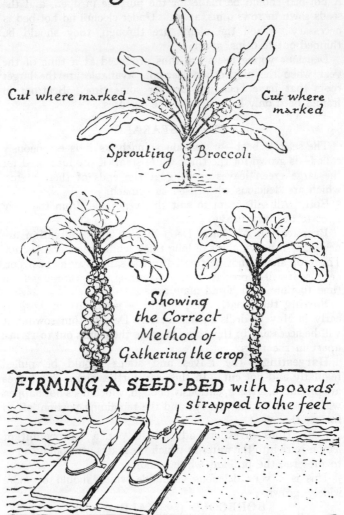

Cut where marked

Cut where marked

Sprouting Broccoli

Showing the Correct Method of Gathering the crop

FIRMING A SEED-BED with boards strapped to the feet

BROCCOLI (or Winter Cauliflower)

There are various types of broccoli, the first producing a beautiful white head similar to the cauliflower, and sometimes called the winter cauliflower, the second producing a large number of purple sprouts, and the third yielding a profusion of agreeably flavoured white "sprouts." The cultivation of the two latter types of broccoli will be described under the heading of "Broccoli, Sprouting."

So intermingled have the cauliflower and broccoli become that it is almost impossible to-day for an expert to say where the cauliflower ends and the broccoli begins. In the old times the broccoli was not so pure in texture and quality, but to-day, particularly since the introduction of the French varieties, such a statement is not true.

The hearting broccoli may be divided into four divisions, the first for autumn use, the second for winter or early spring use, the third for spring use, and the fourth for late spring or early summer use.

By careful planting and sowing it should be possible to produce broccoli for the table from Michaelmas Day one year to the middle of June the following year.

Soil. Broccoli will grow in most soils, but it seems to prefer a clay or a heavy loam. The light sandy soils should be made firm, because, if they are not, open curds result.

Preparation of Soil. On the whole, broccoli prefer firm soil, and so the wise gardener will plant his crop on land that has been well prepared for a previous one. In this way the land will have had the chance to settle down, and there is no need to do any special preparation in consequence. Apart from this the treatment can be generous, but not so generous that a soft, succulent condition is produced, which in cold districts may cause the partial loss of crop owing to the hard winter. If the soil for the previous crop was bastard trenched, single digging will usually do for broccoli.

Manuring. The light lands should have well-rotted farm-yard manure or compost added at the rate of a barrow-load to 10 sq. yards. After this has been dug well in, firming can take place.   On heavy soils farmyard manure is not necessary, and, in fact, its use is to be deprecated.   The crop should follow a well-manured summer crop, and this should leave the land in just the right condition for broccoli.

Artificial manures may, however, be applied, though, in order not to let the plants grow soft, nitrogenous manures are omitted.   Superphosphate may be used at $1\frac{1}{2}$ oz. and sulphate of potash at $\frac{1}{2}$ oz. to the sq. yard.   These may be supplied just before planting.

Sowing the Seed.   It is usual to sow the seeds of most of the varieties of broccoli during the second week in April, though in southern districts those who want to get good heads early in the autumn may sow at the end of March.   The sowing of the main June varieties also may be delayed until the middle of May.

There is no need for the seed-beds to be wide or for the drills to be deep.   A narrow seed-bed is easy to look after, and one 3 ft. wide will generally do.   The seed is sown in the drills from $\frac{1}{4}$ to $\frac{1}{2}$ in. deep.

After sowing, some protection from birds must be given. Black cotton strung from short pieces of bamboo is usually very effective.   If the seeds are in danger of being taken, they may be soaked in Horticule, and this will prevent both birds and mice from touching them.

The little rows in the seed-bed need only be 6 in. apart.   The soil should be raked down finely before sowing, and watered with mercuric chloride (see p. 250) should club root be prevalent.   Once the seeds are through the rows should be hoed continually, so as to keep down weeds and provide a mulch. The young plant has need of plenty of light and air.

Before the seedlings get too long and lanky they should be thinned and transplanted into further seed-beds, 6 in. between the rows and 3 in. apart in the rows.   This pricking out of the seedlings ensures first-class plants, and in consequence better heads in the autumn.

Planting.   As has already been stated, broccoli is a useful crop for following those crops that have been harvested early. They grow well after early potatoes, French beans, or even peas. It is not advisable to plant this crop after any other member of the cabbage family.

As soon as the land is ready, the plants should be put out, as to leave them in their seed-bed too long makes them lanky.

Generally speaking, they may be planted in rows 2 ft. 6 ins. apart, the plants being 2 feet. In the case of some of the small varieties, the rows may be 2 ft. and the plants only 18 ins. apart. The advantage of close planting is that the plants give some protection to each other. The disadvantage is that they never grow as large as when given the wider spacing.

When planting, the ground should be firmed well, as loose soil is apt to produce loose curds. Watering-in of broccoli should be avoided, as, if this is done, heavy waterings are necessary subsequently.

Gapping up may be done a fortnight after planting out, and for this purpose a few plants in the seed-bed should always be saved.

General Cultivation. One of the most important things is to make certain that the plants are not damaged during the winter. In the milder districts nothing need be done, but in cases where the soil is wet and the winter hard the plants may be pushed over so that the heads incline to the north. This can be done by taking away a little soil from that side and, after pushing the plants over, placing this on the other side. If this is done during November, the plants will be helped over the frosty periods of the next few months.

Sometimes during this heeling over process the plants seem to flag, and, if they do, they should be given a thorough watering.

It is possible also to give some protection to a small plot of broccoli by using plenty of straw or bracken, but the disadvantage of this is that it gets very sodden in the rain and has to be removed. The plot can often be protected by placing some kind of temporary barrier around the outside to keep off the cold winds.

Apart from this, hoeing should be carried out until the weeds cease to grow and until the soil gets impossible to work satisfactorily.

D*

Harvesting. The curds should be cut directly they are ready, and should too many " turn in " at a time a leaf or two should be broken and put over the white head in order to keep them back.

It is necessary to make a few special remarks about the four groups mentioned earlier on, and these are outlined under special headings.

Autumn Broccoli

The seed of such varieties may, as has been suggested, be sown earlier, and some growers prefer to sow in February or March in a frame. These are often planted out on specially prepared, deep-dug land which has been well manured. Planting may take place in May or early June.

Spinach is then sown in drills in between this crop just before it comes into cutting.

Winter or Early Spring Broccoli

The seeds are sown at the usual time, and planting may be carried out whenever the land is free. There is, with reasonable limits, little difference in the time of turning in whether the plants are put out early or no.

Spring Broccoli

These are, perhaps, the most difficult of all broccoli, because they are so much affected by weather. The seeds may be sown at the usual time, though sometimes gardeners prefer to make two or three sowings at intervals of a fortnight or so in order to make certain that they have a constant supply.

Late Spring or Early Summer Broccoli

A crop sometimes in demand and sometimes which comes in so late as to compete with peas. As a whole the varieties in this group are hardier than those in the previous group, but on the whole they throw smaller heads. They can be grown in a more open situation than the winter or spring broccoli.

Varieties

AUTUMN :

Veitch's Self-Protecting. This produces pure white, close heads which are generally well protected.

Extra Early Roscoff. One of the new French broccoli ; it turns in in November and December and is specially suited in the south and south-west.

WINTER OR EARLY SPRING :

Winter Mammoth. A favourite variety in the southern districts, and one which is good where there are no severe frosts.

New Year. Turns in in late December or early January, throwing large white curds.

Early Feltham. Turns in in the middle of January to the beginning of February and seldom fails to give good results, even in cold districts.

Roscoff No. 2. Of a delicious flavour, and particularly suited for the south and south-west.

Mid Feltham. Similar to the Early Feltham, but is used during March and April.

Snow's Winter White. A robust and hardy variety which matures in December, throwing large heads.

Roscoff No. 3. Cut in February and March.

SPRING :

Roscoff No. 4. May be cut in March or April in the south-west and some time later in other areas. This is the last of the Roscoffs, and it produces really beautiful pure white heads.

Satisfaction. A large type of broccoli which usually stands well under northern conditions. It produces medium-sized heads, pure white in colour.

LATE SPRING OR EARLY SUMMER :

Late Feltham. Another hardy variety suited for the midlands and north ; it comes into cutting in May.

May Blossom. Turns in in mid-May. Good southern variety.

Late Queen. A dwarf and compact grower, rarely affected by frosts ; it may be cut May and early June, and is one of the really well-protected types.

Clucas's June. A very hardy variety, suitable to be grown under northern conditions ; it is somewhat of a dwarf grower, but throws a good curd.

Whitsuntide. A late variety for the south, which throws a large, pure white curd at Whitsuntide.

BROCCOLI, SPROUTING

This was mentioned under the general heading " Broccoli," and no garden should be without this delicious winter crop.

The sprouting broccoli should not be expected to throw a pure white curd, but instead throws a large number of elongated flower-heads which are much prized by the connoisseur.

The sprouting broccoli is hardier than its cousin the ordinary broccoli, and there is no need to protect the plants during the winter.

The seeds may be sown in April and the plants put out in rows 2 ft. square. They should be well treated and they will produce an abundant crop as a result.

On the whole the purple variety is preferred to the white type, and there are both early and late purple varieties. Of the two the late purple is perhaps the hardiest, and it is seldom attacked by pests and diseases.

Harvesting. Sprouting broccoli should not be cut until the flower-shoots are found to be growing out from in between the axils of the leaves. These are then cut down to within two-thirds of their length, and as a result more shoots are thrown out on the same little stem. The main leaves are not cut until the majority of the sprouting tops have been removed, as these give some protection to these tender delicious shoots. At the end of the season practically the whole plant will have been consumed. It is a most economical crop to grow.

Varieties

Calabrese. An Italian type of sprouting broccoli which has a particularly good flavour. It is one of the earliest to turn in, and is used during September. The shoots should be gathered immediately, as they quickly run to seed. Sow in March.

Early Purple Sprouting. A very compact grower, and one which will often be fit to cut from December—February. Shoots should be cut when 9–12 inches long.

Late Purple Sprouting. Will withstand the most severe frosts and yet will grow away quickly directly the weather gets milder; it comes into cutting in April and gives a beautiful green colour.

White Sprouting. Comes in at the same time as Early Purple — but is not so hardy.

BROCCOLI, STAR

Latterly the Star Broccoli have been given a good deal of prominence in the Press. This is generally sold under the name of Nine-Star Broccoli, and the plants produced throw a large number of small cauliflowers on one stem. It is said to be a cross between a sprouting and an ordinary variety. As many as a dozen little cauliflowers can be cut from a plant.

The seed may be sown as for sprouting broccoli.

BRUSSELS SPROUTS

The Brussels sprout is one of the crops that must be well grown if it is to be profitable. There are five points that should always be borne in mind when attempting to cultivate this crop, and these are as follows :

(1) They should be sown early and grown on carefully, as they need a long season of growth.

(2) They should be planted widely apart, as they need plenty of room for development.

(3) They should be heavily manured, and a liberal quantity of well-decayed farmyard manure or compost may be incorporated during the preparation of the ground.

(4) They prefer firm ground, and so the soil preparation should be done early, leaving the land rough so that it may settle down. Very often a Brussels sprout crop may follow another crop that has been specially well manured, and in this case the soil will not be dug over deeply.

(5) The initial cultivation that is carried out should be deep, as the roots of this crop go down low.

Soil. This crop is not particular as to soil, though very often it throws heavier and better sprouts on firm land than on loose land.

Preparation of Soil. The soil should always be deeply prepared, and bastard trenching is always advisable. Despite the deep digging, the ground should always be made quite firm, so that the sprouts that form will really be large, firm " buttons." Firmness of soil cannot be over-emphasised, and the author has seen successful growers put sprouts out into land in which it was very difficult to make the holes for planting !

For this reason sprouts often follow a deeply cultivated, well-manured previous crop. In this way there is little need to do special deep cultivation.

Manuring. It would be difficult to advise too heavy a dressing of well-rotted farmyard manure, as Brussels sprouts are always hungry. A well-piled-up barrow-load of well-rotted manure or compost should be used to 8 sq. yards.

Artificials may be applied also, superphosphate at 1½ oz. per sq. yd. and sulphate of potash at ¾ oz. to the sq. yd. in addition. If the sprouts are not growing satisfactorily, Chilean potash nitrate may be applied at 1 oz. per yd. run.

Seed-Sowing. It is a good plan to try to produce a succession of Brussels sprouts throughout the autumn and winter, and to do this seeds may be sown from February (in a frame) till early in April. Sowings can be made also the previous year in August, and the plants thus raised planted out 3 ins. square in a sheltered border. In this way they live throughout the winter and can be planted out very early in the spring.

The first sowing of the year is done at the end of February or early in March, in a frame in light, well-raked soil. The seeds can be sown broadcast and the plants transferred to further frames and planted out 3 ins. apart when they are fit to handle.

The next sowing is made in March or early April, and in this case the seeds are sown thinly and the seedlings transplanted into their permanent position directly they are fit to handle. Whenever plants are raised in a seed-bed in this way it is quite a good idea to pick out the largest plants at the first transplanting and then to go over the original bed a fortnight later and pick out the largest that are left, and to do this three times. In this way successive batches of plants of different sizes can be obtained from one sowing. It is necessary to water the seed-beds with mercuric chloride (see p. 250) if club root is feared, and to dust with Gammaxene (see p. 236) to check flea beetle attack.

Planting. The plants should be put out during May, or perhaps early June, in rows 2½ ft. apart, the plants being at least 2 ft. apart in the rows. For the tall, heavy cropping varieties the plants need 3 ft. square. If the planting can be done during a showery period, so much the better, but, if not, the plants must be watered in ; mercuric chloride should be used as well if necessary.

Because the rows are far apart, it should be possible to sow intercrops between the rows, and spinach, radish, or lettuce are quite suitable for this purpose.

Hoeing should continue throughout the summer, to provide a good tilth, but during hoeing injury to the leaves should be avoided. The leaves of the sprout plants should never be removed until they are turning yellow and decaying. The head of the plant should not be removed until the end of February, as this not only helps to manufacture plant foods to feed the plant, but it does give some protection to the plant as a whole.

Harvesting. When the sprouts are gathered it is quite a good plan to cut them off, leaving a short stalk on the main stem, rather than to break them off. These little short sprout stems will then throw further loose open sprouts, and in seasons of scarcity of greens these are very useful. Gathering should be done systematically, starting from the bottom of the stem and working up. All the plants should be gone over. It is a bad plan to pick the sprouts from one or a few plants and to leave the others untouched.

Varieties

It seems very difficult to get a really true variety of Brussels sprouts. There are many strains available which are really selections from plants that have shown desirable characteristics. There is much to be said for getting hold of a reliable strain that suits your particular district. Latterly, however, the Cambridge University Research station have produced a number of definite varieties which are worth while growing :

Cambridge Early No. 1. An early variety which produces large solid sprouts that cover stems of medium height.

Cambridge Main Crop No. 3. Produces fine solid sprouts on a strong growing stem. A splendid general purpose variety.

Cambridge Late No. 5. A handsome tall-growing kind which produces fine sprouts from the ground upwards. Although a later sprout, can be picked fairly early when of moderate size, but will retain large sprouts until late in the season.

Other varieties which are worth growing for the reasons mentioned are :

Harrison's XXX or **XXXX,** a medium-sized strain which is excellent in the midlands.

Timperley Champion, a tall variety—first-class for the north.
Clucas' Favourite, another tall northern variety studded with solid sprouts. An abundant cropper.

Laxton's Improved, a tall strain, much liked in Bedfordshire and adjoining counties.

Rearguard, the latest variety of all. Usually picked 3 weeks after any other kind.

DWARF STRAINS:

There are two dwarf strains which only grow 15 inches high and which therefore can be planted much closer together than the mediums or talls.

Dwarf Gem, produces small, solid sprouts, much liked by French chefs.

Darlington, an early variety which does well on light sandy soil, produces medium-sized sprouts.

MEDIUM SIZED STRAINS:

Rouslench Early, grows 15–24 inches high.

Rouslench Late, grows at a similar height, but later.

CABBAGE

There are a large number of types of cabbages, many of which will be dealt with under their special heads. The main crops, however, refer to the spring, summer, and winter varieties, and it is quite possible to keep up a supply of cabbages all the year round.

There is no reason at all why cabbages should not be grown in all gardens now that the club root disease (see p. 249) and the cabbage caterpillars (see p. 241) can be kept down.

Soil. Cabbages will grow in any soil, though the spring cabbages prefer a light soil to a heavy one. Perhaps the ideal soil might be called a retentive loam.

Preparation of Soil. Deep cultivation is necessary, together with the addition of manure.

Manuring. All cabbages need heavy manuring, except perhaps the spring cabbage, which, because it has to live through the winter, should not be given too much nitrogen. A liberal dressing of farmyard manure or compost may be used. Artificials to use during the preparation of the soil should be superphosphate at 2 ozs. to the sq. yd. and sulphate of potash at $\frac{1}{2}$ oz. to the sq. yd. During the growing season Chilean potash nitrate may be applied at 1 oz. to the yard run as is necessary.

On the very light soils, kainit may be used instead of sulphate of potash, and in this case 1½ oz. should be applied, while for the September-planted spring cabbage on heavy land basic slag may be applied instead of superphosphate, at 4 ozs. to the sq. yd.

The ground for cabbages should be well limed if there is a tendency for it to be at all acid: 7 ozs. to 8 ozs. of hydrated lime should be used to the sq. yd., and this should be applied to the surface of the ground before the plants are put out.

Spring Cabbage

This should not be confused with spring-sown cabbage, as the latter produce crops for summer or autumn use. Spring cabbages are sown in the summer and planted out in the autumn.

Seed-Sowing. The seeds should be sown some time during the month of July, though in the southern counties it may be preferable to delay the sowing until early in August. Those who are in doubt as to the best time should make two small sowings. The seed-bed should be prepared as for broccoli and the ground raked down finely, the seed being sown in drills 9 ins. apart and ½ in. deep. If the seed is sown thinly there is no need to transplant, and it should be possible to put the plants out into their permanent positions some time in September. In the case of the August sowings, planting may be delayed until October.

Planting Out. Spring cabbages follow conveniently after such crops as early potatoes, peas, or beans, and the manuring for these should be sufficient for the cabbages with the addition of the special artificials outlined. The plants should be put out 18 ins. between the rows and 12 ins. between the plants. The stronger growing varieties, such as Durham Early, may need 18 ins. by 18 inches.

General Remarks. On heavy land tending to be acid, nitrochalk may be used in March to hurry spring cabbages along, though as a general rule Chilean potash nitrate will be found most suitable.

The stalks of the cabbages should be removed directly they are cut, and be put on the compost heap to rot down as manure.

Bash them up with the back of an axe on a chopping block first. If they are left in the ground they will rob the land.

Summer Cabbage

The seeds for the summer varieties are usually sown in March, and further sowings may be made if necessary at fourteen day intervals. If this is done, a succession of plants will be provided which may be put out whenever the land is free.

Winter Cabbage

Winter cabbage are sometimes preferred to savoys and other " greens."

Seed Sowing. The seed may be sown in March with the summer varieties if desired. This is what is usually done in the north and south midlands.

In the south, two sowings may be made, one in the first week of April, and the second early in May.

These later sowings are seldom pricked out into further seed-beds, but are *sown* as for broccoli (see p. 104).

Planting Out. The winter cabbage, particularly the Drumhead types, need plenty of room, and so the rows should be 2 ft. apart, and the plants 2 ft. apart in the rows. More compact types may be as close as 18 ins. in the rows.

As these plants have generally to be put out during dry weather, watering is usually advisable. Shallow furrows may be drawn out, and these are given a good soaking. The plants may be " swished round " in a bucket containing mud and a little lime, and thus the roots get covered with mud and are kept moist. It is surprising what a difference this makes to the recovery of the plants.

After planting, the rows should be hoed regularly and a dust mulch produced. This will help the plants to " get away " quickly.

General Cultivation. Hoeing must be continued throughout the season. Caterpillars and the blue aphis should be watched for (fly or bug), and the plants dusted or sprayed with derris (see pages 239–240), when an attack threatens.

Varieties

There is no doubt that certain varieties do better in certain districts. For instance Durham Early is excellent for the north, and Early Evesham first-class for Worcestershire. The great thing however, is to buy good seed from a first-class seedsman and the following should fit the bill well.

SPRING CABBAGE :

Clucas's First Early. One of the earliest varieties of cabbage known. Dark green in colour, forming a good heart.

Durham Early. An earlier variety than First Early, but perhaps not quite as hardy ; this forms a very large cabbage indeed.

Flower of Spring. A compact variety with few outer leaves which produces full-sized hearts of delicate flavour ; it seldom bolts.

*Harbinger. A bright, early cabbage ; the hearts make delicious eating, and the heads mature early.

SUMMER CABBAGE :

In the summer cabbage group there are *very quick maturing* varieties suitable for sowing under cloches or in frames in February, such as :

Velocity, round-headed, will cut in 12 weeks if not transplanted.

*Harbinger, pointed heart, moderate firmness. This variety when sown in July and covered with cloches in October, can be cut in December.

QUCK MATURING VARIETIES ARE :

Primo, which if sown in frames in February is ready 4 months later. Firm, tender and excellent flavour. The market-gardeners' favourite variety.

Early Paragon Drumhead, a drumhead type which also does well from February or March sowings.

Golden Acre, a round-headed type which will produce heads 6 inches across and 5 lbs in weight.

The Swift is a small, compact type, much liked in the Midlands.

MID SEASON TYPES :

All the following varieties are sown in March and they fall naturally into three sections, July, August and September.

JULY SECTION :

Greyhound, perhaps the quickest growing variety there is.

Cotswold Queen, said by the R.H.S. to be the most delicious spring sown cabbage.

AUGUST SECTION :

All the following are larger cabbages than in the July section, and if these are not required successional sowings may be made of the July varieties.

Utility, a round-headed, large and heavy type of Primo.

Simpson's Long Standing, excellent where gardeners only want to cut a cabbage now and then, for the hearts remain in good condition for a long time.

* Can, in fact, be both!

Winningstadt, a conical variety. Very popular for showing. Remains in condition for a considerable period.

Autumn Queen, a variety to follow Winningstadt, a drumhead of moderate size.

WINTER CABBAGE :
Early Paragon Drumhead. Throws a drum-like heart, which is firm and of good flavour.

Christmas Drumhead. A much later variety, it is large and very " hearty," and needs plenty of room.

January King. Sown in May, it cuts in February. Extremely hardy.

Red Cabbage (Pickling)

The red cabbage is usually grown for pickling, though in some districts it is stewed. The epicure insists on it as *the* vegetable for serving with partridge.

Seed-Sowing. The seed may be sown in March on a seed-bed, as in the case of ordinary summer cabbage. The plants thus raised, when planted out should come in for use in the autumn.

Those who require larger heads should sow in the month of August, and these plants will be fit to cut about the same month the following year.

Those who like it stewed may make a sowing in April.

General Cultivation. As for other cabbages.

Varieties

Ruby Red. This is one of the earliest varieties and should be sown in the spring. It does not grow so large as some, and is a good variety for the north.

Danish Stonehead. A variety that can be used either for pickling or cooking ; it throws heads of a deep red colour with a firm heart.

Lydiate. One of the largest red varieties known ; it throws a firm heart ; it is late and quite hardy.

Coleworts

Too often coleworts (or " collards," as they are often pronounced) are thought of as just any type of cabbage which is cut when small and undeveloped.

Coleworts are quite an interesting type of cabbage, being useful because of their hardiness.

Seed-Sowing. The seed may be sown in seed-beds in the spring, but more often the seed is sown thinly in rows where the plants are to grow. In this case the rows are 18 ins. apart.

Planting Out and Thinning. When the land is suitable, the plants may be put out 1 ft. square. Those that are sown in rows are generally thinned to 6 ins. apart first of all, and then, when the plants have grown to a usable size, a further thinning may be done to 1 ft. apart.

In this way an early succulent crop is obtained.

Time of Sowing. At almost any time in the Spring and Summer.

Varieties

> **Rosette.** Generally used in the winter. Bears rosette-shaped heads, crisp and of a good colour.
> **Hardy Green.** This has larger hearts on the whole ; it is hardy and very suitable for the north.

CABBAGE, SAVOY, (*see* SAVOYS p. 176)

CARROTS

It should be possible to have carrots as a vegetable all the year round. The main crops may be stored and used as desired in the winter, while sowings of "frame" varieties give delicious roots very early in the spring. There are many types that can be grown, and these may roughly be divided into five parts :

(1) Forcing types—those grown in frames on hot-beds.

(2) The Shorthorns. These produce short roots, and so are wanted for early sowings in warm borders and for shallow soils.

(3) The Guerande.

(4) The Intermediate, which are much liked by many people for use as "main" crop, especially on the heavier soils.

(5) The Long. A type of carrot much longer and larger than the others, and often grown by the acre by market gardeners on the deep sandy soils. Such roots keep well, but may be considered by the epicure to be rather coarse.

Soil. Without a doubt, carrots do best on a deep, well-cultivated sandy loam. Heavy soils may be improved by the addition of sandy material, and on such soils the shorter-rooted types should be grown.

Preparation of Soil. All root crops need deep cultivation, but especially the fine pulverisation of soil. If carrots are to grow with straight, clean roots the soil should not be " cloddy."

Even with types that require no great depth of soil, heavy land may be left rough in the winter so that the frosts and winds can break it down, and so make even the few inches of soil there are, in as perfect a condition as possible.

Sand, wood ashes, burnt refuse, and even burnt soil will do much to improve the texture of heavy land.

Manuring. As already indicated, carrots do not require large quantities of farmyard manure or compost dug into the soil prior to seed-sowing. The heavy soils may appreciate the addition of some organic matter in the form of rotted leaves or spent hops.

The following organic fertilisers may be used for the early crops :

2 ozs. of Fish manure to the square yard, plus Liquinure, applied at fortnightly intervals, should the growth not be considered quick enough.

For main crops use :

4 ozs. of a good Fish manure to the sq. yard.
Apply ten days or more before sowing the seed.

Seed-Sowing, Earlies. Early sowings can be made in south borders and in other warm spots. These can take place in March in drills 9 ins. apart. The rows may even be 6 ins. apart for very small varieties. Protection may be given to these beds by using continuous cloches, or a frame light or two. (For sowing in January, see p. 58). It is difficult to get good germination unless the soil is warm.

Seed-Sowing (Main Crop). It is for the main crop that deeper digging may be necessary, though on heavy soils it is possible even to grow short-rooted varieties for main-crop production.

As was suggested under the heading of " Manuring," it is

better to manure the previous crop heavily and not to apply special manure other than compost and ' Fish ' when preparing the seed-bed.

The seed may be sown in April onwards in drills ¾ in. deep and 12 to 18 ins. apart, according to the variety. Some gardeners like to mix the seed with a little dry earth, as this makes thin sowing easier to do. After sowing the drills, the soil should be raked over so as to cover the seed and produce a level bed.

Seed-Sowing (Late Crop). A further sowing of early varieties may be made in July, so as to provide tender young roots in the autumn and winter. These sowings should be carried out in exactly the same way as described for the early sowings. For these later sowings it is possible to broadcast the seed and just to pull the plants when they are large enough to use.

Thinning. There is no need to thin the early sowings, providing a really thin sowing is carried out. The roots should be pulled early, when the roots are young. The same holds good with regard to the July sowings, and, in fact, when broadcasting is done thinning is impossible to carry out.

The main crops, however, should be thinned to 6 ins. apart, depending on the variety. It is usual to thin at two periods, the first thinning to be done to half the distance required and the second thinning to the final distance. It is during these thinnings that the greatest care should be taken to prevent an attack of carrot fly. Whizzed naphthalene should be applied along the rows before thinning and immediately afterwards (see p. 242).

General Cultivation. There is little to do other than thinning and hoeing, though the latter is necessary at regular intervals all through the season. Carrot seeds do not germinate easily unless there is sufficient moisture present, and, in dry seasons, after sowing the seed it may be necessary to give the rows a good flooding from time to time.

Harvesting. Before the autumn and winter frosts appear the roots should be lifted and stored in sand or dry earth. The tops should be cut off neatly first of all (these being rotted down for compost), and the roots stacked neatly in a shed or a clamp, as described for potatoes.

Carrots can be grown in cold frames In this case the seed is not sown until say mid-February. See that the frame faces south.

Varieties

It can be said that carrots fall into 3 main classes—The Short carrots, the Intermediate or Half-Long carrots and the Long carrots.

These again may be sub-divided into groups as shown below:

SHORT CARROTS.

1. Forcing, out of season, in heated frames.
   Extra Early French Shorthorn. Delicious quick growing.
   Demi Longue a Forcer, probably the original name of the above variety, much used by market-growers.
2. For cold Frame or under cloches or even for catchcrops in the open.
   Early Horn, cylindrical, 4 inches long. First-class.
   Early Gem, 5 inches long, 3 inches in diameter. Coreless. Oval.

INTERMEDIATE OR HALF-LONG CARROTS. (STUMP ROOTED).

1. **Early Nantes,** keeps well, medium sized roots.
   Amsterdam Forcing, cylindrical, coreless, best of the last carrots for frame growing.
2. MAIN CROP.
   Chantenay, the most popular main crop half-long type.
   Autumn King, said to go on growing longer into the autumn than any other variety.
3. NORMAL POINTED ROOTS.
   James' Scarlet Intermediate, small core, bright and clean, one of the most popular varieties, and rightly so.
   St. Valerie, another first-class variety of similar type.

LONG CARROTS:

Altrincham. A very hardy variety, good roots of fine texture.
Long Surrey. Very long straight roots of good colour.

CAULIFLOWER

Cauliflowers are one of the most popular summer vegetables, and, though they may be likened to the broccoli already described, they are said to be more delicate in flavour, and for this reason are much in demand.

Soil. The cauliflower seems to do best on a somewhat rich loam which has been heavily manured, and whose moisture content is kept up.

Whatever the soil may be, it should be well worked and liberally manured if a good crop of cauliflowers is to result.

Preparation of Soil. The land should be bastard trenched and farmyard manure or compost incorporated well below the top spit. If this can be done in the autumn with the heavier soil, so that the land can be left rough, it will be easier to get the soil down into a fine condition in the spring. Just before the plants are ready to put out, the ground may be forked over and the artificials incorporated in this way. Finally, lime is applied to the surface of the ground.

Seed-Sowing. There are various times of the year when seed may be sown if an unbroken supply of white curds is aimed at from early June to the end of October.

Autumn Sowing. The first sowing should be done in the autumn—round about the middle of August in the northern counties, and early in September in the south. The seeds may be sown in warm seed-beds outside and the seedlings thus raised pricked out in quite poor soil into cold frames 4 ins. square. It should be seen that the seedlings are quite near the glass, so that they do not become drawn, and liberal ventilation may be given throughout the winter on bright days. During the more frosty periods, mats should be used to cover the glass so as to protect the young plants.

It is most important, when pricking out these young plants, to see that they are not buried. When seedlings are planted too deeply, blind plants result the following summer.

The seedlings thus raised can be planted out in March and April in a sheltered part of the garden.

Another method is to sow the seed thinly in boxes and to place these in a cold frame or cool greenhouse. Poor soil is again used, the surface being given a good sprinkling of hydrated lime after the sowing has taken place. The plants raised in this way are then pricked out 4 ins. apart into frames for the winter.

January and February Sowings. Those who do not prefer or find it inconvenient to sow in the autumn may raise suitable plants from sowings made in January or early February. In this case the seeds are usually sown in boxes, and these are put into a greenhouse or frame with sufficient heat on to keep out any frost. When the young seedlings come through, the plants are pricked out as before, this time into light, rich soil. The plants thus raised are usually ready to put out early in April.

The advantage of such a method of sowing is that all worries of over-wintering are eliminated, but the disadvantage is that the crops produced are never as large as those from autumn sowings.

Spring Sowings. The seed of the later varieties may be sown in March or early April in specially prepared seed-beds out of doors. The seed rows may be 6 ins. apart, and when the plants are through they may be thinned out to 3 ins. apart, the seedlings being transplanted into further seed-beds if necessary.

These seed-beds should be watered regularly if dry, to get the plants growing, and should be hoed every other day if possible.

Later Sowings. Still later sowings may be made late in April or early in May. Here again the seeds are sown out-doors in a fine seed-bed, and the young plants thus raised are pricked out when they are fit to handle in rows 6 ins. apart with 3 ins. between the plants. The late cropping varieties are obviously chosen for this purpose.

N.B. With any of these sowings the mercuric chloride treatment must be used (see p. 250) if the land is infected with club root.

Planting Out. The autumn sowings may be planted out in early March in the south in a sheltered situation, the plants being 1 ft. square. On very rich soil it may be necessary to plant them 18 ins. by 1 ft.

For the later sowings, the distance between the rows may be increased to 2 ft., the plants being 18 ins. apart in the rows. It much depends on soil, climate, and the manuring whether these greater distances are necessary or not. For the late summer sowings the rows may be as far apart as 2½ ft., the cauliflowers being 2 ft. between the plants.

Planting should always be done firmly, mercuric chloride solution being poured into the hole if necessary. As this treatment keeps both club root and the cabbage root maggot at bay, it is well worth carrying out.

The roots must be spread out, and the hole should be made large enough so that this can be done. The plants should be planted out before they get too big, as in this way better crops result.

General Cultivation. Hoeing regularly between the plants is necessary, and during dry weather copious waterings should be given in addition. This is very necessary, especially in the early stages, as to get large curds no check in the growth must occur.

When the plants are curding, should the weather be warm, one or two of the inner leaves may be bent over the " flower " to prevent it from opening up or turning yellow. It is quite easy to break the centre vein of a leaf without severing the leaf altogether.

It is to be hoped that the season will not be too dry, but if it is, and the plants need water, heavy drenchings are really necessary. These should always be followed by a good hoeing.

Harvesting. The curds should be cut as early in the morning as possible, and brought into the house while they are still wet with dew.

In cases where too many heads become ready to cut at one time, whole plants may be pulled up with soil attached to the roots, and these may be hung in a shed, upside-down, and used as desired.

Growing in Frames. It is possible to make up a mild hot-bed in a frame any time from mid-November to the end of February. Four inches of light soil should cover the manure. After a week the soil may be raked down fine and the seed broadcast. The soil is again raked and firmed with a presser. Radish seed may be sown at the same time thinly— these are up and are cleared before the carrots need the room.

After sowing close down the frame. After germination

ventilate if the temperature of the bed rises above 60 degrees F. in the day, and after four leaves have been made ventilate whenever possible. At this time thinning may be done to 1 in. apart. Water sparsely and carefully. Try and see that the original soil is sufficiently moist before sowing.

At the beginning of April the lights may be removed altogether on fine days.

Varieties

1. V. EARLY SUMMER CAULIFLOWERS.

   Types to be sown in the autumn and overwintered in frames or for sowing in the greenhouse in January and February.

   a.   For growing in the greenhouse or frame throughout.
   Feltham Forcing, delicious, quick growing, snow white curd.
   Presto, similar to above but must not be sown before November.

   b.   For sowing in the autumn and planting out in April for cutting in early June.
   Early London, the earliest type. Sow September.
   White King, a good all-round type. The largest curd. Sow October.
   Magnum Bonum, the latest of the three. Sow September.
   All the Year Round, sow early September. Neat compact growth.

2.   For sowing mid-February, for cutting mid-June—early July.
   Leader, withstands drought better than any other type.
   Early Snowball, quick growing, small, very early.
   King of Cauliflowers, dwarf, medium size.
   Forerunner, forms a curd 10 days before any of the above types.

3. LATE SUMMER AND AUTUMN CAULIFLOWERS.

   a.   For sowing in March to crop in August and early September.
   Majestic, very large and fine type of cauliflower.
   Early Giant, one of the earliest large-headed. Comes into use early in September. Very popular with Exhibitors.
   Dobbie's 6-weeks. Curds turn in 6 weeks after planting out.
   Orion, usually turns in next to Dobbie's 6-weeks.

   b.   For sowing in April to crop in October, November.
   Veitch's Autumn Giant. Produces huge white heads of excellent quality.
   Clucas's October. A first-class variety for this month.

CELERY

Celery is an excellent vegetable to grow, not only because it is very popular, but also because in the production of this crop the land is left in the best possible condition for succeeding crops. Where celery trenches have been prepared it is obvious that deep cultivation is necessary, and the exposure of such a large surface of soil to all kinds of weather does much to improve it.

This is one of the vegetables that can be used either as a salad or when cooked.

Soil. The main desideratum in connection with celery soil is that it should be deep. Many market gardeners prefer peaty soil for celery production, because of the high amount of organic matter present. Acid soils seem to grow better celery than those that have a high lime content. A soil which retains moisture easily is important, because plants have a tendency to go to seed if they receive a check owing to dryness at the roots. Much of the acreage of celery in this country is, therefore, grown on soil with a high water table.

Preparation of Soil. This consists principally in preparing special trenches in which the celery is grown. Normally these are prepared 16 ins. deep and 18 ins. wide. It is not that the celery should be planted deeply, especially on heavy soils, but the preparation of the trench makes it easier to blanch the celery subsequently, and to ensure that the plants get sufficient moisture throughout their growing season.

The soil is taken out when the trenches are being prepared and is then thrown on either side of the trench in equal proportions, and this makes ridges of equal height. If several trenches are being prepared, a distance of 2 ft. 6 ins. is generally allowed between the trenches, and in these areas catch-crops are often grown.

Some growers prefer to make wider trenches, so that they may grow two or three rows of celery in a trench. This does save time in the initial preparation, but it is not so easy to carry out the earthing-up operations afterwards. The general rule with regard to the width of the trench is that for every extra row one wishes to grow another 6 ins. width should be added. The beginner, however, should certainly use the single row trench.

The ridges thus made at the sides of the trenches should be flattened, and on these, various catch-crops can be grown. Lettuces, radishes, and shallots are most suitable for this purpose. The earlier the trenches are dug the earlier can the ridges be used for growing a catch-crop, and, further, the better will the trenches be weathered.

Manuring. Horse manure is preferable if it can be obtained, but well rotted compost is first class, and the bottom of the trench should be filled with a good layer of either of these materials, so that it is at least 6 ins. deep when it is trodden down firmly. On this a 5 ins. depth of good friable soil should be placed.

In addition to the large quantities of organic matter which are placed in the bottom of the trench, regular " feeds " may be given with liquid manure. This can be purchased already made up as Liquinure and after dilution is poured into the trench every ten days or so with a watering-can.

Seed-Sowing. Beginners are apt to sow seeds too early, and as a result the plants tend to bolt (i.e. throw up a flower-stem) during the summer. The earliest seed to be sown should be about the middle of February, and from such sowings good sticks should be ready to use late in August and at the beginning of September. These earlier sowings are made in boxes, and a compost rich in organic matter is used. Celery seeds on the whole germinate readily, and so thin sowing is necessary. After the seeds are sown, a little of a similar compost may be sifted over them and the soil then pressed down lightly with a wooden presser.

The boxes are then put in the greenhouse with a temperature of 60–65 degrees F., and they may be covered with a sheet of glass on top of which is placed a piece of brown paper. Once the seeds have germinated the glass and paper should be removed and the boxes set on a shelf near the light. A fortnight or so later the seedlings may be pricked out into further boxes, placing them 3 ins. apart. This time a slightly " heavier " compost may be used.

Main Sowing. The main sowing is usually carried out early in March, either on a hot-bed or in boxes in the greenhouse as before.

To make a hot-bed in a frame, good horse manure is placed in the frame, treading it down until it is 1 ft. deep. This should then be covered with 4 ins. of compost rich in organic matter, and it is useful to see that this soil is sterilised before using. This can be done either by steaming or by soaking it with 2 per cent solution of formaldehyde a week or so beforehand. A pint of formaldehyde should be dissolved in six gallons of water and stirred well, and the soil in the frame watered with this solution. Four gallons of solution should be sufficient for a frame 6 ft. long by 3 ft. wide. After watering, the soil should be covered with sacks to retain the fumes, and then, four or five days later, the soil forked over well so as to release them. In this way the soil will be partially sterilised and the seedlings will grow better in consequence.

Half an ounce of seed will be sufficient to sow a frame of this size, and this should raise some thousands of seedlings— far more than the ordinary garden owner needs.

Those who prefer may sow their seeds under continuous cloches and really hardy plants may be raised this way.

During frosty periods it may be necessary in the north to cover the glass up with some old sacks, and, directly the seedlings are through, they may be removed during the day.

Celery seeds do not germinate quickly, but once they have germinated the plants should grow steadily. When they are 2 ins. high they may be transplanted.

Later Sowing. Another sowing may be made at the end of the second week in March, under cloches as before.

The last sowing is usually made the second week of April in a sunny border. A little protection may be given by means of cloches, should the weather be cold. It is advisable to do these sowings in light, rich soil, and the seedlings raised in this way may be transplanted in two or three batches.

The advantage of these various times of sowing for those

who are particularly fond of celery is that a constant supply may be achieved from the end of August to the following March. Those who have no greenhouse may carry out the sowings in frames, or under cloches, and those who have no frames or cloches may at least raise seedlings in a warm corner outside.

Planting Out. When the plants are ready, either from the frames or in the open border, they may be planted out into the trenches. At this time they will usually be 3 or 4 ins. high. The plants are lifted carefully with a trowel and then planted in the trenches 1 ft. apart. Some growers have them as close as 9 ins., and this smaller distance may be sufficient for the weaker-growing varieties. After planting, the soil is made firm around them and then the trench is given a thorough soaking with water and the soil at the bottom of the trench hoed thoroughly the next day.

General Cultivation. During the whole of the growing season the trenches must be kept moist by regular waterings. These waterings will probably alternate with the feeds of liquid manure outlined in the paragraph dealing with manuring. Throughout the season the ridges should be kept well hoed ; the catch-crops should be harvested as soon as possible.

Any side-growths that come from the base of the celery plants should be removed. These suckers only rob the main plant and are of no value. The plants should be sprayed regularly with nicotine and soft soap to keep down celery fly, and if necessary with Bordeaux (see p. 250) for the prevention of celery leaf spot, also known as celery blight.

During the winter it is necessary to protect celery from frost. There are one or two ways of doing this. The tops may be covered with straw or bracken, and the tops may be bent slightly to one side at the last earthing so as to prevent the moisture from trickling down into the heart of the plant during a sunny or rainy period.

On the other hand, during the summer celery benefits from having the foliage sprinkled every day during the hot weather. This should be done late in the afternoon.

Earthing-Up. In order that celery may be fit to eat it

A sweet corn ready to eat, with the sheaths pulled back to show the cob. Note the male bloom at the back.

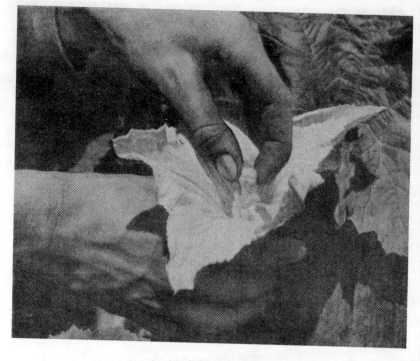

Pollinating the female bloom of a marrow plant.

must be blanched, and this may be done at regular intervals ; it is not advisable to earth higher than the base of the leaves.

It is usual to do the first earthing-up with the handfork and to bring the soil up to the base of the plant in a somewhat loose manner. This allows the plant to expand, and all that it is necessary to do is to bring some earth half way up the plant and all round it.

The earthing-up should always be done with the hand grasped firmly around the plant while the soil is put into position. It is necessary to avoid allowing any soil to get in between the stems, and so an hour or so before earthing-up the soil is chopped down finely and allowed to stand before it is worked into its new position.

The first proper earthing-up is done when the plants are ovei 1 ft. high. This may be about the middle of August. Another earthing is carried out three weeks later, and the final earthing some time during the month of October. It is at this last earthing that the soil is brought up to the top of the stem as high as the bottom leaves. When earthing-up, the ridges should be made smooth and steep, as in this way the rain is carried away and does not get down into the plants.

It is possible, when earthing-up, to wrap the celery plants with brown paper or with corrugated cardboard. This is tied into position and prevents the soil from reaching the stems. It is said, however, that plants blanched in this way are not so well flavoured as those that come into contact with the soil. An alternative is to use a cardboard tube which can be slipped into position, but the writer has not found these satisfactory. Loose ties can always be made if necessary, and some growers use wide rubber bands, which they slip up the plant as the earthing-up process proceeds.

It may be as well to reiterate some of the important points in celery production, and they are as follows : Grow the plants slowly, without any check. Do not allow them to become frozen or dry in the frames. Always arrange for plenty of organic matter to allow a free root run. Be on the look-out all the time for celery fly, especially when the plants are in the frame. Be willing to spray with nicotine whenever

E

necessary. Earth-up so as to blanch, and if the beginner finds it difficult to hold the plant with one hand while he is pushing the soil around the plant with the other, another helper may grasp the plant with both hands. Another method is to give a loose tie of raffia round each plant. Earthing-up should never be carried out when the plants or the soil are wet.

Harvesting. About eight weeks should be allowed after the first earthing-up before the sticks are sufficiently blanched to be used in the house. When the necessary period has elapsed, the celery stick may be dug up from the trench, the soil being placed around the dug-up portion so as to prevent the sticks on either side from greening.

Varieties

WHITE :

White Perfection. A strong-growing white celery. Produces solid, firm sticks. Is crisp and of good flavour.

Darragh's White. Popular because it is fairly resistant to septoria blight. Has not the same length of stem as White Perfection.

Blundell's White. One of the best for early purposes. Tall, crisp, and of good flavour. It has the advantage of blanching quickly.

PINK :

Clayworth Prize Pink. A large early variety of excellent quality. Keeps well and seldom goes to seed.

Clucas's White Pink. An old and heavy winter celery. Though truly a pink it blanches nearly white. The stem is very wide at the base and hardly tapers up to the foliage.

Resistant Pink. Similar to Darragh's White in its resistance of septoria. Tall, late, and of good flavour.

RED :

Standard Bearer. Throws very solid sticks of good size and flavour.

Covent Garden Red. An excellent flavoured red-coloured variety. Excellent for table use.

CELERY, SELF-BLANCHING

Those who have not the room for trenches, or do not care for one reason or another, to prepare them, should concentrate on growing celery on the flat, choosing one of the self-blanching varieties.

The soil where this crop is to be grown should be bastard

trenchèd and enriched with plenty of farmyard manure if possible. The celery plants, which can be raised in the ordinary way, are then planted out in rows 18 ins. apart, the plants being 1 ft. apart in the rows. Dwarfer varieties need only be 1 ft. square. When the plants are put out on the flat the ground should be well soaked afterwards, and the following day the bed should be hoed over so as to leave the surface rough.

This celery is called self-blanching, though it is usually necessary to place straw among the plants in order to ensure that the stems are really white. It is possible in small gardens to blanch each individual plant by tying stiff paper collars into position. The use of mats or sacking is sometimes advised, placed as a kind of fence right round the plants and over the top of them.

Varieties

Doré. Probably the best pure white dwarf. Has an excellent flavour.

KALE

The kales, though not perhaps the most delicious of vegetables, are invaluable because they are so hardy and ensure a good supply of green vegetables throughout the winter months.

As in the case of parsnips, the kales as a whole are improved by frosts.

Soil. There is no need to worry about special soil condition, as kales will grow well in practically all gardens.

Preparation of Soil. There is no need to make special preparations, as they usually follow a well-manured crop and are quite content with the soil preparation and manuring given to the previous crop. Occasionally mustard or some other quick-growing crop is sown and then is cut down eight weeks or so after sowing and dug in as a green manure.

Manuring. See Cabbage.

Seed-Sowing. It should be possible to make a sowing of seed during the first week of March in the south, and towards the end of March in the north. Further sowings can be made during the second and third weeks of April. A fine seed-bed should be prepared by raking the soil down well, and if an open situation can be chosen, so much the better.

The drills should be 9 ins. apart, and if the plants are to be thinned and transplanted they should be put out 6 ins. apart in the rows.

Asparagus kale may be sown as late as June and July.

Transplanting. Should the plants get rather large and the rows somewhat crowded, it is possible to transplant or prick out the young plants into further seed-beds. If this is done, stouter, firmer plants are produced; these give a better crop in the long run. The final transplanting into their permanent positions is usually done towards the end of June or the beginning of July onwards. They are a very useful crop to follow early potatoes, early peas, or even French beans.

General Cultivation. When the plants are put out, they must have plenty of water to start with. This can be achieved by puddling the plants in, and if the mercuric chloride treatment is used for the purpose of keeping down both club root and the cabbage root maggot the amount of this liquid that is put into the hole at planting time is sufficient to start the plants off.

Harvesting. Kales may be harvested as desired, but it is inadvisable to use them until the other green vegetables are scarce. In this way they are able to grow unrestricted and build up a good plant. Early in the new year the heads of the kales may be removed, and in this way dozens of side-growths will break out. These prove very useful.

Varieties

Hardy Sprouting. A type that will withstand the most rigorous weather. Large shoots are produced all down the main stem. They are delicious.

Extra Curled Scotch. A Scotch kale which is robust and compact in growth. The leaves are densely curled, and prove most acceptable on the table. A very hardy and productive variety.

Asparagus Kale. One of the later varieties. Hardy, producing, as it does, a large number of shoots in the spring. Is sometimes sown where the crop is intended to be grown.

Thousand-Headed. A very hardy variety which is strong and branching in habit. Is excellent for use in the spring, and is remarkably productive.

Russian Kale. Extremely hardy. Produces dense head of foliage in November and then abundant delicious young shoots in the spring. Should be more grown.

Drumhead Kale. Forms loose, cabbage-like head. Good flavour.

Hungry Gap Kale. Withstands drought, wet and frost. Very hardy. Is better sown where it is to grow.

Variegated Kales. Extremely decorative, ranging from Ivory-white to bright rose and crimson. Colour disappears in cooking, and leaves become appetising green.

LEEK

The leek is essentially a north-country vegetable for some reason or another, though of course it is the national emblem of Wales. The Emperor Nero was very fond of leeks, and said that they helped to clear his voice !

The leek has become deservedly more popular year by year, largely because even the severest of winters cannot harm the plants.

Soil. Leeks can be grown on practically all soils providing these are deeply worked or special trenches are prepared. They naturally prefer a well-drained loam, and do not particularly like a very light sand or a badly drained clay. Leeks like soil in which there is plenty of organic matter present, either in its natural form or which has been specially added. They also prefer soils that retain moisture readily without being sodden.

Preparation of Soil. The best results may be obtained by growing leeks in trenches as has been described for celery. In this case the trenches are taken out 9 ins. to 1 ft. deep, and manure or compost is then placed in position. If this can be done a few days before planting, so much the better. The organic matter should then be forked into the bottom of the trench and 3 ins. of good soil put on top of this. This leaves the trenches about 6 ins. deep. It is quite convenient on certain soils for them to be 18 ins. apart from centre to centre, and this leaves a distance of 1 ft. between the trenches when they have been dug out. The plants are put out in these trenches 1 ft. apart (see illustration, page 39).

Manuring. The farmyard manure or compost that is dug into the bottom of the trench will be the main requirement of this crop. Many growers like to use a little dried poultry manure as well, and apply this along the rows when they apply the top soil at the rate of about 1 oz. to the sq. yard.

Those who cannot get hold of poultry manure should use 2 ozs. of a good fish manure per yard run instead once a month, and nitrate of soda may be given at the rate of $\frac{3}{4}$ oz. per yard run.

If leeks are grown on the flat or in trenches, the same kind of manurial dressings should be given.

Seed-Sowing. The seed may be sown in gentle heat under glass towards the end of January. A fairly light compost should be used, and quite shallow boxes with good drainage are useful for this purpose. The seed is sown thinly, a little light soil sifted over it, pressed down lightly with a wooden presser, and then watered with water at the same temperature as the house, through a fine rose. The boxes are covered with a sheet of glass and with a piece of brown paper, and after the seedlings have appeared the boxes are stood on a shelf near the glass.

When the baby plants are an inch or so high they may be pricked out into other boxes 1 to $1\frac{1}{2}$ in. apart. A good compost for this consists of 2 parts of fibrous loam, 1 part of finely divided, well-decayed leaf-mould, 1 part of old horse manure passed through a fine sieve, and $\frac{1}{2}$ part of silver sand. These materials are mixed together and the boxes filled up to within $\frac{1}{4}$ in. of the top, pressing the soil down firmly.

The boxes are watered, placed on the shelf of the glasshouse, and kept at a temperature of about 55 degrees F.

When these plants are growing well, at 5 or 6 ins. high, they should be hardened off gradually by placing them in a cold frame. This usually takes place towards the end of March. By airing the frames regularly it should be possible to remove the lights by the third week of April, when the leeks can be planted out.

It is possible also to sow the seed under cloches about the middle of February. The drills may be as close as 9 ins. apart.

There are two main groups, the cos and cabbage lettuce, but for the winter it is the cabbage varieties that are principally grown.

Few people realise that lettuces can be cooked in the same way as cabbage, and taste similar to spinach. One of the best ways of preparing them for the table is to parboil them and to simmer them in milk.

Soil. It is important that the soil for lettuce should be rich in organic material. This ensures that the moisture is retained during the warmer months. On the whole a light, rich soil is preferable, especially if this is liberally manured.

Preparation of Soil. It is here where the good gardener can score, as he will dig in large quantities of organic material—well rotted compost and the like—one spade deep. In this way the roots of the plants will reach this layer just at the time when they need it most. In addition, he will use organic forms of fertilisers such as fish or meat or bone in the top 3 or 4 ins., lightly forked in.

Manuring. The advice given in the previous paragraph should be borne in mind. It is as well to give lettuce a dressing consisting of 2 ozs. fine meat meal, $\frac{1}{2}$ oz. precipitated bone phosphates, and $\frac{1}{2}$ oz. sulphate of potash. 1 oz. of Chilean potash nitrate may be applied to the sq. yd. as a top-dressing and lightly hoed in a week or ten days before the plants are due to heart.

Seed-Sowing. Lettuce seed may be sown at various times of the year, both in the open and under glass.

Spring Sowings. From the beginning of March onwards it is possible to make sowings of lettuce at fortnightly intervals until the middle of April, and at three weekly intervals from the middle of April until the beginning of August. The plants raised from these sowings may either be allowed to grow where they are sown, or may be thinned out and transplanted to further borders.

The drills for the earliest sowings are usually 6 ins. apart, and as soon as the young seedlings appear they are thinned out to 2 ins. apart. The sowings that are done in the open for growing where they are sown should be made in rows 1 ft.

E*

apart, the plants being thinned to 10 ins. apart. Even in such a case, any thinnings that are required may be transplanted.

August Sowings. During the third week in August in the south, and about the second week in August in the north, it is possible to sow seed thinly on a specially prepared, moist seed-bed. It is here where the use of damped horticultural peat comes in "handy." Use this at ½ a 2-gallon bucketful to the square yard. Special varieties are used for such sowings, and the plants thus raised are put out in rows 1 ft. apart, and 10 ins. apart in the rows.

Again, it is possible to sow the rows where the lettuces are to grow, and to thin the plants out to 5 ins. before the winter sets in. A second thinning to 10 ins. may be carried out in the spring.

Frame Sowings. About the second week in October in the north, and the third week in October in the south, another sowing may be made in frames. When the plants are large enough they can be pricked out into other frames 2 ins. apart, and are left in these frames growing sturdily until the turn of the new year. As soon as the soil is fit to work, these lettuces are planted out 12 ins. by 10 inches.

The plants, when in frames during the winter, should be given protection from frost by covering the lights with sacking, and air should be admitted on every possible occasion.

November Frame Sowings. Lettuce seed may be sown in frames in November, each seed being dropped separately ½ in. apart. A light compost is used in the frame, and a little of this is sifted over the seeds after sowing. The lights are then put into position and kept there until the plants are through. After this, during the fine weather air is given and the whole light may be removed. It should, however, be replaced during wet periods.

The soil in which the lettuces are sown should be thoroughly soaked after seed-sowing takes place. If this is done, there should be no need to water further, once the plants are through.

Continuous Cloches. Continuous cloches are useful for growing lettuces, as they give the necessary protection and yet are perfectly ventilated and let in light all round. Cloches can be used to cover salads at any time of the year, and quicker growth thus results. They are, however, of the maximum value for the sowings made during the middle of August or the middle of October, for it is possible by using them to obtain lettuces up to the end of the year in the case of the August sowings, and for an early spring supply in the case of those sown in October.

It is usually unnecessary to cover lettuce rows sown in the summer. See the author's book " Continuous Cloche Gardening."

Thinning and Transplanting. It is practically impossible, except for the single-seed-sowing method, to guarantee that lettuces are sown thinly enough. Many gardeners affirm that lettuces cannot be thinned and transplanted early enough, and under the French gardening system the lettuces are pricked out when only two little seed-leaves are showing.

Lettuces must be given plenty of room to develop, and kept growing quickly, and a crisp appetising salad results. It is those that are crowded, and so are slow in growth, that tend to be soft and unpalatable.

Lettuces should be handled carefully, as they are tender and can easily be damaged. The roots also dry out quickly, and for this reason they should not be left out of the soil longer than necessary. They must not be transplanted deeply, as otherwise " peaky " plants result, but should, however, be planted firmly. If the land is at all dry there is a danger of botrytis.

General Cultivation. The hoe must be kept going between the rows whenever possible. It is not so necessary or advisable to go on to the land in the winter, but even under these conditions, when the soil is warm enough, surface cultivation will do a great deal of good.

Cos lettuces do not heart naturally as easily as the cabbage varieties, and for this reason they are often tied round with raffia when they have made three-quarters of their growth in order to help them to heart properly. The cos lettuces, too, seem to need far more moisture, and so should be regularly watered.

Harvesting. Lettuces should be cut as soon as they are ready. If they are not they will quickly go to seed, and then are of little value except for cooking.

VARIETY CLASSIFICATION

The two main groups of lettuce are, of course (a) the Cabbage and (b) the Cos, but in addition there is an Intermediate type generally known as the Density Group, the best of which is perhaps Osmaston Gem. The cabbage lettuces themselves can be divided up into three types—(1) what are known as Butter-Heads, those with ordinary smooth leaves and smooth hearts ; (2) the Icebergs, the most popular type in America, which have crisp crinkly leaves and huge white hearts ; and (3) the Gathering lettuce which doesn't heart at all but has crispish leaves, a typical variety being Green Jade.

Now in the cabbage lettuce group as a whole, will be found a number of sub-sections which arise because of the different times in which seed may be sown. It is important to know which type and variety to sow at differing periods of the year. It is important also to realise that certain types of lettuce prefer the short days of the winter and do well under glass while others insist on the long days of summer and do better during the summer months.

Varieties

Study the following carefully.

Varieties for :—

(a) Heated greenhouse or frame for growing in the winter.

Cheshunt Early Ball, raised by the Research Station for the heated frame, but does not do badly in unheated frames and under cloches.

Blackpool, Early French Frame. A light green lettuce, ideal for frames, especially in the north. Quite good for cloches also. Always insist on the Blackpool strain.

Gotte a Forcer, used principally in French Gardening, i.e. in frames over hot-beds. Delights in no ventilation.

Loos Tennis Ball, a slow growing looser leaved type of lettuce, popular in the north. Is said to be immune from mildew.

(b) Varieties for the unheated greenhouse in winter, the cold frame or the Continuous Cloche. May do well from spring sowings in the open.

May Queen, sometimes called May King. Insist on a good **strain**. Produces a large lettuce with a good heart, loves air.

Delice, a lovely light green lettuce, much liked in the Midlands.

Victor, a medium green type ; hearts well. Can be got to turn in in April in the south and May in the north.

(c) Varieties for sowing in September, for cutting in November, or for sowing in October for standing the winter in the open.

Stanstead Park, very hardy, dark green leaves, large stained reddish brown. Very coarse.

White Maderia. Very similar to above. A poor eater.

Imperial, produces a solid heart of a good size, hardy, probably the best of the clear green-leaved types.

Arctic King, much recommended but really too small. Is of good quality and very hardy.

Winter Crop, the largest in this group but is particular as to soil and district.

(d) Varieties that only succeed when sown in the autumn for standing out of doors in the winter and cutting in the spring.

McHattie's Giant, a good old-fashioned type with large spreading puckered leaves and a loosish-heart. Though very hardy is apt to be coarse.

Whitsuntide, similar to above.

Green Winter, leaves edged with yellow, dull and unblistered. Medium size and fair flavour.

Lee's Immense, commonly known as **Hardy Hammersmith**, a very large old-fashioned type, but coarse.

(e) Varieties for sowing very early in spring, for cutting in the spring, for cutting out of doors.

Borough Wonder, a good lettuce with solid heart of a pleasant colour. Stands drought well. Leaves pale green with a S-shaped folding of the edges as they get older.

Market Favourite. Similar to the above.

Trocadero, the original type of this group, but tends to have red margins to the leaves. A medium to large well-shaped heads

(f) Varieties for sowing in spring or summer but which are not hardy.

All the Year Round ; firm heart, well flavoured, medium dark green puckered leaves. Insist on a good strain.

Standwell. Has large dark green leaves, crumpled in character, but a particularly good variety for dry soils and drought years.

Continuity, an excellent lettuce for those who do not mind the brownish or purply leaves. Produces a good tender heart, stands the drought well.

Feltham King, shiny mid-green leaves. Solid compact hearts An excellent drought resister, popular with market growers.

(g) Varieties with the crisp curled leaves known as Iceberg. Sown any time during the spring or summer.

Webb's Wonderful, perhaps the best of the group. Grows really large with waxy green foliage.

Sutton's Favourite. Compact, fairly large with yellowish green puckered foliage.

(*h*)   The Gathering Group, to be sown any time during the spring or summer. Should never be transplanted.

American Gathering, loose, crisp curled leaves which should be picked like spinach.

Green Jade. Similar to the above but has a very striking bright green colour to the leaves.

COS LETTUCES

It is not possible to divide cos lettuces up as easily as cabbage lettuces into various groups. There are however, four main types (*a*) the miniature, (*b*) the winter type, (*c*) the summer and (*d*) the semi-cos or Density group.

(*a*) The Miniature.

Little Gem, usually sown in January under cloches or in the greenhouse, hardened off in February and planted out in March for hearting in May. A delicious little baby cos.

(*b*) Winter type.

Hick's Hardy Winter White, sown in the autumn for hearting in the spring, rather spreading in habit and should be tied up with raffia or have a rubber ring put round it to get it to heart well.

(*c*) Summer type.

Lobjoit's Green Cos. May be sown in the autumn under cloches or in frames and with some protection will then stand the winter. Best all-round variety. Dark green, self folding, large.

Balloon. Its name suggests what it looks like when growing. Has big outer leaves that enclose the heart with balloon-like effect.

(*d*) Density Group.

Winter Density, glossy dark green leaves, hardy, very delicious. Lovely firm, semi-cos hearts.

Osmaston Gem, perhaps the best strain of this group. May be sown in spring as well as the autumn. Delicious yellow hearts, firm and tender.

MARROW

The marrow is the vegetable crop that is often grown on the rubbish-heap and in any odd corner of the garden. It is not realised very often that it may be grown trailed up a fence, a shady one being most suitable for the purpose, and that it may be grown in its bush form in rows like any other vegetable.

During wet years it will appreciate being grown on a mound,

because its roots will be drier, but in dry years it likes growing on the flat.

In the northern and more smoky districts it may be necessary to grow this vegetable in a cold frame.

Soil. Marrows can be grown on almost any soil, providing they are (*a*) well drained, and (*b*) rich in organic material.

Preparation of Soil. If this crop can follow one which has been liberally manured, then there is little special cultivation to be done. Crops that are off the ground in May usually leave the land in a good condition for marrows.

Manuring. As much organic material as possible should be incorporated into the soil where the marrows are to grow. Some gardeners make furrows 9 ins. deep and half fill these with well-decayed compost or manure. They tread this down well and then replace the soil, forming a ridge over the compost or manure. In this way a certain amount of bottom heat is generated, and the plants get away quickly in consequence.

In addition a good fish manure or meat and bone meal should be forked in a fortnight before planting at 3 ozs. to the sq. yard.

Seed-Sowing. It is possible to sow the seeds outside in a little pocket of specially prepared soil where the plants are to grow. This is especially true of the rubbish-heap, where little soil-pockets may be made at intervals. In this case it is advisable to cover these pockets with a four sided cloche, in order to help germination and give the seedlings some protection when they come through. It is inadvisable to sow the seed much before the first week in May. The plants raised in this way will be later in cropping than those raised under glass.

Under Glass. It is usual to sow seeds in 3 in. pots which are filled with a special compost consisting of equal parts of well-chopped-up loam or good garden soil and old rotted manure. The pots should be well crocked and filled up with the compost to within $\frac{1}{4}$ in. of the top. One seed is then placed in each pot point downwards, and after watering, the pots are placed in a greenhouse of a temperature of about 55 degrees F.

If a greenhouse is not available, the pots may be plunged in soil over a hot-bed in a frame. The cloche method in situ seems ideal.

In the ordinary way plants raised are hardened off, the ones in the greenhouse being taken out into frames, and the ones in frames being given more and more air. In this way they should be quite ready to be put out in the open ground during the third week of May. (Again, this emphasises the advantage of the cloche method).

In the frame and in the greenhouse too, the greatest care should be taken not to over-water.

Planting Out. Where numbers of marrows are to be grown, the rows should be set out 4 ft. apart, the plants being 3 ft. apart in the rows. Bush marrows are preferable for this system.

When growing " trailers," these may be kept pinched back, or they may be planted on the rubbish-heap or any similar corner and allowed to ramble as they like.

General Cultivation. Those that are grown in the rows should be regularly hoed, and, in order to conserve moisture and to increase the crop, mulchings may be given with grass mowings, rotted leaves, or spent hops during June.

Harvesting. Marrows should be cut when they are young and tender. If they are they are not only more delicious, but the plants will produce a heavier crop. It is said that regular cutting may treble the crop.

Varieties

Clucas's Roller. A long white trailing type, bearing a large smooth marrow with no rib or neck.

Long Green. A very prolific type of marrow. Dark in colour and ideal for the table.

Bush-shaped Green. Bears medium-sized fruits, bright green in colour, early in the season.

Bush-shaped White. Similar to the previous variety, but the fruits are of a beautiful creamy-white colour.

Rotherside Orange. Bears flattened globe-shaped fruits of a beautiful golden colour and of a delicate flavour.

MUSHROOMS

It will be impossible under this heading to conform to the

regular headings used for vegetables. The publishers have asked that mushrooms may be included, and it is for this reason that they appear.

Selection of Place. Mushrooms are being grown to-day in all kinds of places—cellars, greenhouses, frames, caves, and even out in the open. Generally speaking, it is necessary to have a shed or some brick structure, and if this can be insulated, so that the temperature never falls below 50 degrees F. and does not rise above 70 degrees F., all should be well.

Some may find it possible to build special outbuildings for the purpose, and to see that these are heated by means of hot-water pipes. In any case, draughts should be excluded, and even cold buildings may be planted from September onwards. The beds thus " impregnated " usually crop well the following spring.

There must be many a railway arch, disused tunnel, vault, or quarry that could be converted quite cheaply into a mushroom shed.

Those who intend to grow mushrooms in a glasshouse will need to give the necessary shade. This may be done either by growing this edible fungus underneath the staging, and screening this round with hessian, or, if the whole house is used, the glass should be whitened or painted with clay and oil. If necessary, the beds can be littered with a 6 ins. depth of straw instead of shading, as is practised in the open.

In frames, similar rules hold good, and the depth of the frame should be about 2 ft. · A sunken frame keeps warmer in winter and cooler in summer.

When mushrooms are grown outside, the manure is placed in ridge beds 2 ft. 6 ins. wide at the base and only 6 ins. wide at the apex. These beds are generally 2 ft. 6 ins. high.

Soil. It may seem extraordinary to write about soil in connection with mushroom culture, but beginners must be warned of the importance of the right soil for casing. It is not that good cultivated soil is necessary, or that rich soil is required. As a matter of fact, this is undesirable. A friable sandy loam is perhaps ideal, but this should be obtained about 1 ft. below the surface of the soil. If such soil can be stacked for some time before using, it may be sprinkled with hydrated lime during the stacking process : 20 lbs. of hydrated lime is generally used to each cubic yard of soil.

Manure. At the present time it is difficult to expect very heavy crops of mushrooms unless horse manure is used. Fresh horse manure is necessary, and this is all the more valuable when wheat or oat straw has been used for bedding. Old manure, or manure mixed with wood-shavings, peat, or sawdust, is not suitable. If possible, the manure should be from horses that have been corn fed. The horses should not have been under veterinary treatment, nor should the stables have been washed down with disinfectant.

When the manure arrives it must be " made." This usually has to be done under cover, especially during the autumn and winter, for if the manure becomes sodden it is practically useless. The manure is then shaken forkful by forkful, and any refuse found should be withdrawn or any large lumps that appear should also be broken, and it should be stacked into a neat pile.

If the straw has the appearance of not being saturated with urine and being rather dry, it should be sprinkled with water so as to damp it. In four days to one week's time the heap may be turned, and this is usually done by making the outside of the heap the inside and the inside of the heap the outside. The straw is shaken out with a fork as before. Subsequent turnings are done at intervals of three or four days, and a good rule is that another turning should be given after the heap starts to sink appreciably.

After three or four "turnings" the manure should come into the right condition. It is then nut brown in colour, free from any unpleasant odour, and when a quantity is squeezed in the hand it should not exude moisture, but just feel damp. Another test is to take a proportion of the strawy material into both hands, and then to give a slight twist. If the straw snaps easily, without any effort, then the compost should be ready. This condition naturally takes place owing to the fermentation of the manure during the various turnings and stackings.

Beginners always wish to be given instructions about definite time, number of days, and so on. This is impossible in the case of composting manure for mushroom growing, and if the heap of manure smells of ammonia it should be turned again and again until the odour has disappeared. Then, when it is sweet-smelling and uniformly brown in colour, the tests suggested may be carried out and the manure will be ready to use.

The Beds. The beds can be made in various ways. It is possible to place them flat on shelves, flat or in ridge form, either double or single, on the ground.

The Flat Bed. This is usually about 8 ins. deep before the casing soil is put into position. Winter beds may be as deep as 12 inches. The manure is laid into position forkful by forkful and is trodden down firmly. It is when it is fully trodden down that the 8 ins. depth is required ; generally speaking, 14 ins. of loose manure will tread down to 8 ins. of compacted manure. If, during this treading down, hollow places appear, these should be filled up with a little compost and trodden down firmly.

The Ridge Bed. A ridge bed may be prepared in the same way, though it is rather more difficult to do, as it is triangular in section. It should be 2 ft. 6 ins. along the base, 2 ft. 6 ins. high, and 6 ins. across the top, as already described. Smaller ridge beds are made indoors. One ton of fresh manure will make enough compost for 2½ yds. length of such a ridge bed. The manure is spread evenly over the length required and well trodden down. A further layer is then added and trodden down in the same way. If treading has been well done, the bed should be about 2 ft. 6 ins. high, with a certain proportion of material hanging down the sides. This material may be taken off with a fork and placed on to the top of the bed, and this should bring the height up to 3 ft. or so. Then a good deal of beating has to be done with the back of the spade, and the apex is thus rounded off and firmed. Such a ridge bed is usually made for growing mushrooms in the open.

If ridge beds are used indoors, they may be 22 ins. wide, 17 ins. high, and have a somewhat flat top 9 ins. wide at the apex.

The method of construction is similar to that already described.

Inserting the Spawn.   Outside it is necessary to cover the beds with straw to prevent evaporation, especially if the compost is on the dry side.   This is rarely necessary indoors. If beds tend to sweat too much, the ventilators and doors may be opened to create a good draught, though opening ventilators in a cold house in winter makes them sweat still more owing to condensation.   If, on the other hand, the beds tend to dry out, they may be syringed with water a day or so before spawning is carried out.

After the beds are made, a soil thermometer should be used to test the temperature.   This should rise to round about 130 degrees in the ridge bed and up to, say, 110 degrees in the flat bed.   If heating does not take place, something is radically wrong.

Once the bed has reached this temperature, in two days it should commence to fall, and the spawn may be inserted at round about 70 degrees F.   In exceptional cases, when the temperature falls quickly, it may be necessary to spawn at 80 degrees F.

Pure culture or sterilised spawn should be used, as this on the whole gives more regular results than the old-fashioned brick spawn.   Small pieces are broken off the size of a walnut and inserted 10 ins. square all over the bed.   A hole is made 1½ in. deep and the spawn pushed into position.   The compost is then put back and pressed down tightly, and in this way the spawn will be buried 1 in. deep.   If the compost is pressed tightly round, the mushroom mycelium (or " roots ") when it grows will come directly into contact with it.

Five days later the bed should be examined, and the little white threads of mycelium should be found spreading in the compost.   If this occurs, then the bed may be cased from ten days to three weeks after the spawning day.   On the whole, it is better to case a little late than too early.

Soiling.   The type of casing soil has already been discussed, and if it is possible to obtain this from a grass field, and to dig out the 12 in. of soil below the turf, it will be found most suitable.   It should be free from organic matter.   The preparation of this soil has already been described. Growers who use the same soil again and again have to sterilise it by steaming.

The casing soil is usually damped slightly, so that it is moist and will bind over the ridge beds. It should not, however, be wet, otherwise it will stick on to the back of the shovel in an uncomfortable manner when the soil is put into position.

It is more difficult to case a ridge bed than a flat bed, but in either case the casing soil should be approximately 1½ in. deep, though for ridge beds the depth is usually decreased towards the apex. It is usually comparatively easy to case the bottom of a ridge bed, but it is the top half that takes some getting into position. Beginners, therefore, will find it better to case the bottom of the bed for a good length first of all, and after this practice to try placing the top soil into position.

General Cultivation. Indoors, the structure may be kept at a temperature of round about 60 degrees F., and if all is well the first mushroom may appear five weeks from the date of spawning. In many cases mushrooms are not seen until eight weeks after this date, but when no mushrooms appear at ten weeks something is wrong.

It is after the mushrooms have appeared that the temperature should be kept at 55–60 degrees F. Watering may be given, but only as a damping here and there to ensure that the casing soil is uniformly moist. It is easy to see the dry areas if an electric torch is shown on to the beds. Of course, some mushroom sheds are well fitted with electric light.

It is better on the whole to be an under-waterer than an over-waterer, for it is only the casing soil that should be damped and not the manure below. Much may be done to keep the beds moist by just syringing with a very fine rose the walls, the paths, and the air.

Draughts should be avoided, and, as a matter of fact, very little ventilation is needed in the average mushroom shed. The temperature of the house should not exceed 65 degrees F., an equable temperature is desirable.

Growing in Lawns and Pastures. It is possible to grow

mushrooms in grass outside, though this method can never be guaranteed to give successful results. The method adopted is to remove a small portion of turf to a depth of 2 ins. and then to dig out the soil below to a further depth of 8 or 9 inches. This hole is then filled with similar compost as advised for mushrooms inside, except that this is generally mixed with an equal quantity of subsoil such as is used for the casing. The hole is then filled with this material to within 1 in. of the top and a piece of spawn the size of a walnut is then pushed down 1 in. deep. After pressing the compost again into position, the grass may be replaced and the whole surface levelled by beating it with a spade.

This spawning should be carried out all over the pasture or lawn chosen at distances of 18 ins. apart. A period of dry weather at any time from May to July is chosen for the planting. A very rainy summer will probably kill the spawn.

The grass concerned should never be manured with basic slag, but agricultural salt is often found of benefit if used at the rate of 2 or 3 ozs. to the sq. yd. just before cropping time.

Harvesting. The mushrooms should be pulled out of the bed and not cut. The method is to take hold of the mushroom, give a slight twist, and remove it. If a proportion of the stalk is left behind at any time, it should be dug out and burnt. After this a little of the casing soil should be placed into position and smoothed down. Beginners imagine that by pulling the mushrooms the " roots," as they call them, are disturbed. It is better to take a little mycelium up than to leave a dead stalk behind, to become a breeding place for pests and diseases. The ends of the stalks should never be left in the house, but should either be burnt or be sterilised with formaldehyde.

The crop may last from two to four months, the longer crop taking place in the winter and the shorter crop in the summer. Some growers believe that they can prolong the cropping of the beds by watering with a solution of common salt. A small tablespoonful is placed into a 2-gallon can of water for this purpose.

A sq. ft. of bed should give 1 lb. of mushrooms, and successful growers may get 3 lbs.   It is useless to leave a bed in position once it has ceased cropping, however, and it may be removed and used for manuring the soil.

A ton of horse manure as it comes from the stables should, when composted, make 40 sq. ft. of flat bed 9 ins. deep.

Diseases and Pests. Mushroom-growing is not so free from troubles as people imagine.   There are fungus competitors, fungus diseases, insect and allied pests, and these may all of them cause extensive damage (see Chapters XII and XIII).

ONION

The onion has been used as food probably tar longer than any other vegetable.   Two hundred years before the birth of Christ it was written about, and it is known that the Pharaohs had it on their tables.

There is a constant demand for onions, and hundreds of tons were imported annually from abroad.   It is probable that the main reason why it is not cultivated more is because few people know how to keep down the ravages of the onion fly.

Soil. On the whole, onions seem to prefer a sandy, rich loam and one which can be deeply cultivated.   Onions, however, will grow in heavy clay soils providing these can be " opened up " by adding sand, burnt soil, or similar material.

Preparation of Soil. It is the preparation of the soil that is perhaps more important than the soil itself, for most soils may be improved.   Some growers try and obtain clay for their sandy soils, while others with heavier textured soils dig in sand.   Having added the necessary " ingredients," the soil should be dug over deeply so as to make it fine and loose throughout, and this should be done several weeks before the seed is sown.   For the spring sowings autumn cultivation is advised, but for the autumn sowings it will probably be only possible to do the cultivation a week or so beforehand.

The soil should be well drained and yet contain sufficient organic material to retain moisture.   Onions are often grown on the same soil year after year.

It is usual to firm the surface of the soil before sowing the

ONIONS
Showing how the tops are bent over to help ripening

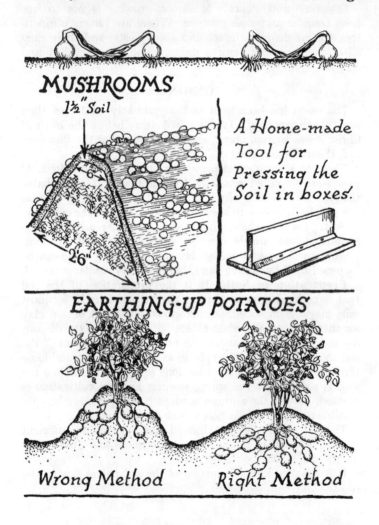

MUSHROOMS

1½" Soil

A Home-made Tool for Pressing the Soil in boxes.

26"

EARTHING-UP POTATOES

Wrong Method   Right Method

seed, and this can either be done by a light rolling, or by treading. This firming should never be done when the soil is pasty, but may be carried out directly the weather improves.

Manuring. When trenching the ground to, say, a depth of 1 foot, 5 cwts. of rotted farmyard manure or compost to the sq. pole may be incorporated deeply. It is a good rule to remember that onions do not like manure within 6 ins. of the soil surface.

For one reason or another, many gardeners have an idea that onions want large quantities of *rank* manure, but if over-doses are used then the bulbs fail to ripen easily and diseases often appear.

In addition, those who like artificials may use 1 oz. sulphate of potash and 2 ozs. of superphosphate per sq. yard.

Poultry manure or fish manure may be used as a top-dressing, at 3 ozs. to the sq. yard a week or so before planting. Wood ashes may be used also if they are available, at the rate of ½ lb. to the sq. yard.

Soot is very popular in some districts, and this may be applied with the wood ashes, if desired, at ¼ lb. to the sq. yard.

During the growing season, Chilean potash nitrate may be used as a tonic if necessary from time to time at ½ oz. per yard run, so as to help the plants along.

Onions, Spring Sown

Seed Sowing. The spring-sown onion is one that is harvested in the autumn, and should not, therefore, be called as it sometimes is, the spring onion.

When the soil is in the right condition—that is, the top inch or so should be almost dry—the soil may be consolidated and the little drills prepared. It is possible in the south to do this during the month of March, and in the north very often sowing may be delayed until April. It is interesting to know that in the south-west the author has seen onions sown in January.

The seed should be sown in rows 1 ft. apart and the drills should be very shallow. To cover these drills up it should only be necessary to do a very light raking, and finally a treading along the rows to firm the soil and so ensure its contact with the seed. Again this firming should not be done if the soil is inclined to be sticky.

General Cultivation. Directly the seeds have germinated and the crop is visible, hoeing should commence, and it should be remembered with onions that hoeing should tend to be away from the rows and not up with them. A few weeks later it should be possible to thin, and an attempt should be made to leave little groups 2 ins. or 3 ins. apart, according to the variety. The intermediate groups will be thinned out a few weeks later, and the onions thus pulled should supply material for salad. Finally the little groups will be thinned down to one plant, which should produce a good bulb.

When an onion is growing properly, it should, as it were, sit on the surface of the soil, and thus receive the benefit of the rays of the sun. If the earth is drawn up to onion bulbs, they tend to elongate and look like leeks !

It is during this thinning process that the onion fly has an opportunity of laying eggs, and so starting the maggots on their career. To prevent this, whizzed naphthalene should be sprinkled regularly along the rows, as this acts as a preventive (see p. 245).

On light land and during a hot dry summer it may be necessary to water, giving a good soaking when necessary. This watering should be discontinued about the middle of August, so as to allow the bulbs to ripen off.

Harvesting. The bulbs should ripen naturally, but to help them the tops are usually bent over at the neck. After this, the necks will commence to shrink, and 10–14 days later, the onions may be lifted out of the soil and left on the surface of the ground to dry off. This drying-off process may be continued by taking the bulbs, shaking any earth off that may cling to the roots, and laying them on a gravel or cinder path in the sun.

If 3 rows of onions are layed in position under continuous cloches—perfect ripening results in the open.

After this the onions may be stored in a cool, dry, airy

place. It is possible to hang them up in ropes under the shelter of the eaves of a building, or on the walls of a potting or tool shed. The main thing is not to allow them to get damp, as otherwise they tend to start into growth again.

Onions, Exhibition

Many people like to grow very large onions, not only for exhibition, but because they are delicious when cooked.

The preparation of the soil must be carried out even more carefully than for the spring sown onion, and on heavy, sticky soil the surface may be forked up rough in the autumn and the real trenching left until February or early March. The final working down of the surface of the soil need not take place until early in April, and when the soil is in the right condition— i.e. not too wet. The seed (and special varieties should be grown for the purpose) should be sown during first week in January in boxes under glass ; the compost should consist of 2 parts of good soil, 1 part of silver sand and 1 part of horticultural peat. To each large bucketful of this mixture should be added 1½ oz. of superphosphate and ¾ oz. of ground chalk.

Shallow seed-boxes may be used providing they make ample drainage, and crocks should be placed in the bottom. The soil should then be put in and firmed well, the boxes being filled to within ½ in. of the top. It is sometimes convenient then to give the surface of the soil a light dusting of hydrated lime. The black seed may then be placed ¾ in. square on the surface of the soil, and the presence of the lime makes this careful seed-sowing easier to do. These seeds should then be pushed just under the surface of the soil and a very small amount of compost sifted over. A good watering should then be given with some tepid water through a fine rose, and the boxes should be placed in a greenhouse at a temperature of 60 degrees F. and covered with a sheet of glass and brown paper.

Directly the seedlings are through, the boxes should be placed on a shelf so as to be near the glass, and the seedlings may grow there until they are ½ in. long. Further boxes are then prepared, using another compost, consisting of :—

Potting Compost

7 parts by bulk good soil (sterilised)
3 ,,   ,,   ,, horticultural peat
2 ,,   ,,   ,, coarse sand

adding ¼ lb. John Innes base* and ¾ oz. ground chalk per bushel.

The preparation of the boxes is done in the same way as for seed sowing—and the young plants should be pricked out 2 ins. apart. Another method is to sow the seeds in boxes at stations 2 ins. apart. It is possible to prick out each onion plant separately into a 3 in. pot ; these are convenient when planting time comes.

The boxes are put back on the shelves and are watered regularly, light syringings being given from time to time also. About the third week in March the plants should be so well grown that they can be transferred to a cold frame. Here they can be hardened off, more and more air being given until the lights can be removed altogether.

Planting Out. About the middle of April, on a showery day, the plants may be put out into their permanent position. They should be removed from the boxes and pots with care, so as to disturb the roots as little as possible. Should the soil be sticky, a board is often placed across the bed for the gardener to walk on. The rows may be 15 ins. apart and the plants 9 ins. apart in the rows. Firm planting is advisable.

When the tops have a tendency to fall over after planting, a little bamboo stake may be put at the side and the tops tied up to this. The foliage may be damped for the first four or five days twice a day, and this will help them to become properly established. It may be necessary to water also should the weather be dry.

General Cultivation. The rows between the plants should be hoed continually and a dressing of organic material such as finely divided peat, old mushroom beds, meat and bone meal, added to the surface of the ground from time to time.

---

*John Innes base consists of :—2 parts hoof and horn (⅛ in. grist), 2 parts superphosphate of lime and 1 part sulphate of potash.

If artificials are given, they should be applied sparingly, as overdoses may encourage mildew, or cause the bulbs to split.

Harvesting. This should be done in the same way as for spring-sown onions, though those who are going in for show bulbs often help the bulbs to ripen off by taking them in under glass.

Onions, Autumn Sown

It is possible to sow onions in the autumn either to produce salad onions in the spring or to produce fair-sized bulbs the following summer. Different varieties are chosen for these two purposes.

Seed-Sowing. The seed is sown either the latter part of July or during the middle of August, depending on the situation of the garden, the further north the earlier the sowing. The rows may be 9 ins. apart for the salad onions and 12 ins. apart for the onions that are to bulb.

The sowing of such onions usually follows the harvesting of a well-manured crop, and it is only necessary to rake the ground finely, draw out the drills, and then sow thinly.

General Cultivation. Hoeing is carried out and continued until the winter makes this impossible, and then in the spring regular cultivations may commence again. In the case of the salad onions no thinning is done, as the plants are pulled out as required. The varieties that are to bulb are often thinned, and the thinnings are transplanted in the spring 12 ins. between the rows and 6 to 9 ins. between the plants.

Many people prefer autumn-sown onions, as they are not attacked in the same way by the onion fly, and, further, in the north, where the spring-sown onion does not get the chance of ripening off properly the autumn sown varieties prove advantageous.

Onions, Pickling

Soil. Poor soil is suited for the sowing of this type of onion, and little preparation of the soil is necessary.

Seed-Sowing. The seed is usually broadcast over the surface of the soil and this is lightly raked in. This should be done in April ; the crop is not thinned, and, providing the weeds are kept down, excellent little pickling bulbs will be formed.

When the seeds are sown shallowly the bulbs are round, but those who prefer long or oval-shaped bulbs should sow the seed 1 in. deep.

Varieties

It is important to know which onions to sow at which times of the year and also to realise that some keep better than others, while there are those that are first-class for salad or excellent for pickling. Unfortunately it is only certain types of onions which really come true from seed, those with red, yellow or brown skins, for instance, can be relied on but the varieties with straw coloured skins vary in shape tremendously and in a row you can have flat bulbs, globe shaped bulbs, round bulbs, oval bulbs and so on. There is a lot to be said for large bulbing strains but the question of largeness is mainly one of manuring and cultivation rather than variety. Except for exhibition the huge onion is to be deprecated, and weight for weight in a row, you get a heavier yield of moderately sized bulbs than huge ones.

Learn to classify onions raised from seed into 7 groups, as suggested below :

1. Autumn sowers for bulbing. This Group produces bulbs which do not keep well but a supply of earlier bulbs in the season is assured. Sow in August or September for harvesting the following June and do not attempt to keep them after Christmas.

Giant Rocca, a flattish-oval type of mild flavour, stout, stiffish light green leaves.

Giant Zittau, similar to above. Bulbs semi-flat shape.

White Tripoli, a mild delicious onion but not a good keeper.

Golden Globe Tripoli, similar to above but golden and of globular shape. The inner skin is green.

Red Tripoli, sometimes called Red Italian has a red outer skin and a white skin inside tinged with red at the margin.

2. Autumn sowing for pulling as a spring or salad onion.

White Lisbon, the favourite silver-skin variety for pulling green for salads. Somewhat subject to disease.

New Queen, a good salad type often grown where White Lisbon is not popular.

White Portugal, really one of the white Spanish type but often used as a salad onion.

3. The oval onion, seldom seen in this country except at Shows, but comes very true from seed.

Trebons, pear-shaped, coppery coloured, leaves dark green and numerous. Not a good keeper.

Coconut. Its name suggests its shape. Has a strawy brown outer skin and white flesh. Keeps well.

4. Spanish or Portugal onion. Normally sown in the spring out of doors for harvesting in late autumn. Must not be confused with the onions that used to come in from abroad and are sold under the name of Spanish onions.

Round Spanish, really a sub-group name which covers a number of varieties, the best known of which are :

James' Keeping, a strong flavoured variety which keeps well throughout the winter.

Deptford, one of the oldest varieties which has flattish bulbs with a reddish brown skin.

Australian Brown, an excellent keeper. In the south maybe sown in the autumn.

Brown Portugal or Straw Coloured Spanish. Seldom seen in this country but *the most* popular variety in France. Has a flat bulb with a thick copperish skin. Keeps well and matures early.

White Spanish, again another type rather than a variety. Sold to-day under differing names :

Improved Reading, straw coloured skin, large bulbs, mild flavour, juicy, solid white flesh.

AI. Similar to above but if anything slightly smaller.

Nuneham Park, another similar type which is difficult to distinguish from Reading.

5. The Dutch Onion, sometimes called the Flanders Onion, includes all the best Exhibition varieties known and is probably the most popular group of onions grown in the country. The Exhibition types have their seeds sown in January, see page 155, but normally the varieties are sown in the spring for harvesting in the autumn.

Crossling's Selected, probably the largest strain of this group known. Generally tops the Trials of large varieties of onions. Is used by the winners at most Shows. The seed, however, is not easy to obtain.

The Premier. Another Exhibitor's variety of pale straw colour. Grows to immense size.

Selected Ailsa Craig produces large bulbs which should be oblong in shape, tapering to the neck. Some strains, however, are flatter.

Bedfordshire Champion, one of the most popular varieties for sowing in the spring. Keeps well. Flesh white and mild. Skin strawy brown.

Danvers Yellow came into this country during the war. Does best when sown under glass and transplanted. Should be globular with a yellow skin.

Reliance. May be a hybrid but fits in here best. Will keep till May. Crops heavily with hard bulbs, mild in flavour. Is conical in shape with slightly rounded base. Best sown in the autumn. Unwins probably have the best strain.

N.B.—For Onion Sets (see p. 196).

PARSNIP

The parsnip is one of the easiest of all vegetables to grow, and one that is perhaps the least popular. Perhaps the reason of its unpopularity is that it is seldom cooked properly, but when baked in beef dripping, or fried after it has been parboiled, it is particularly delicious. Even when boiled properly, so that it is like " a mass of marrow," and covered with a white sauce it takes some beating.

Soil. The parsnip will grow in any soil providing it is not too stony. Those who have difficulty in getting long, straight roots may bore holes 3 ft. deep and 3 ins. in diameter at the top. These holes are filled up with friable sifted soil and three seeds are sown on the top. When the seedlings grow they are thinned out so as to leave one in position, and the result is that a very large, straight, clean root results.

Preparation of Soil. The soil is dug deeply, so as to get it into a good friable condition. If it is possible to trench the ground in the autumn or to ridge it, so that the land can be left rough for the winter weather to act on, so much the better. In this way it is easy to fork or rake the ground down in February or March ready for sowing the seed.

Manuring. Parsnips should be grown on land that was manured well the previous year, and, should the land be thought to be poor, fertilisers may be added as described for carrots (see p. 118).

Seed-Sowing. The seeds are sown in the south at the end of February and in the north about the third week in March, providing the land is in the right condition.

Parsnip seeds do not germinate as well as many others, and so the seed should be sown somewhat thickly. The rows should be 18 ins. apart and 1 or 2 ins. deep, depending on the heaviness of the soil. The lighter the soil the deeper can the drills be.

Thinning. When the seedlings are an inch or so high, they may be thinned out to 8 ins. apart. Some gardeners who want to get their roots to exhibition size should thin their plants to 6 ins. and finally to 1 ft. apart later on.

This is how you stop the growth of a marrow or cucumber, by just pinching out the growing point.

Tomato plants can be raised under Continuous Cloches. Here are the seeds sown in little drills and some in pots. The cloches are then put in position and the ends sealed. Cucumber plants, sweet corn and marrows can be raised in a similar manner.

General Cultivation. There is little else that can be done except to hoe continually to keep down weeds and to provide a dust mulch.

Harvesting. Parsnips are not damaged by frost ; in fact, they are improved in flavour after they have been " touched." If there is any danger of the soil being frozen hard, so as to prevent the roots from being dug out when required, then a certain number of them may be lifted and stored in soil in a shed or clamp. Other than this, parsnips may be left in the ground until required, and under ordinary conditions a little litter placed over the rows will prevent the soil from being frozen hard.

When the land is required the following February, any roots that remain may be lifted and stored in earth or sand.

Varieties

Improved Hollow Crown. An excellent variety in the south-east. Produces a heavy crop of long, well-shaped roots.

Tender and True. Not one of the largest parsnips, but is said to have a clearer and smoother skin than other varieties. Given good conditions, it is certainly perfect in form.

The Student. A large variety of good colour. Suitable for the north, where late sowings have to be made.

PEAS

Peas are one of the most popular vegetables in the garden, though one in which the supply is so often shortlived, for many people fail to realise the necessity of regular sowings to keep up the supply. For this reason detailed suggestions are given in this chapter in the hope that those who care for this vegetable will be able to keep picking them from July to the end of September.

Like beans, they have nodules on their roots containing bacteria which live in harmony with the plant. These extract nitrogen from the air, and, when the roots are left in the ground after the plants are cleared, much nitrogenous plant food is added to the soil.

Soil. It is possible to grow peas on most soils, though they seem to prefer a rich, deep, friable loam. If this is naturally

F

calcareous, so much the better. Other soils can be limed so as to counteract any acidity present.

The early peas will grow well in a light sandy soil, but the varieties that come later will appreciate a soil which retains moisture, thus a strong loam or a well-cultivated clay is admirable.

Manuring. Peas are not in the ground long before they grow and start to crop, and so the period in which they have the opportunity for collecting plant food is somewhat brief. For this reason plant foods should be applied sufficiently early, so that they are in such a form that the roots can collect and absorb them rapidly.

Much farmyard manure, or well-prepared compost should be used when bastard trenching the ground, and this should be placed below the top 8 or 9 ins. of soil. This is quite easy to do while the bastard trenching is being carried out. It is better not to have such manure in the top 5 or 6 ins., because in such cases the root system tends to be shallow instead of spreading out and seeking the food below. Horticultural peat can be worked into the top 2 or 3 inches in the case of sandy soils and should be damped first.

This preparation of soil may be done in the autumn, so that the land may be left rough ; it will then be found that the soil is easy to fork down to a fine tilth in the spring.

In addition to the dung or compost, those who like artificials may use 3 ozs. superphosphate and 1 oz. sulphate of potash per sq. yd., and, directly the plants are through, ½ oz. Chilean potash nitrate may be applied per yard run to help to give the plants a start.

Where, however, it is desired to increase the organic content, fish manure or meat and bone meal may be applied at the rate of 4 ozs. per sq. yd. Potash should be given in addition in the form of wood ashes at 5 ozs. to the sq. yd.

Preparation of Soil. Much has been said already about the preparation of the soil in the paragraphs dealing with manuring and with the soil itself.

The bastard trenching in the autumn, the addition of a good layer of dung or compost in the bottom of the trench, the

forking down in the spring—all of these operations are important. It is necessary to try to get the soil into the condition
that peas require, and has already been described as deep,
rich, and friable.

When the actual time of sowing comes, drills may be drawn
out with a draw hoe 5 ins. wide and 3 ins. deep.

Seed-Sowing. In these flat drills 5 to 6 ins. wide and 3 ins.
deep the seed should be sown as evenly spaced as possible.
If the seeds can be 2 ins. apart each way, the plants have a
chance of growing properly. The later varieties can even do
with 3 ins. distances. Many people sow peas thicker than this
in the hope of getting heavier crops. It is seldom, if ever,
that thick sowing gives better results than spaced sowing.
It is useless to argue that large numbers of peas are taken by
birds and mice, for the good gardener will give the necessary
protection from both these thieves. The seed should be
soaked in a mixture of paraffin and red lead for a couple of
hours. When making up this liquid, it should be of about
the consistency of cream. The rows may be protected when
the plants are just coming through by using home-made or
bought pea guards.

The rows of peas may be spaced at distances one from
another according to the height of the variety sown. For
instance, a 3 ft. variety will need 18 ins. *on either side* of it,
while a 4 ft. variety should have 2 ft.

There are four main times for sowing, and these may be
described as : (*a*) the earliest crop (sown under glass) ; (*b*) the
early crop (autumn sown) ; (*c*) the main crop ; and (*d*) the
autumn crop.

The Earliest Crop

The seed of early and dwarf varieties may be sown in boxes
or pots under glass late in January or early in February.
The soil used should be rich in humus, and if it is mainly
composed of good fibrous loam, so much the better. If in
boxes, the seed should be spaced 2 ins. apart, and if in pots,
6 ins. pots are usually used, 6 seeds being spaced around the
edge of the pot.

After seed-sowing, the boxes or pots may be placed in a frame, and the frame can be closed until the seeds are through. After this, as much ventilation should be given as possible, so that a short, sturdy plant may be grown.

The plants thus raised may be planted out in March or early in April in a warm border. Directly after planting, little twiggy sticks should be put along the rows to keep the growth upright.

Those who have no greenhouse or frames may grow the rows under continuous cloches, sowing the seed *in situ* but covering the ground with cloches 14 days before to warm it.

The Early Crop, Autumn Sown

In the south, and in the very sheltered parts of the north, it is possible most years to make a sowing of one of the round seeded varieties during the winter months. It depends on the district as to which is the best time, and the author has been successful from sowings made both in November and December.

The soil where the seed is to be sown should be on the dry side. For this reason it is a good plan to draw the drill out in the morning on a warm day, so as to let it dry out, and then to carry out the seed-sowing in the afternoon.

Such sowings should be protected in some way from the cutting winter winds. It is usual, therefore, to erect little screens for the purpose and to stick the rows early. Some years it is necessary to place straw along the rows before and during a frosty period.

Another sowing may be made at the beginning of February, though in the north it is usual to wait until the end of March. Again, the varieties chosen should be round-seeded ones, and for dwarf varieties the rows need only be 18 ins. apart.

All these sowings can be guaranteed when made under continuous cloches for these give the ideal protection in winter.

The Main Crop

From the beginning of April onwards, peas may be sown at regular intervals. Most gardeners make a rule to make another sowing as soon as the last one is showing above ground. This is not, of course, possible in small gardens. The wrinkled-seeded varieties, being more tender than the round-seeded ones, may be sown somewhat thicker in the rows. The rows should, however, be at the correct distance apart, as there is no advantage in crowding them together.

The Autumn Crop

The earliest varieties may be sown again late in June or the beginning of July, so as to get good pickings in the month of September. It is usually possible to make these sowings on land from which the potatoes or early cauliflowers have been harvested. When drawing the drills out at this time of the year, they should be given a good flooding, as they are likely to be dry. This will give the seeds an opportunity of germinating quickly, and will help to give the young plants a good start.

General Cultivation. From the time that the peas first come through, hoeing should be carried out regularly on either side of the rows. In the rows themselves, hand weeding may have to be done in the early stages. In addition to the regular hoeings, it may be necessary to water in dry years, as moisture is essential to the roots. Following floodings, mulches may be given along the rows to help to retain the moisture, and lawn mowings are usually available at this time of the year for the purpose. Where these are not to hand, horticultural peat can be used instead. It is better, when watering, to do this in small trenches on either side of the row rather than on the row itself.

To help the plants to climb, little bushy twigs may be inserted in the ground near the peas 3 or 4 ins. high. Whenever possible, staking should be done, though the dwarfer types will grow quite well without stakes. The sticks may be placed 6 in. away from the row and 1 ft. apart, and light, bushy sticks should be used. They should be perpendicular so the air can circulate and the peas do not tend to push through, as they do if the sticks slant inwards.

During the first hoeings, the earth should be brought up to

the rows and not away from them. A kind of earthing-up operation is done as soon as plants are 3 or 4 in. high. This earthing-up gives protection and helps to keep the plants upright.

Harvesting. Peas should be picked regularly and no pod should be missed when ready. It is these few pods that are left on the plants that go to seed, and immediately the cropping power of the plants is reduced. Systematic and regular picking will ensure heavier crops.

Varieties

The first thing to realise in regard to peas is that there are two main groups, (*a*) The Round and (*b*) The Wrinkled, and further, that the Marrowfat peas which have such a delicious flavour, are all Wrinkled. Varieties, then, with Wrinkled seeds, contain more sugar. The Round peas are, however, much hardier.

The next classification refers to season and time taken for the peas to come to maturity from sowing. There are (1) The Earlies (the quickest maturing). (2) The Second Earlies. (3) The Main Crop Peas, and (4) The Late Peas.

Earlies mature in 12 weeks. Second Earlies mature in 14 weeks. Main crops mature in 15 or 16 weeks. Late varieties take 17 weeks.

In addition, peas may be divided up into groups according to their heights but it can be generally said that it is the Earlies which are dwarf, and the Lates which are tall.

Because every seedsman can name any variety he cares with his own name, a bewildering number of so-called Varieties will be found in the catalogues.

Early Varieties

DWARF, ROUND-SEEDED.

8-Weeks, excellent type for cloches or frames. Does well in the greenhouse in pots. Grows 18 inches high, bears dark green, curved pods.

Meteor, very dwarf but very hardy. Can be sown any time from September in one year to June the next. Only grows 1 ft. high.

Early Bird, a very popular variety for sowing in the north. Heavy Cropper.

DWARF, WRINKLED SEEDED.

Early Wonder, a dwarf marrowfat, much liked in the west. 18 inches.

Kelvedon Wonder, perhaps the best of the dwarf Marrowfats. 18 ins. Grand for small gardens and allotments.

Little Marvel. Best flavoured Marrowfat. Quick grower. 8 peas to a pod. May be ready in 11 weeks. 18 inches.

TALL EARLY.

Springtide, a very heavy cropper, 3 feet, one of the earliest talls known.

Forerunner. 3 feet. Very hardy ; an improved type of Pilot.

Foremost, very heavy cropper, may be sown end February in south for gathering end May. 2½ feet.

Laxton's Superb. A grand pea ; the Author has sown it in January with success. Good also for autumn sowing, especially under cloches. 2½ feet.

Provost, the only Wrinkled seeded variety in this group. Strong grower. Hardy. 3 feet.

Duplex. Heavy cropper. Straight pods, closely packed with large peas of good flavour. Award of Merit R.H.S. 2½ feet.

EARLY MAINCROPS.

Miracle, bears good pods from top to bottom. Grand variety for droughty periods. Recommended for lighter soils. 4 feet. Marrowfat.

The Lincoln. One of the Author's favourites. Grows only 2 feet high but crops very heavily. Marrowfat.

Giant Stride bears one of the largest pods. Needs to be grown on well manured ground to get these pods really filled. 2½ feet. Marrowfat.

The Daisy. One of the good old favourites with first-class flavour. Crops heavily ; haulm branches well. Marrowfat.

MAINCROPS.

Onward, perhaps the most popular pea of all. 2½ feet. Produces dark green stumpy pods with peas of a high quality. Said to be the most resistant variety to Mildew. First-class flavour. Marrowfat.

Quite Content, a very tall variety, 6 feet. Large podded, heavy cropper. Well worth growing.

Lord Chancellor, an excellent table variety, 3 feet, long straight pointed pods.

Autocrat. A vigorous very late variety, crops heavily, height 3-4 feet.

Gladstone, a good variety for drought areas. Excellent Exhibition pea. 4 feet. Pods pointed, curved. Peas of good flavour.

Alderman, tall marrowfat. 5 feet. Good variety. Well worth growing.

POTATO

The potato is one of the most important crops in the garden, not only because in this country, at the present time, we eat more potatoes than any other vegetable, but also because it acts as a cleaning crop.

Soil. Potatoes can be grown on all soils, though some

produce those of an inferior flavour to others.   It is said that the heavy clays and the peaty soils produce " waxy " tubers. The ideal soil would be a deep, well-drained medium soil, not a pure clay or too light a sand.   A clay soil could be made friable, but it is difficult to work during wet periods, and so during harvesting and planting times troubles might arise.

Potatoes should not be grown under trees, or where the atmosphere is likely to be stagnant, for under such conditions the foliage is soft, and as a result potato blight will ravage the crop.

Preparation of Soil.   One of the best ways of preparing the soil for potatoes is by deep working, and, except in the case of the very lightest soils, this should be done in the autumn. The land should be left ridged, so that the air, frost, and rain can penetrate and sweeten it.   The ridges should run due north and south, so that the winter sun can fall equally on either side of the rows.

In the spring these ridges may be forked down and further ridges made into which the potatoes may be planted.

Manuring.   The land can be manured in the autumn, though most gardeners prefer to apply the dung or compost in the rows in the spring at planting-time.   Farmyard manure or compost should be applied at the rate of about 1 good barrow-load to 10 sq. yards.

In addition, the following artificials should be applied in the rows : $\frac{1}{2}$ oz. sulphate of ammonia, $\frac{1}{2}$ oz. sulphate of potash, and 1 oz. superphosphate per yard run or a good organic fertiliser like fish manure or meat and bone meal.

In the case of the very early potatoes, there is no need to give artificials in addition, as the potatoes are out of the ground before they can make use of the extra plant food.

Purchasing the Seed.   It is most important to buy " seed " either from Scotland or Ireland.   The main thing is to try and get tubers from plants free from virus diseases. With every pound of " seed " purchased the grower should obtain the certificate number.   This is his guarantee.

The tubers used for seed should be about the size of a hen's egg and weigh about 2$\frac{1}{2}$ ozs.   Those who obtain larger tubers should cut these in such a way that each half contains the necessary eyes. This cutting should take place just before the tubers are planted. It is not a good plan to do this cutting some time before planting, as loss of crop results.

Boxing. Directly the potatoes are bought they should be boxed up—that is to say, placed in shallow trays to sprout, rose end upwards. The rose end is the end where most of the eyes are found, and is the opposite end to that which was attached to the underground stem.

The farmer uses a potato tray 2 ft. 6 ins. long, 1 ft. 6 ins. wide, and $3\frac{1}{2}$ ins. deep. In the corners there are small square posts standing 3 ins. above the sides. These posts are there so that the trays may be stood one above the other while the sprouting process is going on, without injuring the sprouts.

The trays containing the potatoes should then be stacked in a cool, light, airy place where there is no possibility of their being frozen. Some growers use a large type of greenhouse, while others find a loft or a shed quite convenient. Air should circulate freely amongst the trays, and pathways should be left so that the potatoes may be looked over occasionally to remove those that are going rotten.

When the tubers start to grow, some disbudding may take place, only the two strongest shoots being left on at the rose end of the tuber. When the time comes for planting, the trays should be taken out into the garden and placed on top of the furrows. The sets should then be taken out one at a time and placed carefully in the bottom of the furrows without breaking off the sprouts. If planting is done carelessly, the sprouts will break off easily and all the trouble spent on them in the trays will be thrown away.

The object of sprouting the seed is to secure a few weeks' growth before planting takes place. Sprouted potatoes are, therefore, ready to lift several weeks earlier than potatoes planted unsprouted. This saving of time ensures heavy crops also, as the potatoes have, in consequence, a longer season of growth.

Planting. The earliest potatoes may be planted in ridges 18 ins. apart, the tubers being placed 1 ft. apart in the rows.

F*

When planted in this way the tubers should be dug up when they are quite small.

Ordinary early potatoes will be 1 ft. 9 ins. apart, the tubers being 1 ft. apart in the rows. The second earlies may be in ridges 2 ft. 3 ins. apart, the seed being placed 1 ft. 3 ins. apart in the rows, while the latest varieties may be planted 2 ft. 6 ins. by 1 ft. 6 ins. It is quite easy to enlarge the distances should the potatoes be particularly heavy croppers, or the soil exceedingly good.

The potatoes should not be planted deeper than 4 ins., and in the case of the earliest varieties a 3 in. depth is sufficient. The rows will, of course, run north and south, and after the potatoes are in position the soil may be drawn over them, leaving a very slight ridge to mark the row. Planting will take place in the south round about the middle of March, and in the north possibly the second week in April. On the whole, it is better to plant the late potatoes first and the early varieties last. In this way the late potatoes have a long season of growth and are not through the ground sufficiently quickly to be affected by a late spring frost. The early potatoes, on the other hand, being early maturing, give sufficiently heavy crops, and yet, being planted later than the main crop varieties, probably miss the spring frosts.

General Cultivation. Directly the foliage appears through the ground the rows should be hoed, using a Canterbury hoe. If there is any fear of frost, the soil may be drawn up to the plant, then, when the frosty period is over, this may be drawn back again.

When the tops are about half grown the first earthing-up may be carried out, by means of a Canterbury hoe, a 6 ins. depth of soil being drawn up to the haulm on either side. This usually takes place when the stems above ground are 8 ins. high.

The next earthing-up is done a few weeks after the first, another inch of soil being brought up to the haulm. Further earthings-up may be done at fortnightly intervals as seems necessary. The ridges, however, should never be brought up too steeply, as if this is done the tubers may be exposed at the side.

During the growing period a sharp outlook should be kept for the potato blight, and directly, if not before, the disease is seen the leaves and stems should be given a thorough spraying with Bordeaux mixture (see p. 253).

Harvesting. The rows of early potatoes may be lifted as soon as the tubers are of a suitable size. If a broad-tined fork can be used, so much the better, as this does not injure the tubers as much. If the lifting can be done on a fine day, the tubers will come out clean and bright, and they look far more attractive in consequence.

The main crop need not be lifted to be stored until the haulm has died down. It is at this time that the tubers will be at their largest size and are certain to have firm skins.

It is a good plan to cut the haulm off the potatoes before digging up the tubers, especially if they have been attacked by potato blight, as then no spores can drop on them and infest them.

The storing of the main crop may be done in a shed or cellar providing it is frost-proof and dark. Potatoes, however, are often stored in clamps, or " buries." The ground on which these are to stand should be, if possible slightly higher than the general level of the soil, so that the tubers may be kept dry. The potatoes are stacked in a long ridge-shaped heap 3 or 4 ft. wide at the base and 2 or 3 ft. high, and this triangular-shaped mound is then covered with straw 6 ins. deep. On top of the straw is put a 6 ins. covering of soil taken from the ground surrounding the clamp. It is during this earthing operation that a trench may be made all round the clamp so as to carry away water. Ventilating holes should be given by means of a tuft of straw being allowed to project through the soil. If this is twisted hard, it will prevent the rain from percolating into the clamp. Ventilators are needed for every 6 ft. length of clamp.

Varieties

EARLIES :

Ninety-Fold. Probably the earliest potato of all, but apt to be soapy. Non-immune.

Home Guard. White floury potato with good flavour. Attractive appearance.

May Queen. Follows Ninety-Fold quite closely, and is a floury potato. Non-immune.

Duke of York. Bears kidney-shaped tubers. A firm, yellow-fleshed variety. Non-immune.

Immune Ashleaf. A yellow-fleshed kidney variety. Said to be similar to the old favourite, Myatt's Ashleaf. Immune.

Arran Pilot, ready 14 weeks from date of planting. Very heavy cropper, especially in the South. A good light land variety. Can be left in the ground as a second early without secondary growth taking place. Immune.

Arran Crest. Very early. Heavy cropper, delicious potato, immune.

Doone Early, will take the place of Epicure. Shallow eyed, compact grower, grand for small garden.

SECOND EARLIES:

Arran Comrade. A round variety, popular for exhibition purposes. The skin and the flesh are white, while the cooking quality is excellent. Immune.

Eclipse. Much liked in the north of England. A heavy cropping white-fleshed kidney. Sometimes called Sir John Llewelyn. Non-immune.

Great Scot. Often grown as a main crop. One of the best-known white round potatoes. Produces a heavy crop of large-sized tubers. Immune.

Dunbar Rover. May become the best second early ever produced. Crops heavily. Shallow eyes. May be regarded as Improved British Queen.

Dunbar Cavalier, sometimes called the new King Edward. Very delicious. Flavour of King Edward with hardiness of Majestic. Very heavy cropper. Keeps well. Immune.

Doone Star, very heavy cropper, good quality, shallow eyed ; light land variety. Should be eaten in August but will last in the ground till November. Immune.

MAIN CROP:

Majestic. An immune variety, being a heavy cropping white kidney. The tubers are generally large.

Arran Banner. A fine early main crop potato. Immune. A very heavy cropper. The tubers are white, round, and somewhat flattened. The flesh is white and the haulm tall and vigorous.

King Edward VII. Probably the most popular kidney variety grown, the skin being pure yellow flushed with pink. An excellent cooker. A light cropper. Non-immune.

Arran Chief. Bears a white round tuber. Quite a heavy cropper. non-immune.

Arran Cairn. Received Gold Medal. Resistant to blight. Upright haulm. Matures late and crops heavily. Immune.

Arran Victory. One of the most floury potatoes. An epicure's variety. Bluish skin. Immune.

Dunbar Standard. Coarse-foliaged variety. Somewhat subject to blight. Very heavy cropper, however. Immune.

N.B. The use of the words immune and non-immune refer to wart disease, and wart disease only. Under the Ministry of Agriculture's regulations those who have land subject to this disease must grow immune varieties only.

Potatoes, Salad

There are two potatoes that are sometimes grown for salad because they are useful for decorative purposes. They are grown in exactly the same way as ordinary potatoes, and may be dug up and used as desired.

Varieties

The Congo. A purple, almost black-fleshed variety of excellent flavour. Non-immune.

Firapple. Bears knotted tubers, pink skinned, with a lemon flushed interior. They are very decorative when served unbroken.

RADISH

Most people grow a few radishes even though they have quite a small garden. The old idea that the radish was hot, and so brought about indigestion, does not hold good to-day, as the introduction of new varieties, with their great improvements in flavour and form, has done much to increase the popularity of this vegetable.

Soil. Radishes do not need deep soil, and they will grow equally well on heavy clays and sands for the summer, providing these are properly prepared.

The main thing is that the soil should not be left lumpy and that the situation should not be such that the growth cannot be immediate and quick. One should aim at growing the radish in its succulent form, and this can be done on a nice rich loam more easily, perhaps, than on, say, a heavy clay.

Preparation of Soil. Little need be done except to see that the soil is in fine condition. The seeds should not be sown in " lumpy " land. In the case of light sands, the surface soil may be improved by forking in some organic matter such as ground peat or finely divided leaf-mould.

Manuring. Radishes are seldom given special manures,

though in all probability 2 ozs. of fine meat meal, $\frac{1}{2}$ oz. of precipitated bone phosphates, and 6 ozs. of wood ashes forked into the top 3 or 4 ins. would improve hungry land. Horticultural peat if damped first is excellent for dry soils if forked in to the top 2 or 3 ins. at $\frac{1}{2}$ lb. to the sq. yard.

Seed-Sowing. The great mistake beginners make is to sow radish seed too thickly, so that only poor roots result. Broadcasting is usual, but, as this is difficult to do thinly, it is generally better to sow the seed in rows 6 ins. apart and only $\frac{1}{2}$ in. deep. The soil should always be made firm after sowing, as it is impossible to get really firm radishes if the soil is loose.

Frames. In order to get very early crops, radishes may be sown in frames over a hot-bed as described for beetroot. It is usual to sow the seed thinly, give a light watering, and then put on the lights. When the young seedlings come through, every opportunity should be taken of giving air, as otherwise the plants become drawn.

During frosty periods the lights are covered with sacking or some similar material, so as to prevent the young plants from being frozen. Should broadcasting have been done, it will be necessary to thin the plants early, if nice sized roots are to be formed. Sowings might be made early in December, early in January, and early in February, and thus a continuous supply of radishes result.

Those who do not wish to have a whole frame of radishes may sow a row of radishes in between their rows of lettuces. In this way two crops will result, the radishes being pulled first. It is necessary to repeat that radish seed should not be sown too thickly, as to grow a perfect radish it should be 2 ins. from its neighbour.

Cloches. Good crops of radishes may be obtained at almost any time of the year from sowings made under cloches. Plenty of organic matter must be worked into the soil however first.

Outdoor Sowings. It is possible to make a sowing of radishes outside in December in a special sheltered, sunny place. The bed should be a raised one, so as to be certain that the drainage is perfect, and the seed is broadcast on to the bed and raked in. Immediately afterwards the bed should be covered with straw to a depth of 4 inches. When the seed has germinated, the straw may be raked off so as to allow the plants to grow in the light.

When there is any sign of frost or snow, the straw should be replaced to give protection, and as soon as possible when the weather gets warmer the straw may be removed altogether.

These beds should be no wider than 4 ft., so that all the straw-moving, thinning, and other operations can be done without treading on the beds.

The next sowing may be made in a warm, dry border in February, and this can be covered with litter as before. These winter sowings are more possible in the south than in the north, and succeed better on the eastern side of England, where the rainfall is lower.

Further sowings may be made from, say, the middle of March to the beginning of September, and these summer sowings prefer a cool, shady position. A north border of the garden is often convenient for this purpose.

In all cases the rows should be 6 ins. apart, and the radishes thinned and pulled early.

Radishes may always be regarded as an intercrop, and can often be sown between seed-beds, between rows of other vegetables like peas, beans, or carrots. They may be sown in the rows of vegetables, like asparagus, parsnips, and seakale, whose seeds take a long time to germinate, as the radishes then mark out the rows and provide an intercrop as well.

For the early sowings the round and long varieties are perhaps to be preferred, while for the later sowings, that are to withstand the summer sun, the oval sorts may be used.

Radishes for the Winter

It is possible to sow what are known as winter radishes during the month of July in the north and in August in the south in drills 9 ins. apart, and, when the plants grow, to thin them out to 6 ins. in the rows. These radishes are more like turnips, and can either be used in salads or are boiled and used as a cooked vegetable. The roots may be left in the ground and dug up as desired.

General Cultivation. Constant hoeing in between the rows is necessary. Dustings with Gammaxene dust to keep down flea beetle has to be done most years (see p. 236), while occasional waterings during dry periods will help to keep the radishes from going to seed.

Harvesting. The radishes must be pulled regularly while they are fresh and young.

Varieties

ROUND :

Red Turnip. Bright colour. Crisp and tender.
Red Turnip Short Top Forcing. Suitable for very shallow soils. Bulbs quickly. Has very few leaves.
Scarlet Globe. Delicious flavour. Good size and tender.
Sparkler. 50/50 Bright red in colour, tipped with white.

OVAL :

French Breakfast. Deep crimson colour, with white flesh inside. Has small leaves, the root being solid and sweet.
French Breakfast Early Forcing. An excellent variety for a frame. Ready much earlier than the French Breakfast.

LONG :

Wood's Frame. A scarlet early variety. Suitable for the frame.
Icicle. A handsome crisp white variety of good shape and quality.

WINTER :

Black Spanish Long. Has black skin, but firm white flesh.
Black Spanish Round. Similar to the above, but round in shape.
China Rose. A round pink variety.

RHUBARB—and as a fruit—(see p. 233)

SAVOY CABBAGE

The savoy may be regarded as the winter cabbage, as it will stand, and in fact is improved by, frost; whereas the cabbage has smooth leaves, the savoy has dark, deeply crinkled leaves.

Soil. On the whole, this crop grows best on heavy, deeply cultivated rich land. If during cultivation the ground can be firmed, better hearted crops result. The savoy does well following a crop like early potatoes or early peas.

Preparation of Soil. As it is definitely related to the Brussels sprout, the conditions described as suiting this crop will suit the savoy.

Manuring. If the savoys are to follow a previous crop, it is a good plan, directly this has been cleared, to sow calcium cyanamide on the surface of the ground at 4 ozs. to the sq. yard. This should be done about a fortnight before the plants are put out, and in this way any weeds present are killed and lime and nitrogen are applied. It is as well to have a break between the application and planting, as cyanamide may damage the roots of the plants if put in immediately. In addition, and prior to this application, meat and bone meal or a good fish manure may be forked in at 4 ozs. to the sq. yd.

Seed-Sowing. Seed may be sown in three batches, the first during the middle of March on a well-prepared, warm seed-bed. A second sowing may be made at the beginning of April, and another sowing at the end of April.

The seeds should be sown in drills 18 ins. apart, and directly the seedlings appear they may be thinned to 2 or 3 ins. apart, and the thinnings transplanted into further seed-beds 6 ins. square if desired. Even in the seed-beds, the rows should be kept hoed, so as to keep them free from weeds.

Planting Out. The plants may be put out into their permanent position towards the end of June and during the month of July. If this is done on showery days, they will grow away quickly, and should the weather be dry it will be better to puddle them in. The rows should be, in the case of the smaller varieties, 17 ins. between the rows, and 15 ins. in the rows, while the strong-growing varieties need planting 2 ft. square.

General Cultivation. There is nothing to be done except to cultivate regularly between the rows and to remove the stalk directly the savoy has been cut.

Varieties

SMALL TYPES:

Very Early. Sow mid-February, cut August-September.
Belle Ville. A beautiful curled deeply coloured savoy. Is very hardy, and of delicious flavour.

Early Dwarf Ulm. Bears solid hearts which are well formed, the leaves being close and compact.

EARLY :

Sow March. Cut September-October.

Best of All. Drumhead which forms firm, solid hearts generally late in October.

Improved Early Drumhead. Similar to above but with firmer heart on the whole.

Pixie Green, very small kind suitable for small gardens.

MID SEASON :

Sow early April, cut November-February.

Perfection, rich dark green compact savoy.

Christmas Drumhead. Nice late firm savoy. Popular in the south.

LATE :

Sow end of April, cut January-March.

Improved Late Drumhead, typical drumhead type, firm, delicious, southern variety on the whole.

Latest of All. Bears intensely curled leaves. Dark green, delicious.

EXTRA LATE :

Sow end April, cut following March.

Omega, slow grower. Well worth waiting for.

Those who wish to grow a succession may grow :—

Ormskirk Early, which should be ready for cutting in September and October.

Ormskirk Medium. A hardy variety which cuts from November to February.

Ormskirk Late Green. Will withstand very severe weather. Cuts from January to the end of March.

Ormskirk Extra Late. Has a fine, deep colour, and cuts during the months of March and April. Unfortunately, this variety does not root well in a dry season.

SEAKALE

Seakale is not one of the commonest of vegetables, and yet when grown it is much liked.

Soil. The seakale seems to grow best on a heavy soil, though it will grow well on an easily worked sandy loam. Those who intend to lift the roots for forcing them under cover will prefer such a soil, as it makes root-lifting easier.

The soil should be well drained, and the situation should be open and free from shade.

Preparation of Soil. Bastard trenching should be done, and during this operation farmyard manure or well rotted compost should be added. If this deep cultivation can be done in the autumn, so that the soil may be left rough and ridged, it will get the full benefit of the winter conditions. In March the soil may be levelled by forking it over ready for planting.

Manuring. Well-rotted manure or compost should be used whenever possible, and this should be dug in deeply at the rate of one good barrow-load per 16 sq. yards.

In addition, should the soil be sandy, use a fertiliser with an organic base like fish manure, poultry manure, " meat and bone " meal, etc., at 4 ozs. to the sq. yd., though some who like artificials swear by 3 ozs. of superphosphate and 2 ozs. kainit per sq. yard. On heavy soils, 1 oz. sulphate of potash should be used instead of the kainit. In the spring, after growth has commenced, Chilean potash nitrate may be applied at about 1 oz. to the yard run.

Seakale appreciates a manuring with seaweed where this can be obtained.

Propagation. Seakale may be propagated in two ways : either by sowing seed or by means of root cuttings or thongs. It takes two years to produce forcing crowns from seed, though the plants thus raised are generally more vigorous. Thongs are usually used.

When seed-sowing is practised, it is done in a fine seed-bed in drills 12 ins. apart and 1 in. deep. The seedlings are thinned out when they are 2 ins. high to 6 ins. apart. The following February the plants are dug up, and are planted out into their permanent positions early in March. Just before planting, the top may be cut off just below the crown, as this makes flowering less likely.

Thongs are prepared from the clean, straight side-roots which grow out from the main root. The best of these side-roots are selected, of the thickness of a lead pencil or thicker. They are then cut into pieces 6 ins. long, the thickest end of the thong being cut level and the thinner end cut slanting. By this means the gardener knows which is the top of the thongs, in spring, and can plant them the right way up.

After preparation, the thongs may be tied into bundles and put in layers of damp sand. They can remain covered with sand until planting-time comes round, and when uncovered it will be found that the top end of the roots have made several eyes. All these, except the two strongest, should be rubbed off.

Planting. Planting may take place during the third week in March, the thongs being put out in rows 18 ins. apart and 15 ins. apart in the rows. The top of the thong should be 1 in. below the surface of the soil. Planting must be done firmly.

General Cultivation. Throughout the summer, hoeing may be constantly carried out between the rows. The plants should be looked over from time to time and any flowering stems that appear should be removed.

By the middle of October, if the foliage has not already died down, it should be cut off.

Forcing. In the winter, when the foliage has died down, the roots may be dug up and taken under cover to be forced, the side-roots being removed to form thongs for the following year. They can be forced under the staging of glasshouses, in frames, or in cellars. They should be stood upright in soil or rotted leaves and moisture may be given by regular sprayings with tepid water. The roots should be kept in the dark. The temperature should be no higher than 60 degrees F.

It is possible to force also in the open by covering the crowns with a forcing-pot or box and then surrounding it with farmyard manure. This may be put on the beds to the depth of 6 ins., and this will create sufficient heat to cause the seakale to grow. In the course of three weeks or so the well-blanched heads should be ready for cutting.

Those who intend to force the roots outside will do well to plant the thongs in such a way that three crowns may be covered by one forcing-pot. This means planting them on the triangular system.

" Natural " seakale is also liked, and in this case the rows are usually 15 ins. apart. The rows may be raked clean in the autumn and may then be earthed up to a depth of 8 ins. or so.

This earthing-up should be done during a fine period, and not when the soil is wet and sodden. The seakale will then grow through the earthed-up portion, and when the tops of the shoots are seen through the ridge, cutting may begin. This may be done by means of a sharp spade, the heads being cut ½ in. below the crown.

When all the crowns have been cut the soil may be thrown down and the cut stems covered with an inch or so of soil.

The rows should be well manured every year, and it should be possible to grow natural seakale in this way without disturbing the rows for six years.

N.B. Wherever seakale is grown, the greatest care should be taken to dig up all the roots, as otherwise they can be a nuisance by sprouting again and again.

Varieties

Lily White. A delicate, good-flavoured seakale, and, when forced, pure white in colour. Is far superior in flavour to the old seakale.

SHALLOT

The shallot is one of the easiest vegetables to grow, and is used for pickling purposes.

Soil. It grows well on any soil, though it may be said to prefer a light loam, deeply worked and well drained.

Preparation of Soil. The soil may be prepared and manured as for onions (see p. 151), though if small shallots are preferred for pickling there is no need for the manuring to be so heavy.

Planting. The bulbs are planted as early as possible, the old rule being to plant on the shortest day so as to harvest on the longest day of the year. In the south it may be possible to get the planting done in January or early February, though in the north it may be necessary to delay until well on in March. The rows may be 12 ins. apart and the bulbs spaced out, according to the variety, 4 to 6 ins. apart in the rows.

Planting may be done in all kinds of " odd " places—along the tops of celery trenches, as an edging to the garden, or on land that is to be used subsequently for other crops.

Before planting, the soil should be firmed so that the bulbs may be pushed in to half their depth. Any loose skins or dead tops should be removed, for worms have a nasty habit of trying to draw these parts down into the soil and thus may pull the bulbs out. Firm planting is necessary.

A fortnight after planting, the bed should be examined and any bulbs that are loose should be firmed and those that have been removed may be replaced.

General Cultivation. The rows should be hoed frequently but not deeply, taking care neither to cut the bulbs nor to bury them, as the shallot prefers to grow on the surface of the soil.

Harvesting. In July the leaves of the shallot will be seen to be turning yellow, and by the second or third week the bulbs may be lifted and left on the surface of the soil to complete the drying-off. After a few days they may be placed on a path or a concrete yard and turned over two or three times, to make certain that they are thoroughly dry. After this they may be divided and stored in a cool, dry place.

Varieties

The Russian Shallot. Sometimes called the Dutch or Jersey shallot. Throws a larger and rounder bulb than the true variety. The skin is of a coppery-red colour and the leaves are greyish-green. This type yields a heavier crop, but does not keep so well.

The True Red or Yellow Shallot may be obtained in these two colours. It throws a nice firm bulb of the right size for pickling, and keeps well.

SPINACH

There are various kinds of spinach grown for the table. They are the summer spinach, the winter spinach, the spinach beet or perpetual spinach, the seakale spinach, and the New Zealand spinach.

The Annual Spinach : Summer and Winter

Both the summer and winter spinach may be classed as annuals.

Soil. A well-tilled loam will produce first-class spinach, and good crops may be obtained on properly worked clay.

Spinach tends to go to seed quickly on very light soils, and, to prevent this, such soils should be enriched with plenty of moisture-holding material.

As stated in *The A.B.C. of Gardening* by the same author, the main requirements seem to be sufficient moisture, available nitrogen, and well-worked land.

Manuring. When preparing the soil, as much dung or compost as possible should be incorporated, to give the spinach the moisture-holding material it appreciates. In order to encourage quick growth, liquid manure may be given along the rows, at fortnightly intervals, directly the plants have started into growth.

Sowing the Seed. The summer spinach should be sown towards the beginning of March in a warm, sheltered position. Two or three sowings may be made from this date onwards at ten-day intervals. As the weather gets warmer the sowings should be made in the moister situations, and to ensure immediate germination the seed should be soaked in water for twenty-four hours.

The drills should be made 1 ft. apart and 1 in. deep, and directly the seedlings can be handled they should be thinned out to 6 ins. apart in the rows.

Few people realise the importance of thinning spinach, but, like most other vegetables, it appreciates room for development.

The winter spinach may be sown from the first week in August to the middle of September at intervals of a fortnight. It is often necessary with these conditions to make special raised beds, 5 ft. wide, 2 or 3 ins. above the level of the soil around. In this way the rain can get away quickly in the alleyways, and, because of the comparatively narrow width of the beds, the crop can be gathered without treading on the soil.

The rows under this system may be 9 ins. apart, and when the plants are through the seedlings may be thinned to 4 ins. apart.

General Cultivation. The rows must be hoed regularly and if possible mulched during the summer with lawn mowings.

The winter spinach may need protection, and this can be done by using straw over and between the rows. Bracken or heather may take the place of straw where they are easier to obtain.   In the north it may be necessary during a frosty period to cover the rows with continuous cloches or lights.

Harvesting. Summer spinach should be picked regularly, and quite hard. It does not matter removing the majority of leaves from the plant.

The winter spinach should not be picked hard or the plants will be spoilt. The largest leaves should be taken, and they should be gathered singly. Only a moderate proportion of leaves should be removed from each plant.

Varieties

SUMMER :

Monstrous Viroflay. A round-seeded variety bearing large upright leaves. Goes to seed very quickly.

Giant Lettuce Leaved. A round-seeded variety ; it is very long-standing and bears medium green leaves.

Long Standing.

The C.O. One of the broadest-leaved round-seeded spinach grown.

WINTER :

New Giant leaved. A prickly-seeded variety, large leaved and very long-standing. May be sown in the spring as well as in August.

Blatchford's New Prickly. Usually grown for winter and spring use. Is a hardy and abundant cropper.

N.B.—Many people find that prickly spinach sown in the summer stands the drought better than the round.

Spinach Beet

Spinach beet, sometimes called the perpetual spinach, is useful, as it produces a continuous supply of large succulent leaves during hot summers. The leaves being similar to the ordinary annual spinach, they are sometimes a more popular substitute than New Zealand spinach.

Soil. See beetroot (p. 98).

Manuring. See beetroot.

Seed-Sowing. The seed may be sown in April and a further sowing may be made at the beginning of August. In this way succession and regular cropping is obtained. The rows should be 15 ins. apart and the plants should be thinned out to 8 ins. apart.

General Cultivation. Regular weeding, hoeing, and occasional waterings are all that are necessary to keep the plants growing and cropping satisfactorily.

Harvesting. The leaves must be gathered regularly directly they are large enough, and even if they are not required. If this is not done, the older leaves will start to get coarse, and it should be the gardener's aim to keep up a supply of fresh leaves that are young and tender. It is usual to pick the leaf, stem and all, so as to ensure further leaves growing.

Seakale Spinach

This vegetable is listed as seakale spinach, though it is sometimes called the Swiss Chard. The main difference between this and the ordinary spinach is that the leaves are very large, thick, and silvery-white in colour. The stalks are served as seakale and the leaf part is dressed as spinach.

It is grown in exactly the same way as spinach beet, and should be harvested in the same way also. It is most important to pick both the stems and the leaves at the same time.

New Zealand Spinach

New Zealand spinach is not liked so much as ordinary spinach by some people, though when it is served on the table, properly sieved, few people can distinguish the difference in the flavour.

Soil. This spinach grows quite well on the light dry soils and does not go to seed like the ordinary types. As it grows somewhat flat upon the ground, rather like ivy, it creates its own mulch. It will grow quite well on the heavier soils, providing they are well prepared.

Manuring. See ordinary spinach.

Propagation. The plants should be raised under glass by sowing seeds in a light compost in boxes round about the end of March. When the young seedlings come through they may be potted up singly into 3 in. pots and set near the glass on a shelf, where they may grow until they are put out at the end of May.

Those who have frames handy may raise the seedlings by

sowing two or three seeds in a 3 in. pot during the second week of April, and, when the plants germinate, thinning them down to one if necessary. Those who have neither glasshouse nor frames may sow " in situ " under continuous cloches about the third week of March, or the seed can be sown out of doors about the second week of May.

Planting Out. The plants should be put out in rows 3 ft. apart, the plants being 2 ft. apart in the rows. This space will soon be covered, and the plants may become interlaced if they are not cut back and picked regularly.

General Cultivation. The plants should never be allowed to become overcrowded, and so the end growths may be pinched back from time to time, these tops being particularly delicious. The " stopping " will cause further branching to take place, and a prolific little bush will thus be formed.

Regular hoeing may be necessary, until the plants cover the ground. Though it has been suggested—and it is perfectly true—that this spinach will grow in dry soil where ordinary varieties go to seed, there is no reason to suppose that the plants will not grow all the better for copious waterings during dry seasons.

Cloches and Longer Cropping

By covering the rows with cloches it is possible to keep the plants cropping throughout the winter. The cloches should go on about the beginning of October.

Harvesting. There are two methods of harvesting, either the picking of single leaves off the stems or the pinching back of the tips.

SWEDE

Swedes are often preferred to winter turnips, and because they are so hardy they are very popular north of Manchester. Swedes have a delicacy of flavour of quite a different character from turnips, and when grown for household use garden varieties should be chosen.

Manuring. See turnips.

Seed-Sowing. The seed may be sown in drills 18 ins. apart, the plants being thinned out to 1 ft. apart, as in the case of winter turnips. In the south of England it is usual to make a sowing about the beginning of May, but in the north, seed-sowing should be delayed until the beginning of June.

General Cultivation. See turnips.

Harvesting. Swedes are usually left outside throughout the winter, and may be drawn as desired. It is seldom that they are seriously damaged by frost.

Varieties

Purple Top Swede. Clean, well-shaped roots of good colour and flavour.

Bronze Top Swede. Similar to above, except that the foliage is of a different colour. It is said by epicures to be the better flavoured.

TOMATO

The Great War was largely responsible for the great popularity of the tomato to-day. During that time the munition workers had more money to spend, and grew to like this vegetable. Since the war the production of tomatoes has increased in an amazing manner, and the price at which they are sold is generally within reach of most people's pockets during the summer.

This does not prevent the garden owner from wishing to grow a few tomatoes on his own, and numbers of glasshouses have been erected in gardens all over the country for this purpose. Even on allotments, particularly in the midlands and the north, one finds that the allotment-holder has built his little greenhouse.

It is possible to grow tomatoes out of doors, and in dry summers heavy crops can be obtained in the open. During wet seasons it is difficult to ripen tomatoes outside, and they are often attacked also by the potato blight.

Soil. Tomatoes may be grown on both heavy and light soils, the important thing being to see that the drainage is perfect.

Preparation of Soil. The heavy soils should be prepared by deep working during the autumn and winter. If the land can be left in ridges, the winter weather will have an opportunity of acting on it and pulverising it.   In February in the south, and in March in the north, well-rotted farmyard manure or compost may be placed in the furrows and the earth in the ridge pulled down to cover the manure in.   This should be done in such a way that further ridges are made over the organic matter.   These ridges need not be so steep as the winter ridges were, and when the time comes the tomatoes may be planted on these.   In this way the roots will lie in warmer and drier soil and yet they will soon get to the farmyard manure. below.

Manuring.   Farmyard manure or compost should be dug in deeply when preparing the land at 1 barrowload to 12 sq. yards, and, in addition, a " complete " fish manure or other organic fertilizer should be used at 4–5 ozs. to the sq. yard. This should be worked into the top 2 or 3 inches.

During dry seasons it may be necessary to add a little more nitrogen, and this may be applied in the form of nitrate of soda or nitro chalk at $\frac{1}{2}$ oz. to the sq. yard in July.   During wet seasons, however, more sulphate of potash should be given and two applications may be necessary at, say, 1 oz. to the sq. yard late in June and late in July.

Liquid Feeding.   Perhaps the most satisfactory way of feeding tomatoes is to use liquid manure.   This can be applied after each truss has set or if preferred as a regular routine every 7 days after the first fruits have appeared.   Liquinure which is now obtainable in bottles, is organic in its base, and makes it possible to apply exactly the right quantities of " balanced " food wherever desired.

Seed-Sowing.   The seed may be sown either under glass or on a mild hot-bed.   This is usually done during the middle of March, either in boxes or, in the case of the frame, directly in the soil.   Generally speaking, boxes are preferable both in the frame and the glasshouse, as in this way the seedlings may be moved about conveniently when potting-up time comes.

John Innes seed compost should be used.

Tomato seeds should be spaced evenly all over the box $\frac{1}{4}$ in. apart, and then be pushed in $\frac{1}{4}$ in. deep into the soil.   The boxes should be covered with a piece of glass, and over this placed a sheet of brown paper. The boxes should then be placed in the frame over the hot-bed, or in a glasshouse of a temperature of about 55 degrees F. In the frame the boxes should be within 6 ins. of the glass.

Directly the seedlings grow, the glass and the brown paper may be removed, and in the glasshouse they may be placed on a shelf near the light. Watering must be done carefully, and water at the same temperature as the house or frame should be given through a very fine rose. Tomato soil should never be over-wet. Water should be given just before the boxes are covered with a sheet of glass.

Continuous cloches may be used with excellent results, producing strong, sturdy, hardy plants. Prepare the soil where the seeds are to be sown, either by (1) incorporating into the top 2 or 3 inches, horticultural peat, sharp silver sand, superphosphate and lime, in suitable proportions to make the soil as near to John Innes seed compost as possible ; (2) removing the top 2 or 3 inches of soil and replace with John Innes seed compost as made up for the glasshouse sowings.

Put the cloches in position 7 to 10 days before sowing, to warm up the soil. Sow the seeds, from mid to the end of March, in the South, and early to mid April, in the Midlands and North. Space the seeds $1\frac{1}{2}$ inches apart, and $\frac{1}{4}$ of an inch deep. When ready, the seedlings may be potted up into 3 inch pots and placed in a trench 3 inches deep and the appropriate width and length. Cover with cloches and seal the ends.

Another good method is to sow the seed *in situ* under Lantern cloches, these miniature glasshouses should be placed at 18 inch intervals along a prepared trench or on soil level, 2 or 3 seeds being sown per Lantern, and later thinned to 1 seedling per site.

The advantages of this method is that the plants suffer no check from transplanting, and that the larger cloches may be used for covering other crops until the end of April, or of course until such time as the plants have grown to the top of the Lanterns.

Transplanting. About the end of March or beginning of April the plants should have grown well, and they may then be transplanted 2 ins. apart into other boxes, or be potted-up singly into 3 in. pots. The compost should be similar, except that more fibrous loam may be added and less peat.

At this stage the plants should be handled tenderly and the stems should not be pinched with the thumb and forefinger, as otherwise they will damp off. It is easier to handle them by the leaves. When potting, they should be made quite firm and watered in.

The boxes or pots can then be placed back into the frames or into the glasshouse again on the shelf. The frames should be shut down and shaded for a few days until the plants get used to their new conditions. After this, ventilation can be given, and the lights removed altogether on the warm, bright days. In the house, ventilation should be given whenever possible, so as to get them growing sturdily. If they tend to get long and lanky, the slightest sprinkling of sulphate of potash will often tone the growth down.

Towards the end of April and beginning of May the plants in the glasshouses should be hardened off by placing them into frames and by giving them plenty of room also. Those in the frames may then be stood outside, though they will need to be given the protection of hessian or some similar material during frosty periods.

It is possible to put a row of barn continuous cloches over bare ground for a week or so to warm it up and then to plant the tomatoes early, hoping that the cloches will give them the necessary protection. Such early planting does give the tomatoes a chance of cropping heavily, as it gives them a longer season of growth.

Raising Plants under Continuous Cloches

Plants raised under cloches are rather later than those raised in heat but are very suitable for outdoor cropping or for planting as a later crop under continuous cloches. Adapt the natural soil to be used by incorporating horticultural peat and sand as advised for the seed compost. Sterilise the strip to be covered, by watering with a 2 per cent solution of formaldehyde and cover with sacks for two days. Fork over the soil and before sowing the seed work in superphosphate at 3 ozs. per sq. yd. and ground chalk at a similar rate. Firm the ground again and water thoroughly before re-cloching. Leave the cloches in position at least 7 days before sowing to ensure the ground being warm enough.

Sow the seed 1½ in. square, and ¼ in. deep. Transplant into 3-inch pots when the seedlings are 3 ins. high, or when the third leaf has developed. Shade the cloches if necessary by throwing a few sacks over the top here and there till the seedlings are well developed. Water as the plants require it but they will not dry out as they do in a greenhouse. Tend to under-water rather than over-water. Always handle seedlings with great care, and use reliable healthy seeds.

Planting Out. It should be possible to put the tomatoes out, under normal conditions, about the end of May or beginning of June. Those who do not want the bother of raising their own plants may usually buy plants that have been raised under glass by a nurseryman near by. The specimens that are bought should be sturdy and hard and about 8 ins. high. The gardener should never be hurried about planting out tomatoes, for it is better to wait a fortnight or so until the soil and the weather are suitable.

The plants that are still in boxes should be prepared for their planting out by passing a knife both ways in between the plants and cutting the roots right down to the bottom of the boxes. If a good watering is done after this, it will be found easy to lift out the plants with a square mass of soil attached to the roots, and as a result planting can be carried out without much check to the young plants.

The hole for planting should not be too deep, and the grower's aim should be to bury the roots so that they are covered with ½ in. of new soil. Firm planting is necessary, and in order to prevent the plants becoming damaged by the winds they should be supported at once by pushing a bamboo or similar stake into the ground and tying the plant up loosely to it.

Sometimes, where a large number of plants are grown, two good posts should be put at the ends of the rows and wires stretched tightly between them. This enables the plants to be tied up to the wires where they grow. At other times, where there are walls or fences, the tomatoes may be grown against these, and the south border is most suitable for this.

General Cultivation. Directly the plants are in, the land should be hoed over to produce a loose surface, and this hoeing should be continued intermittently throughout the season.

The systematic removal of the side-shoots is necessary, and these always seem to grow at a great pace. If they are removed whilst they are still small, the best results are achieved.

It is possible to grow these plants on one or two main stems.

As new growth takes place, so must tying be attended to, and thick, green cotton twine is very satisfactory for this purpose. When tying, a space should always be left for the stem to swell.

During the first week of August it is usually advisable to stop the plants—that is, to pinch off the end of the main stem and so permit no further growth. It will be found that more side-shoots will push out as a result of the stopping, but these will have to be removed as they appear.

It is difficult to advise about the removal of the foliage. It is obviously a bad thing to allow the leaves to form a dense mass which excludes the sunlight and air, but, on the other hand, the leaves manufacture plant foods which feed the fruits. Those plants which have plenty of room to grow may be allowed to retain all their leaves. When planting is done closer than this, whole leaves may be removed here and there, right back to the main stem. It is better to do this than to cut back a large number of the leaves by half.

The leaves as they turn yellow and become useless should be cut off.

It may be necessary to spray tomatoes when growing outside, as a preventive against potato blight. A Bordeaux mixture is used for this purpose (see p. 281).

Ripening Under Cloches

Lay the plants down complete, under the cloches, or pick the fruits and ripen individually. Spread plenty of horti-

A lovely kohl rabi in perfect condition. It is delicious at this stage. Note its appearance.

Bending a leaf over the white curd of a cauliflower to keep it clean and pure. This is a very good thing to do just as the curd is completing its formation.

cultural peat or straw on the ground and put the fruit on this. When laying the plants themselves down it is usually necessary to cut off some of the foliage.

Harvesting. The fruit should be picked as it ripens, and very often it has to be gathered just as it is turning red if blackbirds and thrushes are taking their toll. It is fairly easy to continue the ripening of the fruit indoors if it is placed in warmth.

At the end of September all the fruits that remain should be removed and ripened by hanging the trusses over a wire indoors. The fruit may be kept, if desired, in a deep box of bran (rather in the way that presents are placed in a bran tub), and they will keep in this way for a long time and ripen off satisfactorily.

Varieties

Hundredfold. Excellent variety for outdoor work and cloche work also, early, good flavour and firm flesh.

Exhibition. Large, firm fruit, less seedy than many other varieties. Heavy cropper.

Stonor's M.P. Good cropper, ripens evenly. Firm skin.

Essex Wonder. Even sized fruits, good flavour, firm flesh. Easy to look after but poor shape.

Harbinger. Produces large trusses. Soft skin. Good flavour.

Woodward's Sensation. Popular in the north. Crops well. Good shape.

Market King. Very good variety. Does not crack. Even size.

Clucas 99. Northern variety, very sweet, late cropper. Rather apt to crack.

TURNIP

Many people look upon a turnip as a large, rather hard root which is used in the winter and has to be mashed to make it palatable. There are, however, many varieties of turnips which grow no bigger than a tennis-ball, and which when cooked are tender and delicious.

Growers should remember that turnips belong to the cabbage family, and so are liable to attacks by the same pests and diseases.

Soil. A sandy loam is said to be the most suitable soil for turnips, though the heavier soils will grow the main crops quite satisfactorily. On shallow soils over chalk which do not

G

retain moisture easily, and under similar conditions, it is difficult to grow this crop because the land is " droughty." The result is that the plants have a tendency to run to seed, and, furthermore, they are usually very badly attacked by the turnip flea beetle.

Manuring. The lighter soils should be kept rich in organic materials, which will help to retain the moisture. Very often when the turnip is used as a catch-crop it depends on the manure given to the main crop for its growth.

When grown as a main crop it may be given the same manures as advised for beetroot, but, in addition, lime should be applied on the surface of the soil at 4 ozs. to the sq. yd. just before sowing the seed.

Seed-Sowing. Early, in Frame. The earliest sowings may be made about the end of January in a frame over a hot-bed. Turnips will not stand a great deal of forcing, and the frames should always be given as much ventilation as possible from the time the seedlings show through. It may be necessary also to give sprinklings with water. The seed is often broadcast, but it is preferable to make holes 4 ins. square and 1 in. deep in the soil of the frame and to drop three seeds into each one. After sowing, the holes are filled in. If all the seedlings grow, they are thinned out to one.

Early Outside. It should be possible to sow turnips in the south of England during the early part of March in a sheltered spot, providing the ground can be got down to a fine tilth and it always can be if continuous cloches are put down for 14 days beforehand over the strip covered. The rows in this case can be 4 ins. apart and the seed sown evenly in the rows. When the seedlings are through they can be thinned out to 4 ins. apart. It is possible to broadcast the seed, and to thin the plants that come up, in a similar manner.

In April another sowing may be made in drills 12 ins. apart, the turnips being thinned to 6 ins. apart when they are 1 in. or so high.

Main Crop. The main crop is generally sown in May, and in a shady position if possible. From such sowings it is possible to pull useful roots in the late summer.

Winter Turnips. In this case a sowing is made from the middle of July to the end of August. The drills should be 18 ins. apart, the plants being thinned to 6 ins. apart in the early stages, and to 1 ft. apart when the roots are fit to use.

Turnip Tops. Many people like turnip-tops as a vegetable, and these are of the greatest value during the time of the year when greens are scarce. For this reason a special variety should be sown early in September in rows 2 ft. apart. This sowing is done fairly thinly, and it is left to grow naturally for its leaves and not for its roots.

General Cultivation. In the case of the earlier sowings, it is of the utmost necessity to keep a sharp outlook for the turnip flea beetle. Regular dustings with Gammaxene should be done, even before the little plants are through the ground.

The rows must be hoed regularly. This will not only kill the weeds, but will help to conserve the moisture so much needed by this crop.

In very dry seasons it may be necessary to water, but when watering is carried out a good flooding should be given, and a hoeing and mulching, or a hoeing alone, given immediately afterwards.

Harvesting. The spring and summer-sown varieties should always be pulled while they are young and fresh. In this way they are used before they get coarse.

The winter varieties may stand outside and be used as desired, though in the northern districts, which experience sharp frosts, main crop turnips may be spoiled when left in the ground. In this case they should be lifted and clamped as for potatoes.

Varieties

EARLY IN FRAME AND CLOCHES :

Early Long White Frame. This variety has a blunt nose and a minute tap-root. It is very tender.

Jersey Navet. Pure white. Has a thin skin, the flavour being excellent and mild.

Sutton's Gem, delicious oval turnip quite different from any other variety. Those who haven't eaten this don't know what a turnip can be.

EARLY OUTSIDE AND MAIN :

Early White Milan. The roots are flat, of medium size, and quite smooth. The flesh is white and the flavour is much appreciated.

Early Snowball. A perfectly formed round white turnip with a short top and a single tap-root. The flesh is white, solid and mild.

Early Stone. An early turnip. Roots somewhat flat.

Golden Ball. A yellow-fleshed garden turnip. Clean in growth.

Golden Wonder. A similar variety to Golden Ball.

WINTER TURNIPS :

Chirk Castle. A good winter variety, firm white flesh.

Veitch's Red Globe. A variety which matures earlier than Chirk Castle. Has white flesh.

Manchester Market. A very suitable variety for the north.

TURNIP TOPS : **Green Globe.** Used for its leaves only.

ONION SETS

It is an advantage to use onion sets on soil where onion seed will not germinate easily, and where attacks of the onion fly are particularly bad. To obtain good onion sets carry out the following directions.

Sow the seed in the middle of May to early June in a seed bed of well consolidated soil, with a fine tilth and of good water holding capacity, these conditions are essential. The seeds should be sown in drills ½ in. deep and marked out with a rake with teeth 1 in. apart. It is found the seed is sown more evenly by this method than if broadcast. Sown at the rate of ½ oz. per sq. yd. a good proportion of usable sets is produced. No thinning is necessary.

Be sure the sets are fully matured before lifting, as early lifting encourages bolting next season. Too large sets are also apt to bolt. Aim to get them ¼ to ¾ of an inch in diameter.

Dry off thoroughly in an airy greenhouse, clean and store on wire bottomed trays in a warm temperature, if possible, as this helps to prevent bolting.

Plant out at the end of March in drills 1 in. deep and 12 ins. apart, with 6-8 ins. between the sets. The ground should be prepared as for spring sown onions. Heavy applications of nitrogenous manures are not advised as they do not make very small sets grow into large bulbs, but produce bulbs liable to Neck rot.

CHAPTER IX

SALAD PLANTS

Many people when they think of salad only remember lettuces, tomatoes, cucumbers and radishes. There are many other plants that can be used, and information is given for instance on :—

1. Chicory and how to force it.
2. Mustard and cress and how to prevent it damping off.
3. Endive and how to blanch it.
4. Sorrel and how to prevent the leaves becoming reduced in size.
5. Corn salad and how useful it is after Christmas.
6. Chives and how they can make a useful edging to a border.

In this country we have not yet learnt the art of making salads, except, of course, with a few outstanding exceptions. Every year, however, more and more salads are grown and used, and for this reason it is wise to devote a chapter to showing which crops may be used as salads, leaving the full descriptions of methods of growing etc. (except in a few cases) to Chapter VIII, in which the cultivation of vegetables is outlined in alphabetical order.

Many plants are used in salads raw, while others have to be cooked before they are found to be satisfactory. Some plants—it may be the stems or the leaves—have to be blanched before they are ready, while others can be used just as they grow.

It should be the aim of the keen vegetable gardener to produce crops suitable for salad purposes all the year round. This is possible to do, especially if a frame or two are available. This can only be done if readers are prepared to grow some of the more unusual plants, or to use in salads vegetables normally thought of as fit only to be " boiled."

The great advantage of eating vegetables raw is concerned largely with their vitamin content. Fresh vegetables, used fresh as they are from the garden, contain far more vitamins

197

FORCING CHICORY

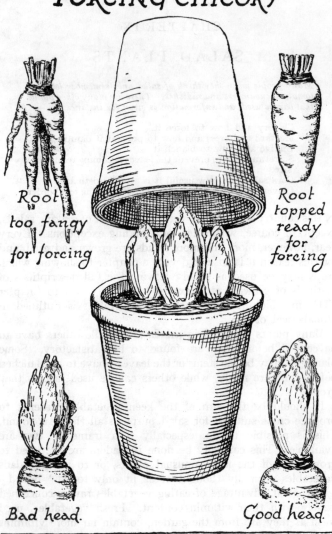

Root too fangy for forcing

Root topped ready for forcing

Bad head.

Good head.

than those that are cooked, or even than those that appear in the shops, owing to the fact that serious vitamin losses occur during travel. Lettuce too, in many cases, provides the vitamins which is now said to be so necessary for human diet.

The following, then, are the principal salad crops.

Beetroot

When this crop is used as a salad, the roots should be pulled before they are coarse, and may either be used immediately or may be stored for use during the winter months.

Celeriac

The method of growing this vegetable is described in Chapter XI. It can be used in salads as is beetroot.

Celery

A very popular salad, both the self-blanching celery, which comes in early, and the main crop celery, which is useful in November, December, and January.

Chervil

Chervil is described as a herb, but small quantities may be used to flavour salads.

Chicory

Plants may be raised if seed is sown on well-prepared land early in June in rows 18 ins. apart. When the seedlings are through they may be thinned to 1 ft. apart. When growing, chicory resembles the dandelion.

Hoeing should be carried out regularly, and in November the roots may be dug up and placed in boxes of sand tightly against the other. The boxes may then be taken into a dark shed or cellar for forcing, or into a darkened frame. They may be forced also under the staging of a greenhouse providing this is kept dark, or be placed under whitewashed cloches with the soil heated below with the electric warming unit.*

---

* The Author can provide details of this if desired.

The yellow leaves thus produced are most tender, and may be in use from October to May providing successional "forcings" are made.   The best variety to grow is the Witloof.

Chives

These prove a very useful crop, and make it possible to have the subtle onion flavouring all the year round.   The plants make a very nice edging to a border, and will grow well under quite dry conditions.   The plants may be propagated by division in the spring.

Corn Salad

A salad crop much neglected, but which comes in very useful from Christmas onwards.   The seeds should be sown in rows 1 ft. apart in September, and the plants thinned out, when large enough, to 6 in. apart.

The leaves of the corn salad resemble the forget-me-not, and should be gathered one at a time from the plants and should be washed before using.   Some people prefer the round-leaved variety, while others like the Regence.

Cucumber

During the summer it is possible to have cucumbers growing out of doors ; and home grown ones are welcomed.   Ridge varieties may be grown, but with the aid of continuous cloches Frame varieties also.

Soil.   Cucumbers like a soil rich in organic matter, moist but well drained.

Preparation of Soil.   Prepare the soil in such a way that there is a 4–5 inch layer of well rotted vegetable refuse or fermenting manure 6 inches down.   Some people dig a hole, for the purpose, where the plant is to grow, making it a spade and a half in width and a similar depth.   After putting the rotting material at the bottom they replace the soil to form a mound.

Seed Sowing.   The seeds may be sown in the glasshouse early April and the seedlings planted out under cloches early

May ; or sown at the end of April and planted out of doors at the end of May, or beginning of June, when fear of frost is over (this applies to the Ridge varieties only). Frame varieties must be covered with cloches throughout.

Seeds may be sown in a prepared seed bed as advised for tomatoes, the seeds being spaced 3 inches apart and ½ an inch deep ; or sown *in situ* on the prepared mounds under Lantern cloches.

Planting Out. When the seedlings have made their first pair of true leaves they should be planted out in the positions where they are to grow, these are usually 3 feet apart.

Stopping and Pollinating. Ridge cucumbers should have the top nipped out when 7 leaves have formed, this is all the stopping that is necessary. Frame varieties should be stopped one leaf beyond the forming cucumber, a lateral will then form, and this, in its turn, will be stopped one leaf beyond the cucumber, and so on. These laterals are usually tied to wires ; but it is possible to let both types to grow at will.

Pinch off the male blooms from the Frame varieties because you do not want the female blossoms pollinated, as this makes the cucumbers taste bitter. Retain the male blooms in the case of Ridge varieties as these are necessary for a good set of fruit.

Watering and Feeding. It is usually necessary to water 3 times a week during hot weather. Cucumbers like moist conditions and these help to keep down the red-spider. The ends of the cloches may be removed in day time, and the tops flecked over with a little limewash, to break up the sun's rays and give a little shade. When the first fruits are about 3 inches long water every 5 days with liquid manure.

Harvesting. Cut the cucumbers as desired but never let them get too old. Keep cutting, therefore, when they are of a good size and the plants will keep cropping. It is possible to get 40 good cucumbers from a Ridge variety, and about half that amount from a good Frame type.

General Remarks. As cucumbers are surfacing rooting they appreciate a good mulch of well rotted compost or peat.

G*

ENDIVE

Blanching Endive under whitewashed cloches.

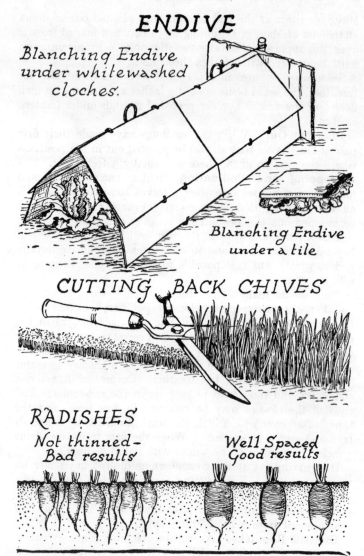

Blanching Endive under a tile

CUTTING BACK CHIVES

RADISHES

Not thinned— Bad results

Well Spaced Good results

Be sure that the roots are not exposed by washing the soil off
when watering, nor let the water collect round the stems as
this may cause stem rot.

Varieties

Hampshire Giant. The best of all Ridge types. Large cucumbers; plants crop heavily. Fruits almost spineless.

Stockwood Ridge. } Two good varieties but neither as
Bedford Prize Ridge. } large as Hampshire Giant.

Conqueror. The best of the Frame varieties for cloche work.

Telegraph. Use this variety when it is impossible to get Conqueror.

Dandelion

The cultivated dandelion is grown in a similar manner to
chicory. It grows well on the dry soils, and there is no need
to give it any special manuring.

The seeds should be sown in May in rows 1 ft. apart, and
plant thinning should be done to 1 ft. apart also.

From November onwards the roots are lifted and forced,
as for seakale. They can also be covered with forcing-pots
and blanched where they grow after the turn of the year. This
blanching is necessary, as the green leaves are rather bitter.

It is quite possible to force roots in boxes in a cellar, covered
with a tent of brown paper or further boxes, or under cloches
as advised for Chicory.

Endive

A salad much used on the Continent, and which is becoming
increasingly popular in England.

The main sowing should be made in a moist border in June
or July, the rows being 1 ft. apart. The seed is slow to
germinate and the seedlings slow to growth. Watering
should be done regularly to encourage growth.

When the plants are fit to handle they may be transferred
and planted out just as cabbage lettuce. In fact, they can be
grown in the same way as lettuce all the time.

They should, however, be blanched, and this is done in
various ways : (1) the outer leaves are tied up over the heart ;
(2) a large flower-pot is inverted over it ; (3) a slate is laid over

the plant ; and (4) the plants are taken up bodily into a dark shed and planted in soil there for a fortnight to bleach.

Much the easiest way of blanching endive is to whitewash the inside of one or two Continuous Cloches and then to stand these over the plants—closing up the ends of the short row thus made with a square of wood or a sheet of whitewashed glass. The plants are thus kept from the light ; not " squashed " and yet are grown in perfect ventilation. The result is they are excellent to eat in 3 weeks time.

There are two varieties :—

Moss Curled, whose leaves are crinkly and crisp ; and Batavian, which has leaves more like a lettuce.

Lettuce

There is no need to extol the excellence of this crop, as it forms the basis of most salads. A full description of its cultivation will be found on pp. 136-142.

Mint

Mint, though not usually thought of as a salad, may be incorporated if it is chopped up fine or used in quite small quantities. It gives that " unusual flavour."

Mustard and Cress

This would seem to be one of the most easily grown crops, and yet on certain soils it " damps off " easily. In such cases the soil should be sterilised before using, either by heating the the soil to 210 degrees F. for twenty minutes, or by soaking the soil with a 2 per cent solution of formaldehyde and leaving until the fumes have gone.

The cress should be sown three days before the mustard seed, and the boxes may be kept dark. It is usually convenient to sow in boxes, and these may be taken into the dark for a few days to ensure long stems. They must come out in the light again five days before cutting, to get the green colouring-matter back into the leaves. They are cut off with scissors when required, as to pull them up by the roots is apt to make the salad gritty.

The best variety for sowing is the white mustard. After the middle of March, mustard and cress may be sown outside, first of all in the south border and then in the north border. Successional sowings may be made until the middle of September.

Nasturtium

Few people think of nasturtiums as a salad plant, though the flowers are often used for garnishing. Actually the flowers can be eaten, and the seeds which form subsequently can be included in salads also, though they are somewhat " hot."

Nasturtiums will always grow well in any poor soil.

Onion

A large number of types of onions are described in this book (see pp. 151-159). It is not necessary to use large quantities of this crop in a salad, as just a " wipe round the bowl " with chives, for instance, is sufficient to give a piquant flavour.

Parsley

Like mint, this is more generally used for garnishing and for flavouring. It is, however, a useful adjunct to any salad, providing it is used intelligently.

Radish

This crop is much liked, not only because of the colour it gives to a salad, but because of its flavour. Radishes should not only be pulled young, but when they are crisp and fresh. There are many kinds, and a trial should be made of the different varieties, as some suit some palates better than others.

Rampion

See Chapter XI. The roots may be used for salads, fresh or cooked.

Sorrel

Sorrel may either be used for a salad or cooked with spinach.

It grows best on a light loam, and the seeds should be sown early in April in shallow drills 18 ins. apart. The seedlings should be thinned early, leaving 3 ins. between the plants in the rows.

The bed should be hoed regularly to keep it free from weeds.

If necessary, all the plants may be transplanted to another piece of ground, this time 18 ins. being allowed between the plants either way. In any case the plants growing on the original patch will have to be thinned to that distance.

Directly any flowering stems appear, they should be pinched out, as otherwise the leaves become reduced in size.

The leaves should be picked off as required, and the younger and fresher they are the better are they suited for the salad-bowl.

Tomatoes

More and more amateurs are growing tomatoes outside, and are finding them comparatively easy to grow (see p. 187).

N.B. For fuller information on Salads see the author's book *Eating without Heating*.

CHAPTER X

HERBS

Herbs, I suggest, can make a great difference in the palatableness of a dish. Did you know that :—

1. Borage attracted bees.
2. Caraway seeds can easily be grown.
3. The curved chervil could be used instead of parsley.
4. The stems of fennel could be blanched and used like celery.
5. Rust in mint can be cured.
6. Horse radish could be grown without its running all over the garden.

THERE are large numbers of herbs that are most useful in the kitchen. Unfortunately, to-day most housewives obtain their herbs, already dried, in little tins or packets. There is no need for herbs to be grown extensively in any garden, but certain of them at least are indispensable. Mint, parsley, sage, and thyme are four of these. Other herbs are, however, useful, and so the general cultivation of a collection of herbs is given later on.

Herbs may be said to differ from vegetables in that they are not themselves used for foods, but they can make a great difference in the palatableness of the dish. It is their aroma and flavour that the chef values.

Balm

This is one of the easiest of all the herbs to grow. It is a perennial, and can be propagated by cuttings or grown as an annual from seed. The leaves are used for making tea for invalids or for those with fever. To make the tea, pour 1 pint of boiling water on ½ oz. of leaves and after twenty minutes the tea is fit to drink.

The plant is herbaceous, and bears circular wrinkled leaves. The seed may be sown in May ; cuttings may also be taken in May.

Basil

There are two forms of basil, the most popular of which is sweet basil.

The seeds are sown in February or March in heat, and the seedlings are planted out in May in rows 12 ins. apart, the plants 8 ins. in the rows. When the plants are in flower the shoots should be cut to the ground and dried for winter use. Some growers lift the plants in September and pot them, in order to obtain fresh green leaves throughout the winter.

Bush basil may be sown outside in April.

Borage

This is always an interesting herb to grow, because it has a great attraction for bees. It grows well on poor soil, while the flowers and leaves are very popular for flavouring purposes. It is a rampant spreading grower. In cider and claret cup, two or three borage leaves impart a delicious flavour.

The plant normally grows 18 ins. high, the leaves being 3 ins. long and bristly. The flowers are bright blue.

The seed should be sown in April or early May in rows 2 ft. apart, and the plants thinned to 18 in. apart. It is possible to propagate also by division or from cuttings of the old stock.

Caraway

Caraway seeds are well known and are used for flavouring cakes, etc. The root of the caraway is also edible, and looks and tastes something like a carrot. The leaves and shoots of this plant can be used for salads.

The plant grows 1 ft. to 15 ins. high, and the seed is sown in May or early June in rows 18 ins. apart. The plant should be thinned to 6 ins. apart in the rows.

The seeds should be ready for gathering in September.

Chervil

Chervil should be used fresh for flavouring both soups and salads. It is often used for garnishing instead of parsley. For this purpose the curled chervil is most suitable.

Seed should be sown any time from July to October in

drills 10 ins. apart, the seedlings thinned to 6 ins. apart. It is essential to get fresh seed. During a hot summer the plants should be watered frequently to prevent them from going to seed. The leaves are picked off as they are required and used.

Fennel

A hardy perennial which produces a quantity of feathery foliage, used either for garnishing or for fish sauces. It is possible to blanch the stems and use them like celery. The seeds, when saved, may be employed for flavouring also.

There are many kinds of fennel, but it is the garden fennel that is grown in this country. It is very popular in the north region.

The seed should be sown in the south in mid-April, and in the north early in May. The drills may be 18 ins. apart and the seedlings thinned 6 to 8 ins. apart.

If the stems are required for culinary purposes, they should be earthed up when the base begins to swell. They are usually blanched ten days afterwards and are then ready to use.

Marjoram

There are several kinds of marjoram, two of which are grown in private gardens, the sweet marjoram and the pot marjoram. The pot marjoram has more branches, and a reddish tinge seems to suffuse the plants. It has, also, violet flowers. The sweet marjoram makes a bushy plant which bears white flowers in June and July. The leaves of the pot and sweet marjoram are used green, and, when dried, for flavouring, while the latter is said to be a tonic.

The seeds should be sown in April out of doors in rows 1 ft. apart, the plants being thinned in the case of pot marjoram to 9 ins. apart and sweet marjoram 6 ins. apart.

Mint

There are many kinds of mint, the peppermint, spearmint, M. longifolia, M. rotundifolia, etc. The spearmint is the variety which seems most used for mint sauce. It is hardy, but susceptible to mint rust. Some epicures prefer M. rotundi-

HERBS

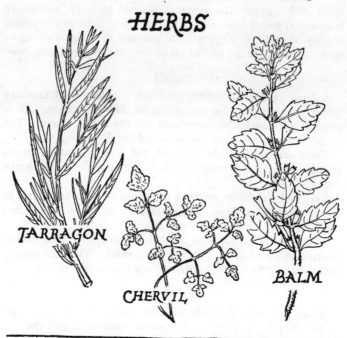

TARRAGON

CHERVIL

BALM

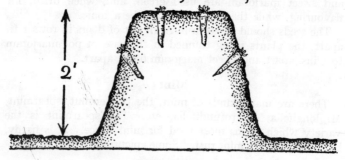

Growing HORSERADISH on a Mound
This ensures a good crop

2'

CUTTING HERBS

Cut Marjoram before
flowers appear

When cutting
Dill for Seed.
Remove head with as
short a stem as possible

CULTURAL HINTS

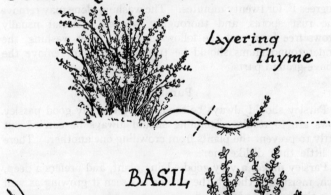

Layering
Thyme

BASIL

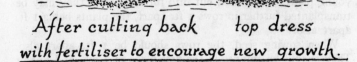

After cutting back   top dress
with fertiliser to encourage new growth.

folia because of its flavour, while others dislike its hairiness. It is propagated by means of the division of roots, and in order to obtain fresh young green leaves throughout the year the roots are often forced during the months from November to May.   This forcing is quite easy to carry out if the roots are chopped up into pieces an inch long and packed tightly in a seed-bed, and covered above and below with an inch or so of soil.   It is possible also to cut stems in the autumn and to hang them up in a cool place to dry for use during the winter and spring.

A damp situation seems to suit mint best, and in order to keep it free from rust a new situation should be made every year early in March.

In cases where the rust is very bad, the roots should be washed before planting out and put in warm water at 110 degrees F. for twenty minutes.   The washing alone may remove the rust spores, and thoroughly washed material usually grows free from rust the following year.   After washing, the underground stems should be trimmed so as to remove the above-ground parts.

Parsley

Parsley should always be sown thinly if really good parsley rows are to result.   Thinning should always be carried out early to prevent the plants from crowding one another.   There is little they dislike more.

Parsley makes a very good edging plant, and prefers a deep, rich, moist soil, though the author has seen it growing as well in a clayey soil as in a sand.

The principal sowings of parsley may be made in March for the summer and June for the winter ; if one sowing is made, this should be done in May.   Those with a glasshouse can make a sowing in heat in February, and, after pricking, the young plants thus raised out into further boxes, they may be transplanted further in rows 1 ft. apart, the plants being 1 ft. apart also.

When sowing seed, the rows should be 1 ft. apart also. They should be thinned in the first place to 3 ins. and finally to 6 inches. These thinnings may be transplanted to other rows if necessary.

By the aid of a cloche or two it is possible to have plenty of parsley all the year round outside. If the plants tend to get coarse, they should be cut down, and the young growth which comes up then will be green and tender. Such cutting down generally defers the flowering which does so much harm to the plants. It is possible to pot up the best plants at the end of September and take them into a cool house.

Varieties

Green Gem. A very compact variety, which never grows more than 5 in. high.

Myatt's Garnishing. This has long leaf-stalks. It is a heavy cropper.

Champion Moss Curled. Produces a very dark-green, tightly curled leaf.

Radish, Horse

This may be said to be a very popular condiment with roast beef. It can become a nuisance in the garden if it is not correctly grown, as it soon spreads like a weed.

Probably the best way to grow it is to make a little mound in December 2 ft. high and 2 ft. wide and as long as is desired, and to see that this mound is on well-firmed soil—a path, or even concrete. Young roots about $\frac{1}{2}$ in. in diameter may then be cut 9 ins. in length, and may be laid in sand until March. At this time of the year the majority of them will have sprouted, and the best may then be planted in the mound at distances of 12 ins. apart and 18 ins. from the normal level of the soil. The thongs should be inserted so as to point downwards.

If the mound is made of good soil, and the crowns are kept disbudded, a good, long, thick, straight root will form which can easily be stored in the winter.

To uncover the horse radish the mound can be razed to the ground and the roots thus exposed. The advantage of the mound method is that it is impossible for the roots to spread throughout the soil, and it ensures good thick sticks being produced. The sticks when dug up are stored in sand.

Sage

Sage is a popular herb, being used as a seasoning either with duck, sausages, or even with cheeses. There are two main sages, the green sage and the red sage. The green sage has wrinkled, velvety leaves and grows like a little shrub. Red sage has violet-coloured leaves and is not very popular.

When purchasing plants of the green sage, it is advisable to ask for the broad-leafed green, as this is regarded as the better type. It is better to buy plants than to sow seed, as seedlings can never be relied on. Cuttings may be taken with a heel in April or May, and may be rooted in a sandy medium. They will generally root quickly in frames, but they will grow quite well in the open ground.

The plants thus raised should be planted out in rows 2 ft. apart, and the plants 1 ft. apart in the rows. After planting they should be hoed regularly, and when plants show signs of flower the flowering stems should be cut back.

Take cuttings, and renew the sage row once every four years.

Savory

This is one of the herbs that has a very strong flavour, and should be used in a similar manner to thyme. The summer savory should be raised annually from seed, while the winter savory is a perennial, usually propagated by cuttings. When growing it looks rather like rosemary. Both of them are cut when the stems are in full flower and tied up in bunches to dry for winter use.

It is possible to raise both kinds from seeds sown in April in drills 1 ft. apart, the seedlings being thinned to 6 ins. apart.

Tarragon

This is mainly used for flavouring vinegar, but is also useful in salads. It can be employed to flavour omelettes also.

The plant is a perennial which grows like a bush 4 ft. high, bears slender shoots and thin, delicate textured leaves. The fresh herb has to be used, as the oil of tarragon disappears when the herb is dried.

The plants should be put out in a well-drained, sheltered situation 2 ft. sq. It is quite easy to propagate by means of division or by cuttings, which should be struck in frames or in gentle heat in the spring.

As in the case of parsley, it is possible to dig up one or two plants and winter them in cold frames so as to keep up a continuous supply of fresh green leaves.

Thyme

This is a useful herb for flavouring stews and soups and is the best adjunct to jugged hare. There are two main types, the common thyme and the lemon thyme. The latter can only be propagated by the division of roots in March and April, or by cuttings in September, while the former can be raised from seed sown in the spring. Actually the division of roots is preferable in the case of common thyme also.

Thyme may be used to form an effective edging, and may be used for this purpose in dry borders where parsley will not grow readily.

It is necessary to ensure frequent division, as, if this is not done, the plants become leggy and may die out. The rows should be 2 ft. apart and the plants 18 ins. apart in the rows.

In exposed situations and under northern conditions it may be necessary to earth the plants up in order to give them some protection throughout the winter. Under such conditions growth may be encouraged by the application of potassic nitrate of soda at the rate of 1 oz. to the yard run, in spring.

CHAPTER XI

UNUSUAL VEGETABLES

This perhaps is the most important chapter of all because it introduces something new to break the monotony of the " meat and two veg."

1. The flavour of Celeriac is like the " heart " of celery.
2. Good King Henry, used as a spinach, is called the Lincolnshire asparagus.
3. Hamburg parsley may be likened to a parsley and parsnip in one.
4. Asparagus peas are delicious.
5. The rampion may be used either boiled or in salads.
6. The Japanese and Chinese eat skirret, but it has a peculiar flavour.

As a nation we are conservative—very conservative. There is proof of this from the fact that we do not take easily to unusual dishes. We are hedged round about with the roast beef and Yorkshire pudding, a few potatoes and a spoonful of soggy cabbage !

To those who are unwilling to grow any other crop than their grandfathers grew before them this chapter will have no appeal, but for those who wish to discover new culinary dishes this chapter should prove of value.

Even here there has been no attempt to include what might be called the very unusual, and to some who may read it all the vegetables mentioned may be well known. It is, however, the author's boast that he has grown all the crops he writes about, and, furthermore, has had them cooked for him at home.

Artichoke, Chinese

Ivory white tubers are produced in abundance, which can be used from November to April either cooked or in salads. They may be boiled, fried, or eaten raw. The plant only grows 18 ins. high.

Propagation. This is done by means of the tubers produced the previous year. Medium-sized tubers should be selected for this purpose.

Planting. This is carried out in April, usually in drills 6 ins. deep. The rows should be 18 ins. apart and the tubers placed 9 ins. apart in the rows. An open, sunny situation should be chosen.

Soil. Probably the most suitable soil is a well-drained free-working loam. The tubers may rot off in badly drained land. Heavy clays should be " lightened," and raised beds may be made to ensure warmth and drainage. Light soils and gravels should be improved by the addition of humus in the form of rotted leaves or peat.

Harvesting. In well-drained soils the tubers may be left in the ground until required, but it is possible to lift them from October onwards. If they are to be kept they should be stored in soil or sand. It is unwise to keep them in a dry place, as in this case the tubers shrivel.

When lifting, all the " roots " that have formed should be removed. The tubers should be kept covered to preserve their whiteness : if exposed to the light for some time they turn a disagreeable yellow colour.

Beans

There are two unusual runner beans which should go in this chapter.

The Blue Cocoa, which bears blue pods, as its name suggests, and The Robin Bean which bears red speckled pods. Both should be grown exactly as the runner bean.

Cápsicum

These fruits always attract by their brilliance of colour when exhibited at shows. They can be used for flavouring pickles, for putting into salads, and for cooking in various ways. They are " hot." The fruit may be likened to a long, queerly shaped tomato, red and green.

Propagation. Seeds should be sown in a lightish compost in pots early in March, either in a glasshouse or in a heated frame. Three seeds may be placed in a 3 in. pot, and after the plants are growing the best one should be retained and the other two removed. They should be grown on in these pots under glass until late May, when they may be planted outside.

In the north of England it will probably be necessary to grow them on in frames or under glass.

Planting. If they can be planted out late in May or early in June the rows should be 18 ins. apart, and the plants 18 ins. apart in the rows. Outside they produce much finer and heavier crops, and will go on fruiting if the first ripened fruits are gathered.

General Cultivation. They should be damped overhead from time to time in the afternoon or early evening to keep down red spider, and hoed regularly.

Harvesting. They are picked regularly as the fruits ripen, and the whole crop is gathered before the end of September, when frosts may be expected.

Cardoon

The author first remembers growing this vegetable in the south of Ireland near Queenstown. It grew far more rampantly than was expected, and was in consequence very difficult to blanch. When growing it resembles the globe artichoke. It has a very delicious " nutty " flavour, and may be used as a vegetable or for soups.

Propagation. The seed may be sown in pots late in March or early in April. There is no need to give the plants a lot of heat. They may be raised quite well in a cold frame. Watering should be done sparingly until the seedlings have grown well. Three seeds may be sown in a pot and thinned out later, as suggested for capsicum.

Some growers sow the seed in the trenches where the plants are to grow in April or May.

Planting. Trenches are made in advance 12 ins. deep, 8 ins. wide, and 4 ft. apart. Manure or organic substitute is put into the bottom of the trench to a 6 in. thickness, and this is dug in. The plants are put out 18 ins. apart in the trench. If sowings are made in the trenches, two or three seeds are placed at 18 in. distances, and these are lightly covered with soil. The plants, when they grow, are thinned down to one at each station.

General Cultivation. The trenches should be given plenty of water, and liquid manure may be given from June onwards once a week or so. Earthing-up should not be attempted before October, and before this is done the lower yellow leaves are cleaned away ; the stems are then tied up together loosely, and if necessary the plants may be wrapped round with brown paper. The soil is then brought up to the plants. A month after earthing-up the cardoons should be ready for use.

Harvesting. Lift as desired and use. In frosty districts, after blanching they may be lifted and stored in a dry place and so kept blanched until required. Cardoons may keep in this way until March.

Varieties

Spanish Cardoon. This is a variety usually grown, as it has spineless leaves. The fault is that it easily runs to seed.

Tours. A very prickly variety, and most difficult to work amongst. It is, however, a superior variety to the other, both in flavour and length of stem. Is a hardy variety also.

Puvis. Quite a good variety, as it has a thick leaf-stalk and is solid. It is well flavoured, and not a prickly variety.

Celeriac

One of the author's favourite vegetables, as it grows like a turnip and tastes just like the heart of celery. It is excellent when sliced into salads or when cooked. It is easy to grow, as little blanching has to be carried out, and the vegetable will keep six months after it is full grown.

Propagation. The plants should be raised in exactly the same way as celery plants, the seedlings being pricked out when large enough. They are planted out in May or early June in rows 12 ins. apart, the plants being put in 12 ins. apart in the rows, on flat ground.

General Cultivation. The rows are kept hoed regularly and fed. Celeriac is a gross feeder, and will need liquid manure from the end of June onwards once a week. A good dressing fo fish manure may be given in September as the roots plump

UNUSUAL VEGETABLES

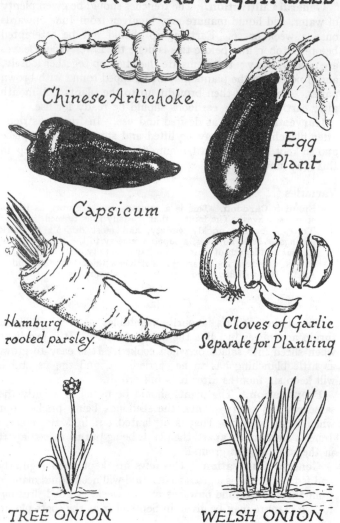

Chinese Artichoke

Egg Plant

Capsicum

Hamburg rooted parsley.

Cloves of Garlic Separate for Planting

TREE ONION

WELSH ONION

UNUSUAL VEGETABLES

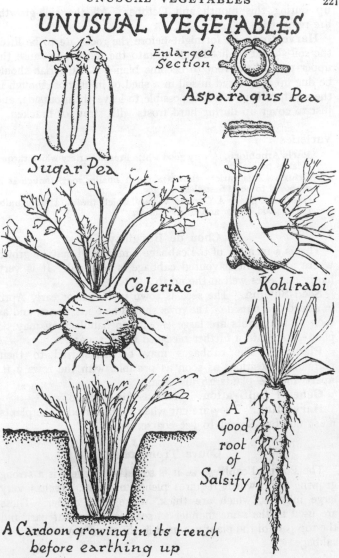

Enlarged Section

Asparagus Pea

Sugar Pea

Celeriac

Kohlrabi

A Good root of Salsify

A Cardoon growing in its trench before earthing up

up during this month and October. All the side-growths are removed.

Harvesting. A fortnight before the roots are to be lifted the soil should be hoed well up into the foliage, to cause the upper part of the root to become blanched. Celeriac should be dug up and stored in soil in a shed or in clamps, though in the south of England it is possible to leave them outside, and just to cover up during hard frosts with straw or bracken.

Varieties

Paris Amebiore. A very good white French variety which throws a large bulb.

Erfurt. This variety throws a much smaller root, though it is supposed to be of first-class quality.

Giant Prague. A German variety which throws a large bulb. It is a good keeper and is very solid.

Chou de Burghley

This is a member of the cabbage family, and may be grown where a different flavoured cabbage is required. It is very hardy and does well in the north.

Seed-Sowing. The seed is sown in March or early April in a seed-bed outside. The rows should be 6 ins. apart, and as soon as the plants are large enough to handle they may be planted out into a further seed-bed 6 ins. square.

Planting. The cabbages may be transferred to their permanent positions as soon as possible, with the rows 2 ft. apart and the plants 18 ins. apart.

General Cultivation. Treat as for cabbage.

Harvesting. They are cut when well hearted ; the plants must not be allowed to get coarse.

Couve Tronchuda

The Portugal cabbage, as it is sometimes called, is a strong growing type which requires plenty of room. It has very large midribs, which are thick, white, and tender. These are used in the same manner as seakale. The leaf part and the top part of the plant are used in the same way as ordinary cabbage.

Seed-Sowing. See Chou de Burghley.

Planting. They are transplanted into rich and well-prepared soil as soon as possible. The plants should be set out 2 ft. each way. They should be watered plentifully during dry weather.

Harvesting. As soon as the bottom leaves are large enough they may be cut off and the leaf portion detached from the midrib. Each part should be cooked separately.

Egg-Plant

Often called aubergine. It is a very delicious vegetable when cooked. It may be stuffed and baked, cut into slices and fried, or flavoured and boiled. The author finds it delicious when fried.

Seed-Sowing. Seed should be sown in January or February in a warm house or in March in a frame. In the house the temperature should be about 60 degrees F. Two or three seeds may be sown to a 3 in. pot ; reducing down to one plant is necessary later on. After a month or six weeks the plants may be potted up into 6 in. pots, and grown on in these until ready for planting outside. It is possible to raise aubergines by sowing the seeds in a frame over a hot-bed, or under continuous cloches—say in April.

Planting. In the north it will be better to grow them on in the frame or glasshouse. In the south they may be planted out on the south border or near a sunny wall. When planted in rows, it will be found the plants need to be put in 2 ft. square.

General Cultivation. The plants should always be grown on a single leg or stem at the start, and when they are strong enough the growing top pinched out to make them branch. Four to six fruits should be allowed to form, and after this lateral growth stopped. They should be syringed on warm days to keep down red spider. They should be hoed regularly and mulched if necessary.

Varieties

Purple. Throws a large fruit, round and purplish in colour. It is of very fine quality.

Blanche longue de la Chine. A long white aubergine of a delicious flavour. Seems to contain more " meat " than the other varieties.

Noire de Pekin. Bears dark violet fruit similar in shape and texture to its white cousin above.

Garlic

A favourite vegetable with the Italians, but not much grown in this country. It is, however, useful in flavourings.

Planting. It should be planted at the same time as shallots, in January or February. The " cloves " should be planted 2 in. beneath the surface of the soil. The cloves may be put in as close as 9 ins. apart each way.

Harvesting. As for shallots.

Good King Henry.

This is known to some people as mercury, and is one of the easiest vegetables to grow. So popular is it in various parts of Lincolnshire that it is known there as Lincolnshire asparagus.

Seed-Sowing. Seeds may be sown where the plants are to grow in April or May in rows 2 ft. apart, and the plants thinned out to 18 ins. apart. Sparse sowing is necessary. It is possible also to divide old plants and to choose the best roots and plant them out.

Seeds, too, may be sown in a seed-bed and the seedlings planted out.

General Cultivation. If this plant is grown on well-manured land, and is treated well, it will crop heavily from April to June. It produces shoots which should be cut in their young stages and tied up into bundles, when it resembles asparagus. If the stems are allowed to get old the skin toughens quickly and then it is necessary to remove this before they can be cooked. The shoots are cooked like asparagus.

Squashes and Pumpkins

Squashes and pumpkins may be grown in the same way as ridge cucumbers or marrows. The plants occupy a good deal of space, and so plenty of room should be allowed.

Propagation. The plants are raised under glass or in frames from seed sown in pots in April or May. Two seeds are usually sown to a 3 in. pot, and, if both grow, the weakest is removed.

It is possible also to sow the seeds where the plants are intended to remain, under continuous or Lantern cloches. Slugs are very partial to the plants, and should be kept at bay with bran and Paris green (see p. 238) or bran and metaldehyde.

Planting out. If any old fermenting material such as grass mowings can be placed in a mound in order to give the young plants a hot-bed, so much the better. This heating of the soil gets them growing quickly from the start.

Harvesting. Both gourds and pumpkins may be harvested directly they are of sufficient size. They are edible, in fact, at all their stages. They can be hung up for use in the winter, and the clever housewife can find a dozen or more different ways of cooking them.

The gourds that throw the smaller fruits are very useful to train up trellis and fences. They then take up little room, and can be got to crop heavily. Many of them are most decorative.

N.B. When pinching back the growing shoots, should this be necessary, these may be saved and cooked as spinach.

Varieties

(a) Squashes.

Hubbard Squash. Should not be eaten till September or October. Will keep till February. Perhaps the most useful winter variety.
Banana Squash. Has the consistency of a banana. Delicious flavour. Will keep on into the winter if necessary.
Acorn Squash. Small variety. Good flavour.
Golden Scallop Squash. Excellent flavour. Quite round. Good keeper.

(b) Pumpkins.

Kohlrabi

Probably the reason why kohlrabi is not more grown is that we prefer our turnips and swedes. On the Continent, kohlrabi is a popular vegetable. There are two types, the green and the purple, the green being the more tender of the two. It is

H

similar in flavour to the turnip, but has that " nutty " flavour that turnips have not.

Seed-Sowing. Seed may be sown at any time from the second week in March to the middle of August. The rows should be 2 ft. apart, and the seedlings thinned to 3 ins. apart in the rows in the early stages, and finally to 6 ins. apart. The young plants pulled at this final thinning should be in a fit condition to use as a vegetable.

General Cultivation. When hoeing, the earth should not be drawn up to the plants, but rather pulled away from them. In every other way they are treated as for turnips.

Harvesting. It may be left in the ground until required, and will usually withstand quite hard frosts. The great thing is not to grow too large roots as they then become coarse. In very cold climates it may be dug up and stored in the same way as other roots.

Sweet Corn

Sweet Corn is becoming more and more popular in this country, and makes a nourishing and welcome variation in diet.

Soil. Sweet Corn will grow well on almost any type of soil, providing it is neither too heavy nor too light. It loves plenty of organic matter in the ground.

Preparation of Soil. It probably grows best on land that has been well manured for the previous crop.

Of course, on light or hungry land it will be necessary to dig in some organic matter. In all cases work half a bucketful of damped horticultural peat into the top 3 inches of soil, with a good fish manure, meat and bone meal, or hoof and horn meal, at 3 to 4 ounces to the square yard.

Seed Sowing. Sweet corn is better not transplanted, sow the seed out of doors under cloches during the second week of April, or in the North at the end of April. If cloches are not available sow during May.

Draw the drills 1½ inches deep and space the seeds 9 inches apart in the case of Canada Cross, and 12 inches apart with the taller varieties. The rows should be 2 feet apart.

General Cultivation. Always give sweet corn full sunshine and, if possible, arrange the crop in a block and not in one or two rows, as this gives a better chance of pollination. There is no evidence that the removal of side shoots is an advantage. In dry weather water well and mulch with damp horticultural peat.

Harvesting. After fertilisation the grains pass through a watery, then a milky, and on to a doughy stage. The cobs are ready for eating at the milky stage, this usually 3½ weeks from the time of flowering. The " silks " will then be brown and withered. To tell the right stage, part of the sheath of the cob should be pulled back and one of the grains pressed with the thumb nail.

The contents should spurt out and have the consistency of clotted cream. Always use sweet corn as soon as possible after picking.

Cooking. Strip off the husks, put the cobs in boiling water with a pinch of salt, simmer gently for 10 minutes, pour off water and serve hot with a smear of butter or margarine, plus pepper and salt for taste.

Varieties

Canada Cross. The earliest and best, ready the third week of July.

Courtland Golden Standard. Taller, later, but quite sweet.

Golden Bantam. Very hardy, medium sized, bright yellow.

Onion, Potato

This is a great favourite in some of the southern parts of England, where it is called the underground onion. It is grown in a similar way to the shallot, and in the south-west is planted on the shortest day.

Planting. In most part of England it is sufficiently early to plant the bulbs out in March and to lift them in August. The rows should be 18 ins. apart and the bulbs set 9 ins. apart in the rows. The soil should be fairly firm before planting, and then the bulbs pressed down into the soil and firmed afterwards also.

The old bulb will form clusters of young bulbs around it,

and, to get large onions, artificial manure may be sprinkled along the rows (see p. 153).

General Cultivation. The plants should be earthed up when the growths are a good size and in this way, good clusters will be formed. There should be no lack of moisture until the bulbs are a good size, and so hoeing and mulching should be done if necessary. Moisture should be withheld when the bulbs begin to ripen.

Harvesting. The onions should be forked up in August and left on the surface of the soil to ripen off. When ripe they should be stored in a cool place.

Onion, Welsh

This is really a herbaceous perennial, and came originally from Siberia. It is very hardy, and on many allotments very popular. There are two types, the red and the white, but neither of them throw bulbs, and the onions they produce always look like spring onions.

Propagation. Seed may be sown in July or August in order to produce a supply in the spring. Young plants may be obtained by the division of the older plants, and each onion plant when put out will produce thirty or forty onion plants around it.

It is a very useful onion to have in the small garden, as it ensures that onion flavouring is available all the year round.

Onion, Tree

This is sometimes known as the Egyptian onion. Stems are thrown up from the bulbs on which clusters of small bulbs are produced. These are excellent for pickling. The author has seen over a dozen small onions on the tops of the stems when the plants are well grown.

Planting. The bulbs formed in the soil or those formed on the stem may be saved and planted out in shallow drills early in April. The rows should be 18 ins. apart and the bulbs 6 ins. apart.

General Cultivation. If well grown, the plants will need some support as the little onions begin to form. The soil should be kept firm around them for the first three weeks or so after planting, as the birds often pull them up by means of the loose skins.

Harvesting in the Autumn. The plant is forked up, and, when dried off, the onions at the base and on the stems are removed.

Oxalis

This is a tuberous-rooted plant, and the aim of the grower is to get as many tubers as possible to form at the base of the stem. The tubers may be the size of a large walnut, but longer and more pointed.

Planting. The soil should be prepared as for potatoes, and the tubers may be planted out in May in rows 3 ft. apart and the tubers 2 ft. apart.

General Cultivation. As the shoots begin to grow the plants may be earthed-up, and these earthings-up should continue as necessary until September, when the tubers should begin to form.

Harvesting. The crop should be dug up early in November and the tubers stored in sand or dry earth in a shed. Damp or frost will cause them to rot away.

Varieties

Crenata has a smooth skin and eyes in profusion. Is rather acid in taste.

Deppi. A variety much liked with lamb or veal. The roots are more tapering, whiter or clearer than Crenata, and it is less acid. It should be grown in a southern aspect. It prefers light soil.

Parsley, Hamburg

Hamburg parsley grows very much like a parsnip, while the leaves resemble parsley.

Seed-Sowing. The land should be prepared as for carrots, and the seed should be sown in March in drills 18 ins. apart, and the plants finally thinned to half that distance in the rows.

General Cultivation. It should be hoed regularly to keep free from weeds, and whizzed naphthalene used along the rows to keep down the carrot fly.

Harvesting. The roots should be in season from November

to the following April, though they may be harvested as early as September if they are required.

It is better to lift in November and to store as for beetroot.

Peas, Asparagus

These are rather fascinating to grow, as they look more like a vetch than the ordinary pea. They do not climb, but grow about 18 ins. high in a bushy form. They have beautiful dark-red blossoms which make them most attractive.

The pods should be picked while they are young and fresh, and this usually means when, say, 1 in. long. The pod is cooked as picked, and the flavour is unique, being something like a cross between asparagus and pea flavour.

Seed-Sowing. The seeds are sown where the plants are to grow at the same time as ordinary main crop peas. They grow quite well in the south border. The rows should be 18 ins. to 2 ft. apart. The seed is small, and so the little drills need be no deeper than ½ an inch.

General Cultivation. Hoe regularly between the rows, and if necessary put a few twiggy sticks in just to keep the branches up.

Manuring. See peas.

Harvesting. Pick regularly, so as to prevent seeds from forming inside the pods.

Peas, Sugar

These, usually called mange-tout in France, are quite different from the ordinary peas. The pods have no tough interior skin, and thus when preparing them for the table all that need be done is to top and tail and then boil. The whole of the pod is quite edible.

Seed-Sowing. The seed may be sown in May in rows 4 ft. apart. The mange-tout peas often grow to a height of 6 ft. and require staking.

Manuring. See peas.

Harvesting. The pods should be picked regularly, as it is the fresh young pods that are so delicious. Further, if any of the pods are allowed to set, cropping ceases.

Rampion

Rampion is really a biennial whose roots are white and fleshy, and may be used either boiled or in salads. In the winter the leaves are useful for salads also.

Seed-Sowing. This crop should be grown on a light soil and in a shady situation. It is a plant that likes moisture, and under dry conditions it may run to seed.

The seed should not be sown until May, and even June and July sowings are quite possible. The drills should be 12 ins. apart and the seedlings thinned to 4 ins. apart.

General Cultivation. The rows should be hoed regularly, keeping the soil free from weeds and the surface loose.

Harvesting. There is no need to dig the roots up until they are required, as they usually over-winter quite well. In severe winters, where it is difficult to get at the plants because of frozen soil, the roots may be taken up and stored in sand or dry soil in a shed.

The roots are usually boiled until tender and served with melted butter.

Salsify

It is difficult to know whether to classify this vegetable as usual or unusual. It is perhaps better known than many of the others in this chapter. It has been described as the vegetable oyster and certainly is a most delicious root crop, having a "nutty" flavour.

Soil. Possibly the best soil is a rather light one but which is deep and moist. It is possible to grow good roots in a heavy soil providing it has been properly prepared. The soil should not have been recently enriched with fresh farmyard manure as this causes the roots to become fangy and to taste earthy.

Preparation of Soil. Bastard trenching or ridging should be carried out in the autumn, and well-rotted compost should be applied well below the top spit. A good fish manure should be used in addition at the rate of 3–4 ozs. to the sq. yard.

Seed-Sowing. The seed may be sown in April, the drills being 12 ins. apart and 1 in. deep. Directly the seedlings are large enough to be handled they may be thinned out first of all to 4 ins. apart and then finally to 8 ins. apart.

General Cultivation. Regular hoeing in between the rows is necessary not only to keep down weeds but to keep the surface soil in a loose crumbly condition. The same care should be taken when hoeing as advised in the case of beetroot (see p. 99).

Harvesting. It should be possible to use the roots first of all during the second or third week of October. Like parsnips they come to no harm when left in the ground until required. Like beetroot they bleed if they are damaged when being lifted. If necessary dig the crop up early and store the roots in sand either outside or in a shed.

Skirret

A rare vegetable, but one which is popular both in Japan and China. The roots, which are eaten, have a peculiar flavour which may take some time to get used to.

Propagation. Propagation may be carried out in the same way as for seakale—by means of thongs.

Seed may also be sown early in April, and to help germination the seed-bed should be kept moist. The drills should be $\frac{1}{2}$ in. deep and 18 ins. apart, and when the seedlings are well grown they may be thinned out to 9 ins. in the drills.

General Cultivation. This is one of the plants that likes deep soil and ample moisture and feeding. Really good-sized roots can only be produced in this way.

Harvesting. The roots should be lifted carefully, as they are much divided, and, once on the surface of the ground or on the path, should be spread out. This lifting should take place in late September or early October, and the roots may be stored as for salsify (see above).

Scorzonera

May be grown in exactly the same manner as salsify. It is quite different in appearance, the root being black and leaves being wider. Actually the two plants belong to different families. The roots are often left in the ground a second year and then they are much larger.

Soya Beans

These have been proved as easy to cultivate in this country

as they are in the United States. They may be sown in drills ½ an inch deep with the seeds spaced out 4 inches apart. The plants grow 2 ft. in height.

A large number of small beans are produced, which may be cooked green or which may be left on the plants to ripen, when, after threshing, the beans may be used as are haricot beans. They are rich in protein. They have a flavour of their own.

RHUBARB

Rhubarb is used as a fruit from a culinary point of view, but it is usually grown in every vegetable garden and so is included in this book.

Being a permanent crop the soil should be prepared as for Seakale (see p. 179). Plants may be raised from seed sown in March in drills 1 in. deep and 1 ft. apart, the seedlings being thinned to 10 ins. Plant out into their permanent position when they are a year old, in rows 3 ft. apart and 2 ft. 6 ins. between the plants. The easier method of propagation is by division, this being done in February or March, the old crowns are divided into roots each bearing a single crown or eye, and these are planted in the same way as given above.

Do not pull any sticks the first year, and only a moderate amount the second year. Keep the beds free from weeds and well watered, and mulched with compost. Feed with Liquinure during the summer and give a dressing of fish manure at the rate of 4-5 ozs. per sq. yd. after the last pulling at the end of July.

Roots may be taken up and brought into a warm dark place for forcing from December onwards. Place in a deep box and cover roots with light soil, keep moist. Plants outside may be hastened on by covering with straw or leaves and a box or cloche placed over them.

Varieties

Hawkes Champagne. Said by some to be the outstandingly good variety.
Dawes Champion. Very good for outdoors.
Early Albert. Good for forcing.
Victoria. Comes true from seed.
H*

CHAPTER XII

VEGETABLE PESTS AND THEIR CONTROL

We must, if we are going to grow vegetables keep down pests.
I therefore tell you what I consider the best ways of :—

1. Poisoning the leather-jackets.
2. Keeping away the cabbage root fly.
3. Killing the celery fly.
4. Preventing the red spider from doing too much damage.
5. Keeping the maggots from attacking the mushrooms.
6. "Boiling" the pea and bean beetles.

TO-DAY one of the most difficult things to do in a garden is to keep vegetables free from pests. The onion and carrot flies are common enough, goodness knows, while the cabbage root maggot every year takes as its toll some thousands of cabbage, cauliflower, and Brussels sprouts plants. It would be impossible in a book of this character to list every single pest that might attack a crop, and so the author has chosen those pests that in his experience are most common in the gardens of this country.

As a county adviser he has had ample opportunity of carrying out trials, and in his travels over the country as garden editor to the B.B.C. he has been able to study pest control in many districts.

The pests are classified under the vegetables they attack, as it is thought that this is probably the simplest way for the amateur to recognise the trouble. In the Appendix on "Miscellaneous Information" at the end of the book, will be found a list of the principal insecticides, with instructions on how these may be made up.

Pests That Attack Many Vegetables

There are a certain number of pests that attack various kinds of vegetables, and it is better, therefore, to list these

first of all before dealing with each crop separately. These
are placed in alphabetical order.

Aphides

Sometimes known as green fly, blue bug, black fly, etc.
A very large family of plant lice which will attack all members
of the cabbage family as well as beans, peas, carrots, etc.

They are sucking insects, and usually attack the under
surface of the leaf first of all. These insects cause the leaves
to curl in many cases, and for this reason they are often
difficult to get at with a spray or dust.

Because they multiply at an extraordinary rate, they should
be controlled in the early stages.

Control. Derris is usually satisfactory if applied either
as a dust or as a spray. In the case of badly curled leaves, a
nicotine spray may be necessary, so that the fumes may
penetrate to the insects. Derris is safe to use at any time, as
it is not poisonous to man.

Beetle, Chafer

It is the grubs of the chafer beetles that damage the plants.
The cockchafer grub has three pairs of legs and is about 1½ in.
long. It is fat, white and objectionable-looking. The summer
chafer is similar to the cockchafer, but is less than 1 in. in
length. The larvæ of these two beetles live in the soil and eat
the roots of plants.

Control. Naphthalene should be dug in at the rate of 1 oz.
to the sq. yd. where chafer beetle larvæ damage is experienced.

Beetle, Chafer, Garden

This beetle is only ½ in. long, and damages the plants as a
beetle. Leaves will be found to be eaten away.

Control. The leaves of the plants should be sprayed with
arsenate of lead, and whizzed naphthalene applied to the
surface of the ground at 1 oz. to the sq. yd., to ac. as a repellent.

Beetles, Flea

Flea beetles are small, and generally black or dark grey.
They damage young plants when they are coming through,

particularly in the case of cabbages, turnips, and radishes, but they will attack the leaves of larger plants also. They can generally be recognised because they hop quickly and hide themselves. Large numbers of them on a plant may cause it to look quite black.

They spend the winter in dry vegetable rubbish such as is found in hedge-bottoms, and may commence attacking plants in May and continue right on into August.

Control. Where this pest is common the seeds of all the cabbage family should be well wetted with turpentine, using it at the rate of ⅛ pint to ½ lb. seed. The seed should then be dried overnight and sown the next day. Just before the plants are through, a good dusting may be given with Gammaxene dust, as it is in this stage that the beetles often do the greatest harm. Further dustings may be necessary at weekly intervals until the plants are quire free.

Caterpillars

Different kinds of caterpillars may be found on vegetables, the most common being those on the cabbage family.

Control. It is easy to control these caterpillars by spraying with strong liquid Derris.

Caterpillars, Surface

Surface caterpillars wander about just above and below the surface of the ground and damage plants by biting through their stems. Some caterpillars are 1½ ins. long and some only ½ in. long, and they are usually grey or brown in colour. They feed at night, and during the day they hide under clods of earth or stones.

Control. Hoe the land regularly, especially during the months of July and August, so as to prevent egg-laying from taking place. This regular hoeing will destroy the young larvæ also.

The bran and Paris green bait may also be used.

Leather-Jackets

This is the young of the daddy-longlegs, and in the north

is called the bot. It is generally about 1½ ins. long, greyish-brown in colour, and has no legs. The skin of the grub is very tough.

Leather-jackets live one or two inches below the surface of the soil, and in this way they are able to feed on the stems and roots of plants below ground. In the night they may come to the surface and eat the leaves also. They sometimes pull these down into the ground.

Control. Bran and Paris green should be applied (see p. 282) all over the surface of the ground in the evening, giving a further application the following day if necessary. Leather-jackets are particularly fond of bran, and the author has never found this method of control to fail.

Millipedes

Millipedes may do a great deal of harm to the roots and stems of plants underground. They have round bodies which, when young, are ½ in. long, and as they grow older 1 in. long. The front four segments of their bodies have one pair of legs each, while the remaining segments have two pairs of legs.

They should never be confused with centipedes, which are carnivorous and do a great deal of good in destroying other pests. Centipedes have flattened bodies, and each segment of the body has only one pair of legs.

Control. Naphthalene should be dug into the soil at the rate of 1 oz. to the sq. yard. This may act as a deterrent.

Large numbers may be trapped if a large carrot is cut into two pieces longitudinally and buried an inch or two into the ground. If these pieces are spitted on a stick they may easily be removed, and the millipedes that have collected may be extracted and destroyed.

Slugs

Slugs may do a great deal of damage in the vegetable garden, not only to members of the cabbage family but to potatoes, celery and so on. They feed above the ground during the night, and below ground at any time. They do not like frost or dry soil, and so burrow down deeply into the ground when these conditions occur.

They often lay eggs in batches of from four to fifty (depending on the type of slug), in damp soil or under stones. The eggs can be recognised because they are white, translucent and glistening. They usually turn yellow and opaque as the embryo starts to grow. Hatching will generally take place in a month.

Control

(1) Make up a mixture consisting of 10 lb. of bran with ½ gallon of water, and add ½ lb. of Paris Green. This is sufficient for a ½-acre garden. The mixture should be applied evenly, and several dressings may be necessary, especially if rain follows each application. Do not apply this poison bait during frosty or dry weather, as the slugs are not near the surface of the ground.

(2) When digging land in the autumn or winter, a mixture consisting of equal parts of finely powdered copper sulphate and hydrated lime may be dug in at the rate of 1 oz. to the sq. yard. This mixture kills any creature it comes in contact with, but chemists fear that the continued use of copper sulphate may injure the soil.

A little sprinkling of this mixture should be made completely round the garden on the surface of the soil to prevent slugs migrating from other parts.

(3) Mix a saltspoonful of powdered meta fuel with a handful of bran (or dead lawn mowings or tea leaves). Little heaps the size of an egg cup may be put along the rows of plants every 3 feet or so. This is the best bait known.

Wireworm

Unfortunately this insect, which is really the grub of the click beetle, may live in the soil for 6–7 years before turning into a beetle. Wireworms, like millipedes, damage plants below ground.

Control. Use Paradichlorbenzine—break this up into portions the size of a French bean and bury these in holes 6 inches deep and 2 feet apart all over the affected ground. It is quite easy to make the holes with a walking stick or iron bar—the holes must be closed up when the piece of chemical is in position. Do this preferably in the Winter when no crops are on the ground—it can cause potatoes to have a bad flavour when used in the Spring and Summer.

ASPARAGUS

Asparagus Beetle

This beetle is very easy to recognise, as it has a black and red body, with black and yellow wing-cases. The small larvæ will be found on the leaves of the asparagus during the summer, eating the foliage.

In the winter the beetles hide amongst rubbish.

Control. The foliage should be cut down directly it starts to turn yellow in the autumn, and burnt. The beds should be sprayed with nicotine and soft soap during the summer if the beetles are seen.

BEETROOT

Mangold Fly

If a fly looking very much like an ordinary house-fly is seen on the beetroot, the mangold fly may be suspected. It will lay its eggs on the under side of the beetroot leaves. The larvæ will tunnel into the leaves and cause blisters, very much like those on the celery. There are often three generations a year.

Control. When the attack is first seen the plant should be sprayed with nicotine, and again a week later.

Other pests that may attack beetroot are black aphis (see broad beans) ; flea beetles (see cabbage).

CABBAGE

Aphis, Mealy Cabbage

This is a mealy mauve-coloured aphis which attacks the under-surface of the leaves of the plants. It is a great nuisance in the case of Brussels sprouts, as it gets into the sprouts themselves.

Control. Spray or dust with nicotine.

They often live on the old Brussels sprouts throughout the winter, and so directly the crop has been cleared the old stumps should be taken up.

PESTS

Carrot attacked by Carrot fly (note grub)

The nibbling around the edge of the leaf by Pea and Bean Weevils

Millipede

Onion Maggot

Cut Worm

Wireworm

PEST CONTROL

VAPOURISER for PYRETHRUM

POWDER BLOWER for DERRIS

META FUEL Slug Bait

Beetles, Flea

For description of flea beetles and their control see " Pests that Attack many Vegetables " (p. 236).

Cabbage Root Fly

The maggots will be found on the stem of the plant just below ground level, and on the roots. The fly lays its eggs just below soil level, and the larvæ burrow down and attack the plants. Often ten or twelve maggots may be found on the roots.

These should not be confused with the turnip gall weevil, which makes a blister and is seen in the autumn.

Control. Mercuric chloride should be dissolved in water at the rate of ¼ oz. to a 2-gallon container. A ¼ pint should be put into each hole at planting-out time. In the case of a very severe attack it may be necessary to give two more waterings with this solution at ten-day intervals.

Dusting around the plants with calomel dust after planting does keep the fly away.

Cabbage White Fly

Minute white waxy flies may be found on the underneath of leaves. They suck the sap, and make the plants unpalatable because of the mess they leave behind.

Control. As for aphis.

Caterpillars

These are the larvæ of the white butterfly which may be found flitting about the cabbage-bed. The eggs are laid in large numbers, and the caterpillars soon eat the leaves.

Control. Spray with Liquid Derris or with liquid D.D.T. In small gardens hand picking is possible.

CARROTS

Aphides

(a) green.

The green aphis may attack the leaves of carrots in the early summer. When suffering from an attack, the foliage will turn yellow.

Control. Spray with nicotine and soft soap.
(b) root.
Control. Water with nicotine (usual formula).

Carrot Fly

A small, shiny, bottle-green fly. It lays its eggs near the surface of the ground along carrot rows. The larvæ then burrow down to the base of the root and tunnel into it. Large numbers of maggots may be found in attacked roots. The trouble is often first noticed when the tops wilt.

Control. Apply whizzed naphthalene at the rate of 1 oz. per yard run just before thinning, and again ten days later.

After thinning, compress the soil to prevent egg-laying and the movement of larvæ. Remove the thinned carrots and burn them. Do not leave them lying about to attract other flies.

CAULIFLOWER. See CABBAGE

CELERY

Celery Fly

Most gardeners have experienced the attacks of the celery fly. The female lays her eggs on the under sides of the leaves, and the maggots that hatch out then make their way in between the upper and lower epidermis of the leaves. In this way whitish-looking blisters are formed. In the early stages these may be picked off.

The attack generally takes place in the seedling stage first of all, but is more evident after the plants are put out into the trenches.

Control. See that the young plants are free from the pest by spraying regularly with nicotine and soft soap. When in the trenches, a regular soaking with the same spray is necessary early in June to control the second generation. A third generation may appear in September, and so a sharp look-out should be kept.

Experiments have shown that a repellent has proved useful. 1 part by weight of creosote to 99 parts by weight of precipitated chalk. This dust is then scattered among the plants thinly, and the creosote smell keeps the flies away. This method of control should be used as a repellent to prevent the females from laying eggs.

CUCUMBER

Red Spider

A small yellow mite may be found on the under-surface of the leaves spinning minute webs. As a result the leaves may turn yellow. It is difficult to see the mite without a magnifying-glass.

Control. See that the under surface of cucumber leaves is syringed regularly with clean water. Red spiders are always at their worst in dry conditions.

The use of a summer petroleum oil may be resorted to in bad cases.

LETTUCE

Aphides

When lettuces are young they are often attacked by a small green aphis. The under sides of the leaves should be examined if the leaves are distorted or stunted, and aphides will generally be found the cause of the trouble.

Control. Spray or dust with nicotine on a warm day. See that the soil all round the lettuces is sprayed also, as then the nicotine fumes may rise and kill the insect.

MUSHROOMS

Mites

There are a large number of mites that may be found in the mushroom-house. The injurious species are usually slow-moving creatures, while the more active ones are normally harmless. Attacks may be noticed as soon as the mushrooms appear, holes being found in the stalks and the caps. These holes, when examined with a magnifying-glass, will be found to contain numerous eggs and mites. The mites may injure the spawn as well, and so cropping may cease.

Control. At the present time no really efficient method of controlling these mites has been found. Fresh manure is probably less likely to contain injurious mites than that which has been stored for a long period.

It is said that D.D.T. has given good results.

Flies

Many species of flies will damage mushrooms, the two most important being the Sciara and the Phorid. These are similar in size; the larvæ tunnel into the mushrooms as they appear, ruining not only the stems but the caps as well. They make the mushroom quite unsaleable, and in the case of bad attacks can easily destroy whole crops.

Control. Relatively low temperatures in the house may prevent egg-laying and retard the development of the flies. The temperature should be kept just below 60 degrees F.

The strictest cleanliness should be observed, as advised in the case of diseases.

Spraying should be carried out as a routine measure with nicotine; 1 fluid oz. of nicotine should be added to 10 gals. of water, but no soap should be added. A good method is to give a spraying after each heavy pick, but excessive wash should not be used or beds may become too wet. An alternative method is to employ one of the pyrethrum fluids now sold for the purpose. These are applied in small quantities through an atomiser, and are much more satisfactory than nicotine because they are non-poisonous to man. Slight staining may occur if the liquid is applied directly to the mushrooms, and it is best blown into the air as a cloud and allowed to settle.

ONIONS

Onion Fly

This is one of the worst pests a garden has to face, and yet it is now one of the easiest to control.

The female of the onion fly, which is rather like a small house-fly, lays her eggs either on the neck of the onion or at the soil level. The larvæ which hatches out burrows to the bottom of the bulb and feeds. The first attack usually takes place some time in May.

Control. Apply whizzed naphthalene along the rows at the rate of 1 oz. to the yard run just before thinning, and again ten days later.

The whizzed naphthalene acts as a repellent and conceals the scent of the oil of onions.

When hoeing among onions, great care should be taken to see that the plants are never damaged, as then the odour that attracts the insects is given off. As in the case of carrots, the rows should be firmed after thinning.

PARSNIPS

Celery Fly

Will attack parsnip leaves as well as celery, though it is perhaps never such a pest on this crop.

Control. See celery.

Carrot Fly

This will often attack parsnips, but will seldom ruin the whole crop.

Control. See carrots.

PEAS

Pea and Bean Beetles

The beetles lay their eggs on the pods and the maggots burrow into the seeds and feed on them. During the time of sowing the little beetles may be found in the seeds.

Control. Plunge the seeds in boiling water for five seconds. To do this they can be put into a little muslin bag which can be hung from the end of a stick.

Pea Moth

The moths lay their eggs on the pods and the larvæ burrow in and destroy the peas. Several maggots may be found in a pod.

Control. Spray the plants with nicotine just as the flowers are setting, as in this way the larvæ may be killed as they are tunnelling in.

As the larvæ drop to the ground when full grown, the soil should be cultivated continually so that they may be destroyed.

PESTS

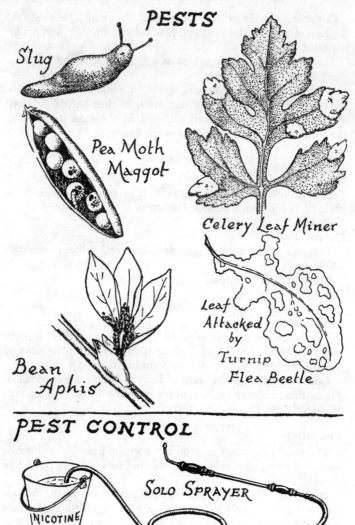

Slug

Pea Moth Maggot

Celery Leaf Miner

Bean Aphis

Leaf Attacked by Turnip Flea Beetle

PEST CONTROL

Solo Sprayer

NICOTINE

Pea and Bean Weevils

The weevil eats peculiar semi-circular holes out of the sides of the leaves and often does a great deal of harm when the plants are young.

Control. Dust with derris either early in the morning or late in the day. Hoe regularly between the rows to promote a fine tilth and to destroy the clods, their hiding places.

Pea Aphis

This may attack the peas when they are young, while a second attack is sometimes experienced a few weeks later.

Control. Spray or dust with nicotine.

Pea and Bean Thrips

One of the most serious pests of peas in some districts. Thrips are black and minute, and are difficult to detect unless the plants are shaken and the thrips made to fall on to a white handkerchief.

They attack seedlings, suck the sap from growing points, and so distort plants and prevent them from growing healthily.

They are generally worse in a dry season, and when they attack the stems, leaves, and pods much damage can be done. Thrip-attacked pods look silver in the early stages, but later turn brown.

Control. See that the soil is limed at the rate of 4 ozs. to the sq. yd. when the seed is sown. When the majority of the flowers have set, see that the rows are sprayed with nicotine and soft soap.

RADISH

Cabbage White Fly
Control. See cabbage.

Flea Beetles
Control. See cabbage.

SPINACH

Mangold Fly

This is perhaps a more serious pest on spinach than it is on beetroot. The blistering of the leaves causes them to be unpalatable.

Control. See beetroot.

CHAPTER XIII.

VEGETABLE DISEASES AND THEIR CONTROL

*Diseases are different from pests, but they are just as insidious.
It is most important to :—*

1. Prevent Club Root—and this is easy to do.
2. Recognise the difference between celery maggot and celery leaf spot.
3. Apply grass mowings to the rows of potatoes.
4. Dig up and burn diseased rhubarb plants.
5. Know the correct formulæ for various spraying mixtures.

WHOLE books have been written on the control of vegetable diseases, and in one American work alone there are over six hundred pages. It will only be possible, therefore, as in the case of insect pests, to deal with the more important diseases, and to suggest methods of control briefly.

As has been suggested in the chapters on cultivation, much can be done to prevent attacks of disease if the plants are grown sturdily and given the right attention. The keeping down of weeds, which act as alternative hosts, is most important. The regular hoeing which creates a dust mulch, and so helps to conserve moisture, should be borne in mind. The land should be properly drained. The plants should be given sufficient room to grow properly. Lime should be applied regularly to prevent the soil from becoming acid.

The chapter on manures gives details of the correct methods of manuring plants, and many of the diseases are worst on plants that are grown " soft." In such cases an application of an artificial manure like sulphate of potash will do much to harden and tone up the plant.

The sowing of seed and planting out should always be done at the right time. Late sowings may be attacked by pests and early sowings may be damaged by weather conditions.

248

Protection should be given when protection is needed, and, in the frame, ventilation should be given whenever possible.

It is important also to see that the vegetable refuse is rotted down properly, and any material like cabbage-stumps and the like which do not rot readily should be destroyed by fire. Directly the leaves of plants turn yellow, and are useless, it is a good plan to remove them, as they may be a potential home of a fungus disease.

It should be remembered that a fungus causing plant disease is a plant growing on another plant.

ASPARAGUS

Asparagus Rust

If the foliage is examined during the summer it may be covered with rusty spots. These spots get darker in colour in the autumn.

Control. When the foliage is cut down in the autumn it should be burnt, so as to prevent re-infection. It is possible to grow resistant varieties, and two good ones are Mary and Martha Washington.

CABBAGE

Club Root

This disease is one of the commonest in the country to-day. The author has had reports of it from almost every county in England. It is known in some districts as finger-and-toe and in other districts as Anbury. The cabbage may wilt on hot sunny days and recover in the evening. When the root system is examined, the large swellings characteristic of this disease will be found to have turned into a club-like mass. Infected plants are much reduced in vitality, and in bad cases plants may be killed entirely.

The spores of this disease can remain in the soil for many years.

Control. In the first place, the soil should be well limed, as the club root disease is always worse on acid soils. Hydrated lime should be applied to the surface of the soil at 7 or 8 ozs. to the sq. yd. during the month of January.

Generally, the infection takes place in the seed-bed, though when the plants are put out they seldom appear obviously clubbed. For this reason few growers realise that they are already diseased.

The seed-beds, therefore, may be watered before sowing the seeds with a solution of mercuric chloride at the dilution of 1 oz. in 12 gals. of water. Ten to fourteen days after, the seedlings should be watered again with a similar solution, and another similar watering should be given seven days after this.

A quarter of an ounce of a similar solution should be poured into the hole when the plants are put out. In bad conditions, the treatment should be repeated again in twelve days' time.

For those who do not care for this *very poisonous* chemical, Brassisan may be used on the seed-bed at the rate of 1 oz. per sq. yd., sprinkling the dust over the soil evenly. Brassisan may also be applied to the dibble holes before putting out the plant. For this purpose, 1 part by bulk of this substance should be mixed with 5 parts of sand. A dessertspoonful of the dry mixture may then be applied to each hole. It is not advisable to apply Brassisan in its concentrated form, as it may damage the roots.

CELERY

Leaf Spot (or " blight ")

Celery leaves turn brown in patches, and little black spots may appear on these. The leaf stalks may also be attacked. If the disease is not controlled, the whole leaf may wither away and the plants can thus be ruined.

The disease is generally seen first of all in July, but in the south earlier attacks have been known.

Control. The plants should be sprayed three times from the end of June, say once a fortnight, with Bordeaux mixture, so as to cover the upper and lower surface of the leaves. In very wet years, four or five further applications may be advisable.

The seedsman should be asked, if he can, to give a guarantee that the seeds supplied have been treated with the correct

solution of formaldehyde to destroy the fungus lurking on
he seed-coat.

MINT

Mint Rust

Little orange cushions may be seen on the leaves and stems
of the plants.   In the case of a bad attack, the shoots become
thickened in a peculiar manner, the leaves are much smaller,
and may be distorted.

Control. Early in October, the mint tops should be burnt
off where they are growing by laying down dry straw on the
mint bed and burning it, so causing a rapid fire. A fire of this
kind should not injure the roots and yet burns up the stems
and kills the disease spores.

Another method that has proved satisfactory in many
districts is to cut down the tops in October and remove them,
and then to water the beds with a 5 per cent solution of a
neutral high-boiling tar oil wash.

MUSHROOMS

Mycogone Disease or Bubbles (Mycogone perniciosa)

The bubbles disease may be seen when the bed comes into
bearing, and may continue to give trouble right throughout
the life of the bed. Whole clumps of baby mushrooms grow
into a shapeless mass and are covered with a white fungus
growth. Single mushrooms may be attacked with a dense
white mould-like growth on the gills, but if they happen to have
become infected at an early stage the stalk remains short and
swollen and the cap hardly develops at all. Mushrooms
deformed by this disease assume all kinds of shapes. They
quickly decay and smell horribly.

Control. See below.

White Plaster Mould (Monolia fimicola).

The white plaster mould often invades mushroom beds, as
does the brown plaster mould as well. The fungus penetrates
the casing soil, and patches of white mould, or brown as the
case may be, appear on the surface.

Control. These diseases are difficult to eradicate because they probably are introduced with the materials of which the beds are made. No methods are known for the control of plaster moulds when they once appear in the compost, but the house, when cleared out, should be thoroughly cleaned.

With the bubbles disease, the strictest cleanliness must be observed when an attack has started. The correct ventilation and the correct temperature control must be maintained.

All diseased mushrooms should be removed directly they are seen, together with mycelium below them, and should be *burnt*. The temperature in the house should be brought down to 50 degrees F. and the parts where the disease appeared may be watered with a 1.5 per cent solution of lysol, or a 2 per cent solution of formalin.

Infected beds, when removed, should not be used for manuring ground which later on may be required for casing soil. In cases of severe attacks, the whole house when empty should be sprayed with a 2 per cent formalin solution. After spraying, the house should be closed down for twenty-four hours, and then given full ventilation.

ONION

Downy Mildew

A greyish-white mildew may be seen on the leaves, and soon afterwards these turn yellow and collapse completely.

Control. In many gardens the dusting of the rows with sulphur dust at the rate of 3 or 4 ozs. to the yard run has given good results. The rows can also be sprayed with Bordeaux mixture (see p. 281).

The autumn and spring sown crops should be kept well apart, as this prevents the infection passing from one to the other.

Those who plant onion sets should only use those that are firm and sound.

PARSNIPS

Canker

The roots of parsnips when examined may appear cracked.

Brown rot then appears, and, soon after, a wet rot destroys the root completely.

Control. Though included in this chapter as a disease, most mycologists do not believe that this trouble is due to any specific parasite.

Two varieties, Large Guernsey and Tender and True, may be said to be fairly resistant.

PEAS

Mildew

The leaves, the stems, and the pods are found to be covered with a white powdery substance. This trouble usually appears on the later sown varieties and towards the end of the summer.

Control. The plants should be dusted well early in the morning, while the dew is still on them, with a good sulphur dust. The dusting must be done in the earliest stages and not after the mildew has obtained a hold.

POTATO

Potato Blight

The leaves of the potatoes are attacked by the disease, and dark green spots or blotches of irregular sizes and shapes appear. These quickly turn brown or almost black, and under warm, damp conditions they may be surrounded by a delicate white mould. The disease may spread at an alarming rate, and the whole of the over-ground parts of the plant may be killed.

The spores may fall on the ground and may thus infect the new tubers. Dark sunken areas appear on the skin, and the potatoes become rotten and useless.

Control. The disease may be controlled by Bordeaux or Burgundy mixture, and, as Burgundy mixture is easier to prepare and is just as effective as Bordeaux, its making up is described here.

Two and half pounds crushed washing soda are added to a $2\frac{1}{2}$-gallon bucket of clean cold water, and stirred until it is fully

POTATO BLIGHT

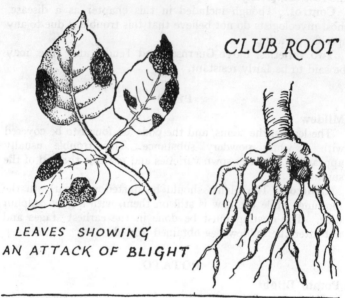

CLUB ROOT

LEAVES SHOWING
AN ATTACK OF BLIGHT

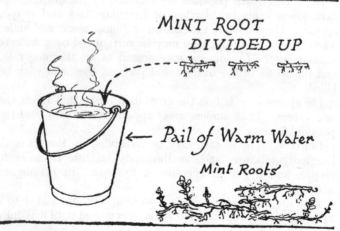

MINT ROOT
DIVIDED UP

← Pail of Warm Water

Mint Roots

RUB PEAS IN MERCURIAL COMPOUND TO PREVENT DAMPING OFF

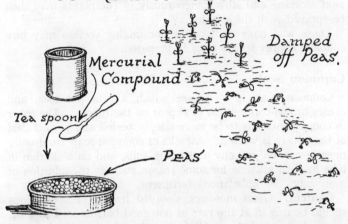

Mercurial Compound

Tea spoon

Peas

Damped off Peas.

WATER SEED BED WITH MERCURIC CHLORIDE TO PREVENT CLUB ROOT

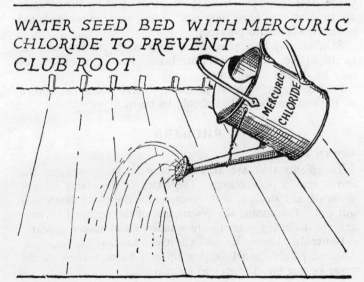

MERCURIC CHLORIDE

dissolved ; 2 lb. powdered copper sulphate are then placed in a wooden tub containing 17 gals. of water, stirred, and left overnight.   The washing soda solution is poured into this tub the next morning and stirred vigourously.   The plants may then be sprayed with the solution.

Those who have no facilities for mixing washes may buy colloidal copper sprays already prepared.

Common Scab

Common scab is a disease which affects potatoes, and causes brown corky scabs to appear on the tubers.   The tuber in consequence has to be more deeply peeled and a good deal of the potato is wasted.   Attacks of common scab are usually more severe on gravelly and sandy soils, and on soils rich in lime or with alkaline for some reason such as the addition of soot, ashes, or unbalanced fertilisers.

Control.   Grass mowings, decayed leaves, or spent hops should be dug in at the rate of one good barrow-load to 4 sq. yards. It is a good plan to fill the trenches up where the potatoes are to grow with grass mowings.   Lime, soot, or ashes should never be applied to potatoes.

Sulphur may be applied along the rows at the rate of 1 oz. to the sq. yd. as the tubers are being planted, or each tuber may be dipped in sulphur.

Peelings from scabbed potatoes should never be thrown on the compost heap, but should be burnt.

RHUBARB

Crown Rot

The plants that are attacked may be recognised, as the leaves turn a puce colour.   The bases of the stems become distorted and swollen, and the crown of the plant develops a soft rot.   This means the destruction of the terminal growth, and the following season only spindly, short spikes appear.

Control.   There is no effective method of control. Affected plants should be dug up and burnt.   They should never be dug into the ground for manure.

SEAKALE

Black Rot

The roots, when examined, will be found to have turned black and to be rotten. This often occurs in wet land.

Control. When planting out the thongs, none which show on them a black streak in the cut tissue should be used. This black streak is the beginning of the disease. Seakale should not be planted in badly drained land.

SPINACH

Mildew

The leaves of spinach are sometimes covered with yellow spots, the under sides of which will be found to be covered with a violet or grey mould.

Control. The plants should be dusted from time to time with a good sulphur dust ; this must be done in the earliest stages.

Spinach should be grown on well-drained land.

TOMATOES

Leaf Mould or Mildew

On the leaves a greyish mould appears, which turns brown later. It will be found in the first place on the under sides of the leaves. As the leaves die the disease seems to take on a purple hue. This is a very common disease, not only in this country, but on the Continent.

Control. The plants should be grown as " hard " as possible by manuring the soil with sufficient sulphate of potash. The plants should be sprayed directly the disease is first seen with the colloidal copper spray. This should be applied so that it covers both the upper and lower surfaces of the leaves, and a spreader incorporated in the wash to improve the fungus-killing properties.

Stripe

The stem of the plants when attacked by this disease will be found to be marked with elongated streaks. The fruit

I

may have brown blotches upon it, and the leaves later on may become mottled and finally will shrivel.

Control. Stripe is a disease of soft fruits, and, in such cases, sulphate of potash should be applied to the ground at the rate of 2 ozs. to the sq. yard. Another dressing may be given fourteen days later. When removing the side-growths and some of the leaves, the knife that is used should be sterilised by dipping it in a solution of formaldehyde before going from plant to plant, otherwise the disease may be transmitted on the blade.

Potato Blight

Will attack tomatoes very badly—in fact will devastate them in a week or so if not prevented or controlled.

Control. Spray with Bordeaux mixture as for potatoes or dust with a copper-lime dust.

CHAPTER XIV

REMINDERS OF WHAT TO DO MONTH BY MONTH FOR VEGETABLES

We are all of us apt to be forgetful and so these reminders month by month the author hopes will prove useful.
Look them up at the beginning of every month, and make the necessary notes.

JANUARY

It must not be thought that there is nothing to do in the kitchen garden during January. Much depends on the weather, of course, and the following suggestions are based on the experience of some sixteen or seventeen varying winters.

General. If the land is frozen, it is a good opportunity to obtain manure and wheel it into position in little heaps. In this way it will be ready where it is required.

Should the autumn digging not have been completed and the weather be open, various, forms of trenching may be carried out on light soils. It is generally unwise to attempt to cultivate heavy soils.

January is a good month to clean out the hedge bottoms, clear out all the odd corners, and *burn* all the rubbish. The ashes thus made should be collected and stored in a dry place.

Ordinary Seed. The catalogues usually arrive this month, and may be perused in the light of the preceding chapters. Some time should be spent in getting out the seed order and sending this away to the seedsmen at the earliest opportunity. An early order makes for early dispatch. A gardener should determine to test one or two novelties each year.

Artichokes, Globe. See that these are protected during the frosty periods with straw.

Broccoli. Heel the plants over if necessary to the north

I*   259

in order to save the curds. In a small garden, straw may be placed among them as well.

Carrots. A sowing may be made in a frame over a hot-bed (see pp. 58–66).

Cauliflower. Look at those that are over-wintering in the cold frames and remove any decaying leaves. Give air on all bright days.

Celery. Prevent the hearts from rotting by covering the tops with straw during hard frosts.

Egg-Plants. Seeds may be sown in heat under glass towards the end of the month.

Leeks. Those who are going in for exhibitions may raise plants by sowings at this time of the year in pots or boxes under glass.

Lettuce should be planted out in the frames over the hot-beds (see p. 58).

Onions. The large exhibition onions are generally raised by sowing seed in boxes or pots this month in heat under glass.

Onions, Potato. Potato onions may be planted towards the end of the month.

FEBRUARY

This is the first month when seeds may be sown outside, at any rate in the south. Should the weather be inclement, various jobs outlined in January may be continued.

General. Make this the month when the paths, edges, and walks will be renovated. It should be possible to put down more gravel, or to renew the paving. Rotting wooden edging may be replaced by concrete and so on. Any labels saved from last year can now be cleaned and repainted ready for use. This is a good job for a wet day.

Look out for annual weeds, particularly groundsel, as this is the beginning of the seeding season.

Forcing. Plants like asparagus, rhubarb, and seakale may be forced now if they are taken into a heated frame or greenhouse.

Artichoke, Jerusalem. These may be planted this

JANUARY

Wheel out Manure

Order Seeds

FEBRUARY

Plant Jerusalem Artichokes

Sprout Potatoes

Force Rhubarb

MARCH

Plant Onions with Dibber

Sow Peas and Lettuce

Sow Marrow under Cloche

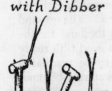

month directly the soil is in the right condition (see p. 82).

Beans, Broad. If the November sowings failed, sow a few more beans in boxes and raise them in a cold frame ready to plant out in April.

Brussels Sprouts. For an early supply, make a sowing of seed in a cold frame.

Celery. Sow seed towards the middle of the month in boxes under glass and raise the seedlings in moderate heat.

Egg-Plant. Sow the seed in a light, rich compost in a heated frame or under glass, temperature 55 degrees F.

Lettuce. Any lettuce raised in cold frames might now be planted out in sheltered beds and covered with cloches if necessary. Further sowings might be made in the frame for planting out later on

Mustard and Cress. Sowings may be made in the frame.

Parsnip. In the south, rows of parsnips may be sown where they are to grow.

Potatoes. Box up the seed potatoes directly they arrive, so as to sprout them.

Rhubarb. The old roots may be taken up, divided, and replanted in well-manured ground. In the south, seed can be sown outside.

Seakale Pots and boxes may be put over the crown out of doors, filled with straw or strawy litter.

Spinach. A small sowing might be made in a south border.

Turnips. A very early sowing may be tried in the south and south-west in a warm border.

MARCH

March is probably one of the most important months of the year from the gardener's point of view. The ground should now be in a workable condition, and the land for the earlier crops may be forked over to produce a good tilth ready for seed-sowing. The frames will be able to be ventilated more and more as the sun gains power, and watering becomes a greater necessity under glass.

Artichoke, Globe. It is possible to sow seed in the open this month or to plant suckers. Any material used for protecting the plants during the winter can be removed as the weather gets warmer, and the finest cinder ashes may be placed around the plants.

Artichoke, Jerusalem. Jerusalem artichokes should be planted now if it is impossible to put them in in February.

Asparagus. Go over the beds or rows, raking them down. Fork up the alleyways between the rows, working in any manure that is to be added. If very early cauliflowers are to be planted, these may be put in now in between the rows after forking.

Beans, Broad. The first sowing of beans outside may be made, and any beans raised in frames should be planted out at the end of the month.

Beans, French. Seed may now be sown in boxes in frames for planting out.

Brussels Sprouts. A sowing may now be made outside in a specially prepared seed-bed.

Cabbage. Seeds may be sown in the case of the summer cutting varieties. Look over the spring cabbage, too, apply potassic nitrate of soda, and remove dead leaves. Hoe the surface soil.

Carrots. Make a sowing of the stump-rooted varieties in a warm border towards the end of the month. A sowing of a main crop may be made towards the end of the month.

Cauliflowers. Raise plants by making sowings in boxes in a frame. Choose varieties like Autumn Giant and Autumn Mammoth. Look over the autumn-sown plants and give the frames as much air as possible, so that they may be ready to plant out at the end of the month or early in April.

Celery. A sowing may be made in a frame by those who have no glasshouse. Seedlings already raised should be pricked out into further boxes under glass.

Celeriac. Sow seeds as for celery.

Chives. Split up the clumps and plant them into a new position. They make a good edging.

Couve Tronchuda. Sow the seeds later on in the month, where they are to grow, in deeply worked soil.

Herbs. Varieties that can be divided should be dealt with this month. Seeds of types that have to be raised, like chervil, fennel, and horehound, have to be sown.

Lettuce. Sow more seed. Plant out any raised in a frame as soon as the weather is suitable.

Onions. Get ready the onion bed and sow the seeds. Transplant the plants of any autumn sowings if necessary.

Parsnips. Gardeners in the north may sow seed this month.

Peas. It should be possible to make a sowing outside the first week, and again the third week. In the north, first sowings may be delayed until the end of the month. Plants raised under glass may be planted out after the middle of the month.

Potatoes. The land where potatoes are to be grown may be got ready by forking, if winter digging has been done, and by working in artificials.

Radish. A sowing may be made in the open.

Rhubarb may be sown or planted.

Seakale. A row or two may be planted this month. Seeds may be sown for next year's cropping. Seakale crowns may be forced.

Spinach. Sow ordinary spinach and spinach beet. Seeds of the New Zealand spinach should be sown in boxes under glass and the seedlings hardened off for planting out in May.

Tomatoes may be sown on a hot-bed early in the month, and the plants raised pricked out towards the end of the month.

Turnips. Sowings may be made of early varieties towards the end of the month.

Vegetable Marrows. Those with cloches or frames may sow seeds thinly in 3 in. pots after the fifteenth of the month.

APRIL

Though March is a busy month, April is even busier. It is during this month that the weeds seem to grow faster than at any other time. The young seedlings, when they come through, need the greatest care at this time of the year, and should be thinned when necessary. Protection from insect pests and diseases. Hoe regularly.

It should be possible this month to remove the lights from the frames containing autumn-sown and winter-sown crops, and to use the frames and lights, if the former are movable, for growing such crops as cucumbers and melons.

This is the month when most of the cabbage tribe seed have to be sown, especially those for use during the winter months. Prepare the seed-beds, sowing one or two rows of each kind.

Artichoke, Globe. Autumn removed suckers which are wintered in frames may be planted out. Give a mulching after planting.

Artichoke, Jerusalem. To get the best crop, remove all side growths, allowing only the main stem to grow.

Asparagus. Beds and rows already established should be kept free from weeds. Sow seeds or put out plants this month in the specially prepared ground.

Beans, Broad. Make a sowing in the open. Plant out those raised in boxes and mulch the rows.

Beans, French. It should be possible to make a sowing outside in a warm border towards the end of the month.

Beans, Runner. Plants may be raised by sowing seeds in boxes in a cold frame.

Beet. Make a sowing of main crop variety towards the end of the month.

Broccoli. Sow seeds in seed-bed for winter cutting. Remember to protect from birds and club root.

Brussels Sprouts. Prick out plants raised last month in seed-beds 4 ins. apart. This produces excellent plants. Make another sowing if necessary.

Cabbage. Sow seed of varieties that are to be cut in late summer and autumn. Give spring cabbage another application of potassic nitrate of soda. Hoe the bed once a week. The majority of the spring cabbage will be cut this month.

Cardoon. Prepare the cardoon trenches. Sow seeds in

the centre, covering them 1 in. deep. Plants may be raised by sowing seed in pots or sowing seed in frames.

Carrots. Sow the main crop towards the middle of the month.

Cauliflowers. Put out the autumn-sown plants in a warm position. Make a sowing of seed about the middle of the month for autumn supplies.

Celery. Harden off young plants pricked out in March. Keep free from celery fly by spraying with nicotine and soft soap. Late celery may be sown in the open.

Herbs. Sowings may be made about the middle of the month if impossible in March. The rows already growing should be hoed.

Kohlrabi. Raise plants by sowing seeds early in the month. Plant out seedlings at the end of the month.

Leeks. Raise plants by sowing seed in frames. Those raised under glass may be planted out towards the end of the month for early crops. Water in well.

Lettuce. Plants raised in frames may be put out. Successional sowings may be made outside.

Maize. Seed should be sown under glass about the middle of the month in boxes. Pot up into 3 in. pots when fit to handle.

Mustard and Cress. Make further sowings.

Onions. Sowings of main crop varieties may be made. Sowings made under glass may be put out into well-prepared ground. Pickling onions may be sown on poor ground.

Parsley. Sowings may be made along the edges of borders.

Peas. Any plants raised under glass may be put out into a warm border. Sowings may be made outside every fortnight to ensure a regular supply.

Potatoes. Planting may be carried out.

Salsify. Seed should be sown in drills 1 ft. apart.

Scorzonera. Sow seed as for salsify.

Seakale. Plant early in the month.

Spinach. Make successional sowings. Spinach beet may be sown.

APRIL

Sow Sweet Corn in pots under glass 3 seeds per pot

Plant Potatoes

Grass
Fertiliser
Manure

MAY

Plant out Tomatoes in trench

Sow Runner Beans

9"

JUNE

Hoe Onions

Mulch where necessary

Water where necessary

I**

Turnips. Thin any rows sown last month. Hoe regularly. Make further sowings.

Vegetable Marrows. Plant out seedlings raised during March. Cover with cloches. Make further sowings in 3 in. pots in frames.

MAY

This is a treacherous month, as very often a severe frost occurs, even during the third week of the month when plants are growing well. Protection may be given, when it is felt that the temperature is likely to drop, with straw, sacking, or mats. Go over the seed-beds and see if there are deficiencies. Make further sowings if necessary. Thin out the seedlings already raised, pricking them out into further beds if necessary.

Keep the hoe going all through the month.

Artichoke, Globe. Plant out suckers to ensure succession.

Asparagus. The sown rows should now be thinned, leaving the plants 1 ft. apart. The older beds and rows should be kept free from weeds.

Beans, Broad. Make further sowings outside.

Beans, French. A sowing may be made either the first, second, or third week.

Beans, Runner. Sowings should be possible towards the third week or end of the month.

Beet. Thin out earlier sown varieties. Make another sowing of a main crop if necessary. Hoe the rows.

Broccoli. Sow seeds for spring and summer cutting next year. Plant out any seedlings pricked out in March.

Brussels Sprouts. Put out the earliest plants into the specially prepared position.

Cabbage. Plant different summer varieties. Hoe regularly.

Cardoons. Make sowings in trenches if not done in April.

Carrots. The earliest sowings may be thinned out and whizzed naphthalene applied along the rows.

Cauliflowers. Make sowings outside of late hearting varieties.

Celery. Prepare the trenches if not already done, and plant out the early varieties.

Lettuce. Keep making successional sowings. Thin out seedlings regularly and plant out. Hoe the rows regularly.

Marrows. Harden off any plants raised in frames early in the month, and plant out during the third week.

Mustard and Cress. Make sowings in the open.

Peas. Make further sowings during the month for August and September use. Protect from mice and birds. Hoe the earlier sown varieties and give them supports if necessary.

Radish. Make a further sowing.

Salsify. Sow seeds this month if not already done.

Scorzonera. See salsify.

Spinach. Continue to sow spinach in the cooler places, and plant out New Zealand spinach at the end of the month.

Turnips. Further sowings may be made, which should be dusted regularly with derris to keep down turnip fly. Use the hoe frequently.

Vegetable Marrows. Cloches may be removed towards the end of the month and the plants kept watered regularly. Those raised later may be planted out after the third week.

JUNE

It should be possible to harvest many crops this month, but, despite this, there is a great deal of work to do with those that are to follow. Keep hoeing all the time, especially if the weather is dry. Mulch where necessary with lawn mowings and straw, and water thoroughly the plants that really need it. Always hoe, and mulch as well if possible, after watering.

Keep down weeds at all costs, and thin the crops out early. It should be possible this month, even in the north, to put out all the tender plants like marrows, cucumbers, and tomatoes.

It should be possible this month to put out many plants of the cabbage family—kale, savoys, broccoli, and Brussels sprouts, for instance. These may be planted whenever land comes available.

Asparagus. The rows or beds should now be bearing well. Cut regularly and evenly. Cease cutting at the end of the month.

Beans, Broad. Make a further sowing in the open. Pinch out the tops of the earlier sowings. Dust or spray with derris.

Beans, French. Make another sowing in the open. Hoe between rows sown earlier.

Beans, Runner. Provide the necessary sticks. Mulch the rows towards the end of the month. Syringe the plants well in the evening, during dry weather.

Beetroot. Thin out the rows that need it. Hoe regularly.

Broccoli. Plants raised from sowings in April may now be ready for planting.

Brussels Sprouts. Plants may be put out into their permanent rows this month.

Celery. Plant out the main crop celery into trenches. During dry weather, water regularly and syringe overhead in evening.

Coleworts. Make a sowing this month after the summer cabbages are over.

Cucumbers, Ridge. Make a sowing on specially prepared ridges. Plant out those raised in pots. Pinch out tip when 7 leaves have formed.

Endive. Rows may be sown on the tops of the celery trenches if desired.

Lettuce. Seeds may be sown on the celery ridges and thinned out. Transplant thinnings to other ground if necessary. Keep lettuce supplied with moisture and hoed regularly.

Onions. Thin out the March or April sowing. Apply whizzed naphthalene to prevent onion fly. Feed exhibition onions well, but with great care.

Parsley. Make a sowing of parsley if the previous sowing has not done well.

Peas. A sowing of the first early varieties may again be made. The earlier sown varieties will now be ready for sticking, and mulchings may be made along the rows.

Potatoes. Earth up potatoes when necessary.

Radishes. Make a sowing once a fortnight. Protect from turnip fly by dusting with derris regularly. Water freely.

Turnips. Make further sowings for successional cropping, taking the precautions mentioned in May.

JULY

One never quite knows what July is going to be. Often it is a very wet month, and if it is the weeds grow apace. If it is a dry month, hoeing and mulching have to be attended to. This is a good month to make a start on a new compost heap. Lawn mowings, the old leaves of plants, hedge clippings, and so on may all be rotted down with calcium cyanamide as suggested (see p. 23).

Artichokes, Globe. Those that are being grown to be used for chards may now be cut down.

Beans, French. Make a sowing the first week of the month for a crop in late September.

Broccoli. Put out any plants that are ready on to ground that is prepared.

Cabbage. Make a sowing of spring cabbage seed about the third week of the month.

Cardoons. Give the strongest growers some support. Water freely, and give liquid manure once a week.

Carrots. Make another sowing of an early variety for pulling young in the autumn.

Cauliflowers. Plant out the later sowings if necessary.

Celery. Plantings may be made, if not carried out last month, either in trenches or on the flat.

Coleworts. Make another sowing of coleworts for winter use.

Cucumbers. Attend to these regularly, thinning out the growths and watering if necessary.

Endive. Make further sowings.

Leeks. Plant out a good batch on flat ground, using a dibber. Plant deeply, leaving the hole open.

Onions, Potato. Take up and use or store.

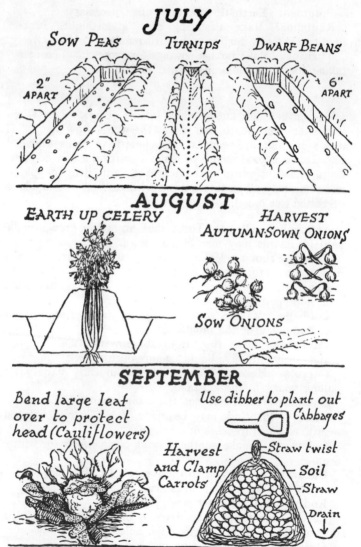

JULY

Sow Peas   Turnips   Dwarf Beans

2" APART

6" APART

AUGUST

Earth up Celery

Harvest Autumn-Sown Onions

Sow Onions

SEPTEMBER

Bend large leaf over to protect head (Cauliflowers)

Use dibber to plant out Cabbages

Harvest and Clamp Carrots

Straw twist

Soil

Straw

Drain

Parsley. Make a sowing out of doors for winter use.

Peas. Hoe the rows regularly. Continue to mulch if necessary, and water if dry.

Potatoes. Earth up the late varieties. Dig up the early varieties as required.

Radishes. Make further sowings successionally.

Shallots. It should be possible to harvest these.

Spinach. Make a sowing for autumn and winter use on well-drained firm land. Hoe regularly. Spinach beet may be sown.

Tomatoes. Tie and dis-shoot regularly.

Turnips. Make further sowings once a fortnight, thinning out the seedlings regularly.

AUGUST

This is the month when more crops may be harvested and when further seed-sowings may be made to ensure a supply of vegetables next spring.

All the winter greens should be planted this month, and should the weather be dry the roots may be puddled in.

Hoeing, mulching, and cultivating, spraying and the general care of crops are all necessary.

Artichokes, Globe. Cut the heads as soon as ready, and use.

Broccoli. If any plants have been put out as intercrops, the main crops should now be removed, and the ground between them forked over.

Beans, French. Harvest all the pods directly they are ready, as by heavier picking heavier crops result.

Beans, Runner. Pick regularly. Water is necessary. Mulch the rows and syringe the plants at night-time.

Brussels Sprouts. Remove yellowing leaves. Dust regularly with cerris to prevent " blue bug attack."

Cabbage. Further sowings of spring cabbage may be made.

Cardoons. Earthing-up should now commence, as for celery.

Cauliflowers. Go over the rows and bend or break a leaf over the curds as they come in to keep them clean and fresh. Dust or spray with derris to keep down caterpillars. Water and give liquid manure if necessary.

Celery. Keep the celery trenches well soaked with water. Remove all side growths. Spray every ten days with nicotine and soft soap to keep down celery fly. Earth-up where early specimens are required.

Endive. Further sowings may be made. Plants raised previously may be planted out in a similar border.

Lettuce. See endive.

Onions, Autumn Sown. These should now be harvested after they have ripened off on the ground. Further sowings should be made for the following season.

Onions, Exhibition. Exhibition bulbs should have the decaying foliage and rough outside skins removed.

Onions, Salad. Make sowings for pulling green early next year.

Parsley. Make a sowing if the July one was not successful.

Peas. If necessary, keep down mildew by spraying with colloidal sulphur. Net rows where birds are troublesome. Hoe, mulch, and water if necessary.

Radishes. Sow seeds freely, choosing the favourite varieties.

Shallots. Harvest, if not already harvested.

Spinach. Sowings may be made for winter cutting on raised beds.

Turnips. Make sowings for pulling in winter.

SEPTEMBER

The summer sown self-sown weeds are usually now very troublesome, and hoeing should be carried out as often as possible.

This is one of the biggest harvesting months, and care should be taken to get many of the crops in, especially in the case of northern gardens, as the first frost usually occurs during the last week of this month.

Artichokes, Globe. Any suckers grown for chards should now be blanched.

Beans, French. Look after the late sown crops and cover with cloches during the third week.

Cabbage. Spring cabbage plants raised in July should now be planted out into their permanent position.

Cardoons. These should be blanched.

Carrots. Lift and store.

Cauliflowers. Continue to protect heads. Make sowings during the second week in cold frame for wintering under glass.

Celery. Earthing-up should commence or continue.

Coleworts. Plant out more rows.

Endive. Give protection to plants growing in the open by frames, and commence to blanch.

Lettuce. Sow winter varieties, both cos and cabbage.

Onions. Lift the main crop, lay on the ground to ripen, then store.

Parsley. Cut back the old leaves to promote sturdy growth. Arrange to cover if necessary.

Radishes. Make further sowings for autumn salads.

Spinach. Make the final sowing for the year on a dry bed. Hoe the other rows regularly.

Turnips. Sow a variety like Green Globe for the tops in the spring.

OCTOBER

Be sure this month, to remove all the dead leaves, and where possible to rot them down for manure, and clear up and burn all the rubbish in every part of the garden.

Asparagus. Go over the beds and cut down the foliage that has turned yellow and burn it. Remove all the weeds, and then give a mulch of stable manure or a substitute.

Cabbage. Plant out another batch of spring cabbages for succession.

Cardoons. Continue to earth-up and blanch.

Cauliflowers. Prick out the plants raised in frames last month 3 in. apart in cold frames.

OCTOBER

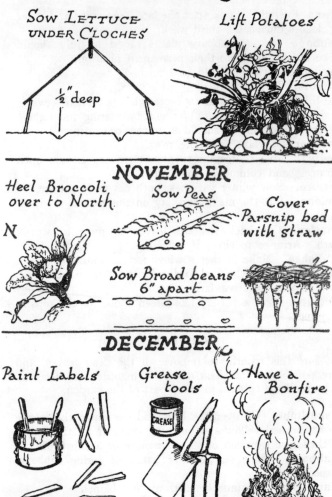

Sow *LETTUCE* UNDER *CLOCHES*

½" deep

Lift Potatoes

NOVEMBER

Heel Broccoli over to North

N

Sow Peas

Cover Parsnip bed with straw

Sow Broad beans 6" apart

DECEMBER

Paint Labels

Grease tools

Have a Bonfire

GREASE

Celery. The final earthing-up should be carried out.

Endive. Any plants outside may be lifted and planted into a cold frame. Continue to blanch as necessary, either by planting out in the dark, or by covering with a pot or box.

Lettuce. Plant out the winter varieties sown in the seed-bed in the middle of September.

Onions. The bulbs on the ground that are ripening off should now be thoroughly dry and should be stored. The first sowing of the exhibition varieties may be made in a cold frame.

Radishes. Make another sowing.

Rhubarb. The first roots may be dug up to be forced.

Salsify. Lift and store.

Scorzonera. See salsify.

Turnips. Lift the roots of the earlier sowings and store.

NOVEMBER

This is the month when the grower ought to do a great deal of the ridging, trenching, and bastard trenching in order to leave the land rough for the winter (see Chapter I).

All crops needing protection should be attended to, and those that are in a district where they can obtain bracken will find this useful.

Every opportunity should be taken of collecting the fallen leaves during this month, either to help to form a hot-bed, or to prepare organic manure.

Any alterations to the paths or to the type of garden should now be made, before the weather gets too hard.

Artichokes, Globe. Stems may be cut down and the decaying leaves removed. Put straw along the rows to protect them from frosts. Remove this during mild periods.

Artichokes, Jerusalem. Dig up tubers as required, or harvest and store in sand or soil.

Asparagus. On heavy land it is usual to cover the beds with the soil from the pathways, so that this will be pulverised by the winter frosts.

Beans, Broad. A sowing may be made this month in a sheltered border, using a long-pod variety.

Broccoli. Heel these over towards the north for protection and cover the stem with a little soil.

Celery. Earth-up further if necessary, and if it was impossible to complete this the previous month. Before a hard frost, lift a few sticks and store them in soil for present needs.

Lettuce. Those in frames should be given air during the mild weather. Keep the surface of the soil cultivated. Remove diseased bottom leaves.

Onions. The bulbs that are being stored should be examined occasionally and decaying ones removed. Turning over is usually beneficial.

Parsnips. Cover part of the bed with bracken or straw so that they can be lifted during frosty periods.

Peas. An attempt may be made to produce early peas next year by sowing a short row on dry soil in the autumn.

Rhubarb. Crowns may be lifted and forced as desired.

Seakale. See rhubarb.

DECEMBER

Complete all the alterations commenced last month. Collect more leaves and store and burn all the rubbish that might breed pests or distribute disease.

Go into the tool-shed, repair and oil the tools. Order any new ones that may be required. See that the shed is in good order. Tar and whitewash if desired. Get ready the labels by cleaning and painting. Store pea and bean sticks and sharpen them on wet days.

Keep a smoulder fire going, so as to produce not only good potash, but an excellent material for improving the texture of seed-beds.

See that all the land drains are working properly, and repair these if necessary.

Go through any inside stores of roots and remove all the decaying ones, to prevent contamination. See that the outside clamps are thoroughly watertight.

Beans, Broad. Give some protection by earthing-up or by bracken.

Celery. Protect the crop with straw or bracken during hard weather.

Endive. Ventilate the frames where these are growing and blanch as required.

Lettuce. See endive.

Radishes. A sowing may be made in a dry, sheltered, warm south border.

Rhubarb. Crowns may be continued to be lifted and forced.

Turnips. Lift and store as required.

Seakale. Earth-up plants in the garden to produce " natural kale."

APPENDIX ON
MISCELLANEOUS INFORMATION

FORMULÆ FOR INSECTICIDES
AND FUNGICIDES

INSECTICIDES

Arsenate of Lead. Arsenate of lead may be bought as a paste or as a powder.

$\left.\begin{array}{l} \frac{1}{2} \text{ lb. paste} \\ 5 \text{ ozs. powder} \end{array}\right\}$ to 12 gals. of water

The use of a spreader in addition will be found an advantage. Use the spreader as advised on the packet.

Never use soft soap with lead arsenate.

Keep this preparation under lock and key. It is poisonous. Never use the wash on a crop that has to be used within six weeks.

Calomel. A 4% calomel dust can be used against cabbage root fly.

Derris. Derris may be used as a spray or a dust.

Dissolve a good liquid derris like I.T.P. in water according to the instructions on the tin.

Derris is not poisonous to human beings or animals. It is fatal to fish, and should not be used near ponds or streams.

Always purchase fresh derris dust of a high rotenone content, i.e., 2 per cent and apply so as to distribute it evenly. A dust gun is the best tool for the purpose.

Gammaxene. This has so far proved to be the most effective control of flea beetles. Applied in the form of a greyish white dust.

Nicotine. This is generally used as a spray, though nicotine dusts are available. When dusts are used, they should be applied on a warm day.

$$\left.\begin{array}{r} \tfrac{3}{4}\text{--1 oz. nicotine} \\ \text{1 lb. soft soap} \\ \text{or a spreader} \end{array}\right\} \text{to 10 gals. water.}$$

Nicotine is a poison, and should be kept locked up when not in use.

Soak the plants thoroughly with the spray and see that the under surface of the leaves is soaked as well as the upper surface. Spraying on a warm day is most effective.

FUNGICIDES

Bordeaux. There are two formulæ, the first one for Potatoes and the second for Celery :

$$(1)\ \left.\begin{array}{r} \text{1 lb. 6 ozs. hydrated lime} \\ \text{1 lb. 6 ozs. powdered copper} \\ \text{sulphate} \end{array}\right\} \text{to 10 gals. water.}$$

$$(2)\ \left.\begin{array}{r} \text{1}\tfrac{1}{2}\text{ ozs. hydrated lime} \\ \text{1 lb. copper sulphate} \end{array}\right\} \text{to 10 gals water.}$$

The crystals of copper sulphate are dissolved overnight in a wooden or china container and then poured into the lime-water in the morning. More water is added if necessary to bring up to correct strength.

Do not use metal vessels with Bordeaux because of corrosion.

Colloidal Copper. This is used very often instead of Bordeaux. It is sold under a proprietary name and is odourless.

Colloidal Sulphur. A fungicide usually bought ready to use under a proprietary name.

It is odourless and does not mark the foliage.

These two colloidal sprays may be mixed together.

Copper Lime Dust. Where it is inexpedient to use a sulphur dust because plants are sulphur-shy, a dust like Bordeaux is very effective.

Sulphur Dust. Special dusts are made for dusting plants where wet spraying is difficult.

Dusting is quicker and cheaper than wet spraying.

Ordinary flowers of sulphur are not suitable for dusting.

POISON BAITS

(1) 10 lbs. bran.
$\left.\begin{array}{l} \text{½ lb. Paris Green} \\ \text{½ gall. water} \end{array}\right\}$ will cover ½ acre.

N.B.—Used for *leather jackets* and *slugs*.

(2) $\left.\begin{array}{l} \text{¼ lb. Paris Green} \\ \text{14 lbs. dried blood} \end{array}\right\}$ applied at the rate of 1 oz. per sq. yard.

N.B.—Used for *wood-louse-control*, particularly under glass.

(3) 2 lbs. sugar
$\left.\begin{array}{l} \text{1/10th oz. tartaric acid} \\ \text{1 pint water} \end{array}\right\}$ mix and boil for ½ hour.

$\left.\begin{array}{l} \text{1/10th oz. sodium arsenate} \\ \text{2 ozs. hot water} \end{array}\right\}$ dissolve

Allow both to cool and then mix thoroughly.

Add 3 ozs. honey.

Dip tiny pieces of sponge in liquid, and place on beds or path where ants abound.

N.B.—Used for *ant control*.

Paradichlorbenzine used for Wireworm control.

TIME TAKEN FOR GARDEN SEEDS TO GERMINATE

	DAYS
Asparagus	14 to 21
Beans	7 to 14
Beet	10 to 18
Brassicæ (all sorts)	5 to 10
Carrots	12 to 18
Chicory	5 to 10
Cress	4 to 6
Cucumbers (in the open)	7 to 14
Cucumbers (in heat)	2 to 4
Endive	5 to 14
Leeks	10 to 14
Lettuce	6 to 10
Melons (in heat)	3 to 6
Mustard	3 to 4
Onions	10 to 16
Parsley	15 to 26
Parsnips	10 to 20
Peas	7 to 14
Radishes	3 to 6
Spinach	7 to 10
Tomatoes (in heat)	6 to 10
Turnips	4 to 10
Vegetable Marrows (in the open)	7 to 14
Vegetable Marrows (in heat)	3 to 5

AVERAGE LONGEVITY OF GARDEN SEEDS

	YEARS		YEARS
Asparagus	3	Mustard	4
Basil	8	Onions	2
Beans	3	Parsley	3
Beet	6	Parsnips	2
Borage	8	Peas	3
Brassicæ	5	Radishes	5
Cardoons	7	Rhubarb	3
Carrots	4	Rosemary	4
Chicory	8	Sage	3
Cress	5	Salsify	2
Cucumbers	6	Savory, Summer or Winter	3
Endive	10	Scorzonera	2
Fennel	4	Seakale	1
Leeks	3	Spinach (all varieties)	5
Lettuce	5	Thyme	3
Marjoram, Sweet	3	Tomatoes	4
Marjoram, Winter	5	Turnips	5
Melons	5	Vegetable Marrows	6

INDEX

285